Why Kids Can't Read

Challenging the Status Quo in Education

Edited by
Phyllis Blaunstein
Reid Lyon

Rowman & Littlefield Education
Lanham, Maryland • Toronto • Oxford
2006

Published in the United States of America
by Rowman & Littlefield Education
A Division of Rowman & Littlefield Publishers, Inc.
A wholly owned subsidary of The Rowman & Littlefield Publishing Group, Inc.
4501 Forbes Boulevard, Suite 200, Lanham, Maryland 20706
www.rowmaneducation.com

PO Box 317
Oxford
OX2 9RU, UK

British Library Cataloguing in Publication Information Available

Library of Congress Cataloging-in-Publication Data

Why kids can't read : challenging the status quo in education / edited by
Phyllis Blaunstein, Reid Lyon.
    p. cm.
 ISBN-13: 978-1-57886-381-5 (hardcover : alk. paper)
 ISBN-13: 978-1-57886-382-2 (pbk. : alk. paper)
 ISBN-10: 1-57886-381-3 (hardcover : alk. paper)
 ISBN-10: 1-57886-382-1 (pbk. : alk. paper)
 1. Reading. 2. Reading—Parent participation. 3. Reading—Remedial
teaching. I. Blaunstein, Phyllis, 1940– II. Lyon, Reid, 1949–

 LB1050.W436 2006
 372.43—dc22

                                                    2005029571

⊗™ The paper used in this publication meets the minimum requirements of
American National Standard for Information Sciences—Permanence of
Paper for Printed Library Materials, ANSI/NISO Z39.48-1992.
Manufactured in the United States of America.

Contents

Part II: Changing the Odds

Appendixes

Endorsements

"This book has the potential to change an appalling statistic—70%–80% of poor minority children cannot read at grade level. This is a national and personal tragedy that cannot continue to exist. Blaunstein and Lyon lay out the facts, solutions, and tools to help parents work to solve this problem. Every parent should know these in order to make the changes needed to eradicate reading failure in our children."—Quentin Lawson, executive director, National Alliance of Black School Educators

"I am the parent of an 11 year old special needs child. She has had a number of problems learning to read. For a parent, navigating the education system can be extremely difficult and frustrating. Everything becomes personal, and the stakes are high. This book was so helpful to me. The resources are outstanding and, frankly, it is good to know we are not in this alone. I will recommend this book as an excellent source for other parents, teachers, and administrators."—Cheryl Kravitz, parent

"Families and parents know the relationship of reading to their children's academic and long-term success. Many, however, are unfamiliar with the nuances of evaluating how well reading is taught in their children's schools. Reid and Blaunstein have made a significant contribution to the tools parents have available to support their children's reading instruction. *Why Kids Can't Read* articulates the challenges parents face with practical solutions and advice on effectively interacting with schools and teachers to support student learning. Parents, teachers, and policymakers will appreciate the no-nonsense stance and strategic resources included in this book." — Brenda Lilienthal Welburn, executive director, National Association of State Boards of Education

"Parents and teachers working together can be an unstoppable force in solving our children's reading problems. This book will guide all who want to strive for a nation of readers." — Robert Chase, former president, National Education Association

Foreword

This book is meant to help the millions of parents who find their children struggling to learn to read. And there is a good chance that you are one of these parents, as almost 40% of our fourth-grade children are not reading at grade level.

There are devastating consequences for children, families, and society as a whole resulting from this epidemic of reading failure, and it doesn't have to be this way. For too long, children have been taught using various methods of teaching based on one particular philosophy of how children learn to read. Those who have used it believed that reading is a naturally learned act, like learning to walk or to speak. If your child is struggling to learn to read, you know this isn't so. This set of beliefs has produced enormous problems for many, many children.

In essence, instructional approaches based on this philosophy ignored the fact that many children, particularly those who struggle to learn to read, require systematic instruction. Yet the philosophy has gone unchallenged for decades, and it has left millions of children as its victims. Fortunately, we now have scientific evidence that a systematic and comprehensive approach to reading—an approach that ensures that all children learn the critical building blocks of reading—is the way to cure this epidemic. So why are we not using it for every child in every classroom in America?

In the following pages you will learn how to determine if your child is being taught to read effectively. The authors explain that to develop reading abilities, children must progress through a series of steps from learning the sounds in our language, to applying phonics skills quickly, and then acquiring the necessary vocabulary comprehension strategies to understand what they are reading.

You will be guided in the process of making change in your schools, and if you need to go higher in the education bureaucracy, you will learn how to do this. You will hear from several parents who have been successful in helping their children, a pediatrician who has worked for years to uncover the scientific evidence about how to best teach children to read, a determined woman who led the charge to change reading instruction in the entire state of California, an expert in using the media effectively to campaign for improved reading, a successful lobbyist who will unveil the secrets of how to influence legislation to ensure that your children learn to read, and more. The knowledge and tools you need are all here. All you have to do is use them.

In 1955, Rudolf Flesch wrote *Why Johnny Can't Read*. In 1981, 25 years later, he wrote *Why Johnny Still Can't Read*. In each book he discussed how using a systematic and comprehensive phonics-based method to teach children to read could solve the problem of reading failure. But somehow we didn't get the message, and millions of children have suffered the consequences. Your child may be among them.

Carol Hampton Rasco, president
Reading Is Fundamental

Preface

While governor of South Carolina and later U.S. secretary of education, I visited thousands of classrooms across the country. I vividly remember elementary school children gleaming with excitement as they proudly read from their books. But, more poignantly, I recall the heartbreak of seeing the children who slumped at their desks, avoiding eye contact in the hope that they would *not* be called upon because they could not read very well, if at all.

We cannot underestimate the seriousness of the reading problem among our nation's children. Most students who are not reading at grade level by fourth grade are missing fundamental skills that will severely limit their options for the future. It is at this point when they must use reading skills to learn other subject matter.

If children do not receive the intensive help they need to bring them up to grade level in the early grades, they lose confidence, motivation, and become overwhelmed. They generally are doomed to falling further and further behind. In later years, these youngsters likely will be among the 1 million middle and high school students who are in danger of dropping out of school or graduating unprepared for the basic demands of college or the workplace.

Individuals who drop out of school or fail to go to college have significantly lower lifetime incomes than those who stay in school and earn higher degrees. A person with a college degree will earn approximately $1 million more in a lifetime than a high school dropout. A person who can't read struggles to understand want ads and instructions on the job, ballots on voting day, and transportation schedules to get from one place to another. The most fundamental tasks become challenges they face each day.

The economic future of our society as a whole demands that we have a literate workforce. In our highly technological world in this 21st century, we depend upon people having good reading skills in order for our nation to remain competitive in the global marketplace. Throughout history, too, denying people the right to read has been a powerful tool of governments that suppress their citizens and control their intellectual growth. These governments take over newspapers, television, and radio and close libraries and burn books. In contrast, America respects the written word and views reading and writing as part of our individual freedoms. For these reasons and more, I believe we all must work together to provide our children with the reading skills they need to succeed in school, get meaningful jobs, and fully participate as citizens of our great nation.

Fortunately, we have the means to do so. *Why Kids Can't Read: Challenging the Status Quo in Education* takes us through research-based steps to help nearly every child learn to read. Research confirms that students who receive intensive, focused reading instruction will learn to read. But this critical task requires the help and good will of parents, grandparents, other caregivers, mentors, teachers, and other educators. Parents and other adults must get involved in their child's education, know what is happening in the classroom, talk to their children's teachers, understand what works, encourage reading, and talk to their kids about their ideas and experiences.

As important as teachers are, we cannot place this responsibility solely upon their shoulders. Children generally know their teachers for one school year—a little over nine months. Parents see their children every day. We as family members have the obligation to do what is necessary and what is right. I urge you to think about the experiences of those in this book, take them to heart, and learn the lessons they teach. Parents and educators who work together to help children read well are rewarded by seeing them become excited, successful learners. There is no greater gift one can give to a child. *Why Kids Can't Read* will help every adult help every child in every classroom experience the pride and thrill of reading well and all of the learning that results from it.

Richard W. Riley
former U.S. secretary of education and
former governor of South Carolina

Acknowledgments

We would like to thank so many people who made this book possible. First, the authors of our chapters, who generously spent the time and effort to share their experiences with parents. We would have had little to say if not for their successes and hard work and understanding of the importance of learning to read.

Next, we would like to thank a group of special parent advocates, Teresa Ankeny, Margie Bell, Penny Marshall, Diane Badgley, and Diane McCauley, who spent many hours discussing with us what would be most helpful to families who are dealing with children who are struggling to learn to read. Their own experiences brought real authenticity to our thinking.

We would like to acknowledge the work of so many researchers whose commitment to only the most rigorous scientific thinking has made it possible to place the powerful tools explained in this book in the hands of educators throughout the country. Thanks must go to the members of the National Reading Panel, who understand the critical nature of their charge to identify the best reading research and make it available for use in classrooms. Their tireless efforts have produced profound change in the nature of reading instruction in our schools.

Patrick Riccards deserves special mention. He reviewed drafts in record time, offered wise counsel and encouragement, and helped us to crystallize our thoughts.

Stewart Davis spent hours above and beyond the call of duty to provide technical support in preparing the manuscript.

Most importantly, we want to thank the children who have inspired us to tell their stories. For too long, children who have difficulties learning to read have not had a voice in the educational process. And it is unfortunate that their voices are heard most clearly through the pain that reading failure has brought into their lives. The youngsters who have received scientifically based reading instruction and are now reading to learn tell us through their confidence and their smiles that with informed teachers providing evidence-based reading programs, failure is no longer an option for them. Their success makes us work all the harder.

And finally, we thank our families for their support, cheerleading, and willingness to help us in so many ways—to Diane Lyon, who is both a blessing and an inspiration, and to Robert Blaunstein, who has been so generous with his support and love for more than four decades, and to our own children, who have taught us many lessons about learning.

Introduction

Phyllis Blaunstein and Reid Lyon

Consider this. In Smithville, there are 4,500 students in elementary, junior high, and high school. In the kindergarten classes, the kids have overcome the first pangs of being separated from their families and bounce into school, eager to see what the day brings. Some of them dive right into the books in their classroom as if they have been provided reading opportunities for some time. Many can write their names and recognize letters of the alphabet. But other students, almost half, hold their books like unfamiliar objects, have difficulties naming the letters of the alphabet, and have no idea how their names look in print. Nevertheless, they, too, are excited to be "in school" and clearly want to learn. However, for many of these youngsters, these positive attitudes toward school will most likely change.

Let's look at the same kids, 5 years later. Our kindergarten children are in fourth grade, but we see that many of them have lost the sparkle in their eyes and are slumped in defeat. Almost 40% of these kids haven't learned to read at their grade level. If they come from disadvantaged environments, failure rates can top 60%. They are on a path to failure, because this year, reading will not be taught as a separate subject. The ante has been raised. Their teachers will expect them to be able to read to learn, and their progress will be based on their ability to gain information through their textbooks in science, social studies, math, and English. Crucial time has passed for them to avoid failure.

Let's fast forward four more years. Our fourth graders are now in the eighth grade. Too many of them are well-known because they are frequently truant, disrupt class time, and generally do anything they can to avoid school. Many of the kids are staying around only until they can legally leave school. Others are classified as needing special education. Four out of 10 of the children who started kindergarten with such eagerness have been failed by their schools in the most fundamental way. For the Hispanic and African American children in Smithville finishing up the eighth grade, the story is the same as it was in fourth grade. Over 60% of these kids have not learned to read. They were not taught to read. They did not catch up on their own. We failed them.

The businesses in Smithville are closing. The clothing manufacturing plant can't find skilled workers, and technology companies that considered locating in Smithville have realized they could not develop an adequate workforce and backed away. The ripple effect has been widely felt. People have lost jobs, and young people have had to locate elsewhere where the economy is thriving. The schools have not had a bond levy passed in so long that buildings are crumbling. The school board can't recruit good teachers and hasn't bought textbooks in so long that according to their social studies texts, the Cold War is still going on.

How did this downward spiral begin? How might it have been avoided and its effects turned around? It began with children failing to learn to read. Reading failure in this country has taken on epidemic proportions. According to the Power for Kids Reading Initiative, more than 21 million students can't read at grade level, and the cost in human lives is unconscionable:

Unemployment: 25% of young adults lack basic literacy skills needed in a typical job.

Substance abuse: 60% of adolescents who abuse drugs also have a reading problem.

Welfare: 76% of children living in poverty can't read at a proficient reading level.

Incarceration: More than 60% of young prisoners are functionally illiterate.

We wrote this book because 90%–95% of these children might have avoided this route to failure. We now have research-based teaching methods and approaches that, if implemented properly, ensure that the majority of our children will learn to read proficiently. This is a wake-up call to parents, educators, and all others interested in the welfare of our children. In the following chapters we tell you how to advocate for research-based reading instruction that will help your children, the children in your neighborhood, and the children in your schools become good readers.

The chapters that follow were written by experts who want to help parents and others concerned with reading education navigate the bumps in the road that are inevitable when people are trying to change a system. Some chapters may be more important to you than others. Please feel free to skip around and choose those that meet your immediate needs.

In the following pages we cover these topics:

- How to work with other parents and community leaders, and to organize and gain strength in numbers
- How to recognize warning signs that your child is beginning to struggle before it becomes a major problem, and what you can do about it
- What the latest scientific findings tell you about reading instruction
- How to do the necessary homework, know what to look for, and demand it
- How to approach schools with the conviction that things will change, and the tools to make that happen
- How to use the media to gain public support
- How to transform your impatience into action
- How to check your child's progress and your school's progress
- How to form coalitions that work to influence lawmakers
- How to help your principal and teachers make needed changes

Part I reveals the stories of families who beat the odds, and part II tells you how you can do the same.

1

BEATING THE ODDS

1

The Crisis in Our Classrooms

Phyllis Blaunstein and Reid Lyon

Brad is 21 and is in prison because he stole a car and totaled it. While most of the people from his high school are graduating from college, or working, Brad is in prison, serving the last 2 years of a 4-year sentence. His problems started when he began school, and he became more discouraged as he went on to fail continually in high school. He dropped out of school at 16, and, looking back, his problems at school seem minor compared to the trouble he's in now. A major reason: Brad never learned to read.

Jennifer is 12. She's a quiet girl, never gets into trouble, and never passes a course. Her report cards look like a series of dittos; D, D, F, F. She reads at the second-grade level and seems stuck there while many of her classmates are reading typical teen books. Jennifer is angry, has no self-confidence, and tries to fade into the woodwork at school. Her mother can't get her up in the mornings or get her to do her homework, and Jen says she hates school. The problem: Jennifer can't read.

> I tried to explain to Jen's teachers that she was falling behind. Each day she came home from school vowing she'd never go back. I am scared to death that she might make good on this threat.

Luis is 16. He just reached the legal age to drop out of school, and so he did. His parents, having immigrated from El Salvador, are not familiar with the school system and found their limited English a barrier to helping Luis get the help he needed. Luis plans to join the military in a couple of years, but he's in for a disappointment because he has no high school diploma. He's already found that he's having trouble getting a job and is a little worried that he'll be sitting at home alone. Although many of his friends have dropped out also, and are wandering around or hanging out on street corners, he hopes life will be different for him. The problem: Luis never learned to read.

Shanisa is 8 years old. She lives with her mother and baby brother. Her mother works two shifts and has had little time to help Shanisa learn her ABCs or write her name. When she started school, Shanisa had never had her own book or been read to. So everything she's learning in school is new and strange. She's not the only one who started school this way. A lot of kids in her class are also struggling to pick up many of the skills children learn before they start school. Now in third grade, Shanisa is falling behind even more. Her teachers are concerned that in 4th grade, when she will need good reading skills to learn other subjects, Shanisa will give up in frustration. And unless someone teaches her to read this year, that's exactly what will happen. The problem: Shanisa hasn't learned to read.

UNPROVEN TEACHING METHODS

For too long, reading programs have been chosen without any evidence that they work, except for the "manufacturer's guarantee" accompanying the program. While many of these reading programs have claimed that they are based on "research," they have not been put through careful studies similar to the ones health scientists conduct to make sure that a drug prescribed for an illness will make you well and not harm you. Nor is it typical in education research to use a method of reading instruction with one group of children and not with another and to compare which group learns better.

The scientific research used in medicine and other professional fields that have a responsibility for the health and welfare of our citizens seeks to obtain evidence from a number of studies that a particular treatment works for people with a certain medical, dental, or psychological problem. If this were not done, a new medication, for example, could make a claim like, "You'll lose 20 pounds in 10 days with this drug," without any solid evidence to back this up. The drug would not have been tested on a large group of people who are struggling with their weight, and their weight loss would not be compared with another group of people who had not taken the drug. You could certainly not count on its delivering the promised result.

COMPETING METHODS OF TEACHING READING HAVE HELD US BACK

Since the early 1970s, many children were expected to learn to read with an approach called *whole language*. Actually, whole language is more of a philosophy of teaching and learning than an instructional method. In essence, proponents of whole language claim that learning to read should be as natural as learning to talk. That is, critical skills like phonemic awareness, phonics, vocabulary, reading fluency, and comprehension strategies can be learned through exposure to reading and writing activities, not through systematic instruction.

Basically, children are expected to learn phonics and other basic reading skills on their own with only minimal guidance from the teacher. Many advocates of whole language actually believe that too much phonics instruction is harmful to children, that it will turn them into "word callers" and will destroy their love for reading. The role of the whole language teacher is to help students "discover" how our writing system works without providing systematic instruction. Their goal for reading instruction is to instill a love of reading, not the ability to read, seemingly without the realization that the latter is the pathway to the former.

Whole language–based instruction, no matter how well intentioned, was not based on any scientific evidence that children will learn to read naturally on their own. Unfortunately, its implementation in many classrooms led to reading failure in many children; they did not develop the critical reading fundamentals on their own.

But it did not have to be this way. For the past several decades, we have had scientific research that would clearly point us in the right direction for how to successfully teach nearly all children to read using a comprehensive reading approach that included systematic phonics instruction to ensure that children can learn to read unfamiliar words. So why have so many schools not used this research to develop and implement evidence-based methods and curricula in your children's classes?

First, education research has not been given the same attention and funding as medical research. This may be because people more acutely feel the immediacy of life and death than we do with learning issues. But should we? Reading can be a life-and-death issue in a figurative sense. When we fail to work within a young child's window of opportunity for learning to read, the child's life course is permanently affected.

Second, there has been a belief that a whole language approach will be successful with most children, and that not all children need to learn the basic fundamentals upon which reading proficiency depends. And while whole language may work for some children who have been exposed consistently to the basics of reading through early language and literacy interactions in the home, it does not work for the 40% of 4th-grade children who do not read on grade level—the millions of children who are struggling!

> Effective reading programs teach children not only systematically, but explicitly as well. There is no subtle subliminal teaching here; children are not left to their own devices. . . . This is in contrast to "whole language" reading programs . . . in which it is assumed that reading is acquired naturally, just as speech is. . . . In this view, letter-sound relationships will be learned naturally, seemingly by osmosis, as children are surrounded by literature and exposed to printed materials. (Shaywitz, 2003, p. 202)

What happens to these students? Many drop out of school, fill our prisons, can't find work, and have trouble reading newspapers, magazines, signs, contracts for cars, loans, credit cards, bills, instructions for appliances and tools, and other information that is critical for all of us to become successful as workers, parents, and full participants in society.

TEACHERS NEED HELP

Large numbers of today's teachers went to school when whole language was the accepted way to design reading instruction. Understandably, they have used this approach to teach reading for many years and are comfortable with it. One would think that with so many children failing to learn to read, teachers would question the effectiveness of whole language approaches. However, the whole language philosophy also suggests to teachers that the use of objective assessments to monitor reading progress was inappropriate. Instead, measures of enjoyment, motivation, and self-esteem were more important.

To avoid implementing invalid and ineffective reading approaches in the future, we must provide our teachers in training and those in the classroom with the best scientific research that helps them understand how reading develops, why so many of our kids have difficulties learning to read, and what we can do about that. They need information about how to determine whether a program or an approach is really "scientifically based." They need to be provided clear information to understand that some research can be trusted and some cannot be trusted.

Given these tools, they can make better decisions about which programs are most effective for which children. We must also make sure that our teachers understand the critical value of measuring how well our students are responding to the reading instruction. You can't modify your instructional strategies to meet the needs of individual children unless you know that the program is breaking down. All too often, it is not until the end of the school year when teachers and parents realize that a youngster actually has a significant reading problem.

In many cases, when children were having difficulty learning to read, teachers had few alternatives other than referring them to special education, where they were often classified as having a learning disability. We now know that if these children had been taught using research-based reading methods, most of them would have learned to read without struggling. Many of these children do not need a learning disability label.

HOW CAN WE PREVENT READING FAILURE?

The good news is that the majority of children who enter kindergarten and elementary school at risk for reading failure can learn to read at average or above average levels, but only if they are identified early and taught using systematic and intensive instruction in phonemic awareness, phonics, reading fluency, vocabulary, and reading comprehension strategies. If they are not identified early, we will have missed a window of opportunity to help them. We know from research carried out and supported by the National Institute of Child Health and Human Development (NICHD, a part of the National Institutes for Health) that the majority of at-risk readers rarely catch up to their classmates if they are not reading by the time they are 9 years old. Instead these struggling readers face a lifetime of illiteracy. It does not have to be this way!

WHO ARE THESE CHILDREN WHO HAVE DIFFICULTY LEARNING TO READ?

These children are from families with parents with graduate degrees and those without high school diplomas. Reading problems affect all children, but, to be sure, kids growing up in poverty are the most at risk. For example, when we look at some subgroups of students, reading problems are more the rule rather than the exception. Only 12% of African American students and 15% of Hispanic students are reading proficiently or better in the 4th grade. In New York City alone, over 60% of minority students cannot read at a basic level.

To be clear, it is not race or ethnicity that causes such great numbers of our kids to have reading problems. It is poverty, and minority students happen to be overrepresented among disadvantaged families. It's difficult to sit by and allow this serious problem to continue when we have the evidence that most children can learn to read when provided with three things: well-trained teachers, effective instructional programs, and strong educational leadership.

We have a moral responsibility to eliminate this shameful reading deficit that affects the quality of life of hundreds of thousands of children. The system is failing our children, and we sorely need to apply proven methods of teaching based on the scientific method—a method that has solved many of the world's thorniest medical mysteries that are at least as complex as reading.

How many more children need to fail before we realize that human potential and life are too precious to risk on the basis of untested beliefs and solutions? This book shows you how to be sure your child is getting the reading education he or she needs and deserves—now.

2

Armed With the Facts: The Science of Reading and Its Implications for Teaching

Sally E. Shaywitz, MD, and Bennett A. Shaywitz, MD

This chapter explains how children learn to read and what they must be taught if they are going to be successful readers. There is now carefully developed research that can guide every teacher in every school to help nearly all children learn to read. Read on and you will discover the five fundamental skills children must learn in order to read and how they can be taught. In language every parent can understand, Sally and Bennett Shaywitz, codirectors of the Yale Center for the Study of Learning and Attention, one of the world's leading centers on reading and dyslexia, discuss the scientific basis for a phonics-based reading instructional method and give you the clues to look for if you suspect your child has a reading problem. Consider sharing this chapter with your child's teacher and principal.

THE READING CODE: SPEAKING AND READING

Reading is a code that must be unlocked if a child is to make sense of the assorted letters on a page. Following intense study by a diverse group of scientists, the nature of the code and the key to deciphering it are now known. One of the most critical clues in solving the reading code comes from understanding and comparing differences between spoken and written language.

As parents we marvel at our children as they successively learn to utter words and then say sentences and then express a range of ideas. In truth, we are witnessing the unfolding of a very natural process, one that is inherent in all of us as humans. Spoken language is built into our genes; all societies on earth have a spoken language. While no one knows exactly how long spoken language has been with us, we do know it is hundreds and hundreds of thousands of years, a very long time. In fact, we are genetically programmed and our brains are hardwired for language. Once children are exposed to a speaking environment, hearing and responding to spoken language, they will learn to speak. Speaking is natural; it's instinctive; most importantly, it does not have to be taught directly and systematically.

Written language is very different. Humanity has been using written language for only 5,000 or 6,000 years, from an evolutionary perspective a relatively short period of time. Even today, some societies continue to communicate solely through oral language. In contrast to spoken language, we as humans do not seem to be genetically programmed for written language; our brains are not hardwired for reading. So, as opposed to spoken language that is automatic and natural, reading is acquired and must be taught. For many years, the question challenging scientists and educators alike was, How do children break the reading code? Or more practically, What must be taught to children to help them learn to read? How do children acquire written language?

In contrast to spoken language, we as humans do not seem to be genetically programmed for written language; our brains are not hardwired for reading. So, as opposed to spoken language that is automatic and natural, reading is acquired and must be taught.

A SCIENCE OF READING

Happily, these questions are now being answered. For the past two decades or more, the National Institute of Child Health and Human Development (NICHD), a branch of the National Institutes of Health (NIH), has devoted considerable resources to supporting rigorous research into how children learn to read and into the nature, course, and remediation of reading difficulties. This means that the research in reading has met the same high standards of scientific inquiry that characterizes research in other important areas that affect the health and well-being of children.

As a result, there is now a science of reading to which parents and educators can turn for guidance in identifying potential reading problems early and accurately. This science has resulted in proven, effective methods of teaching all children to read and to help struggling readers become good readers. Extraordinary progress in our understanding of the nature of reading and reading difficulties provides exciting new knowledge with direct application for the classroom teacher for teaching reading. Never before have rigorous science, including neuroscience, and classroom instruction in reading been so closely linked.

There is now a science of reading to which parents and educators can turn for guidance in identifying potential reading problems early and accurately. This science has resulted in proven, effective methods to teach all children to read and to help struggling readers become good readers.

EVIDENCE-BASED EDUCATION

Today, we are in a new era in education—an era of evidence-based education. This represents a true paradigm shift for education and is one of the most important developments in teaching reading in the last half century. Just as parents are knowledgeable about the importance of childhood vaccinations, parents of school-age children must become aware of these important new developments in teaching reading so that they can help ensure that their child will become a reader. Evidence-based education offers the potential to ensure that children will be taught by methods and programs that are proven effective, rather than by ones that often do not work.

Let me explain. Pediatricians practice evidence-based medicine. When parents bring a child to see me for a medical problem, they expect that I will select the very best treatment, one that will effectively treat their child's condition. To do that, I will look to the evidence, that is, consult the scientific literature and read published studies where different treatments for the child's condition will have been compared, one to another. Based on this scientific evidence, I will choose the treatment that was proven to be most effective. This approach, now the gold standard in medicine, is referred to as evidence-based medicine. We expect no less from our physicians. Experience has taught us that without evidence of effectiveness, many of our assumptions about what works and what does not are often incorrect.

Experience has taught us that without evidence of effectiveness, many of our assumptions about what works and what does not are often incorrect.

For example, for decades there were many opinions about the source of stomach ulcers and many approaches to treatment reflecting these opinions. But none of the opinions considered the possibility of an infectious agent as the culprit. With time, rigorous scientific research replaced opinions, beliefs, and hunches, have brought dramatic and positive changes to the treatment of ulcers. The evidence proved that many of the previous beliefs (and treatments) about the etiology of gastric ulcers had been wrong. Based on strong scientific evidence we now know that a bacteria, *H. Pylori*, is the culprit, and treatment of the offending bacteria will alleviate the problem. This is but one example of the positive influence evidence-based practice has had on medicine and on our health and well-being.

Incredible as this may seem, until very recently, such an evidence-based approach had not been applied to or practiced in education. Rather, when asked how a particular reading approach was chosen, an educator was likely to respond, "In my heart I know it works," or "I believe in this philosophy," or "I've always used it"—decisions based on subjective opinion and not objective evidence. We would not find this kind of decision making acceptable in matters involving the health of our children, nor should we allow this sort of thinking to characterize how our children are taught to read. This unscientific and ineffective approach to teaching reading must change. Children deserve better. Too often parents do not know that their child's instruction is not meeting the criteria for proven methods of teaching. I have seen too many instances where parents are told, for the first time, on the last day of school, "I hope Emma has a better year next year." Children are 7 or 8 years old only once in their lives; we cannot tolerate a child spending a year or years with an ineffective program, particularly when there are highly effective, scientifically proven reading approaches now available.

When asked how a particular reading approach was chosen, an educator was likely to respond, "In my heart I know it works," or "I believe in this philosophy," or "I've always used it"—decisions based on subjective opinion and not objective evidence. We would not find this kind of decision making acceptable in matters involving the health of our children, nor should we allow this sort of thinking to characterize how our children are taught to read.

EVIDENCE-BASED EFFECTIVE READING INSTRUCTION

In 1998, Congress, concerned that there appeared to be a near-epidemic of reading failure, mandated the director of the NICHD, in consultation with the secretary of education, to appoint a National Reading Panel (NRP) to "assess the status of research-based knowledge, including the effectiveness of various approaches to teaching children to read" (Departments of Labor, Health and Human Services, and Education, 1997), with the goal of guiding effective reading instruction in America's classrooms. The NRP was mandated to develop rigorous scientific criteria for evaluating reading research and apply these criteria to the existing reading literature. Accordingly, the panel established strict scientific standards to determine which reading studies to review, using the methods that reflected the high standards adhered to in medical (and psychological) studies to test the efficacy of new treatments and medications. One critically important standard the panel adopted was to focus on experimental investigations; these are research studies specifically designed to show cause and effect—that any change in reading performance was causally related to a particular reading intervention. Experimental studies are the only kinds of studies that can confidently claim, for example, that the use of a specific reading program is responsible for an increase in reading scores. Such standards have not generally been used in evaluating reading research or in selecting reading programs.

Adhering to these criteria, the NRP was able to identify the most effective teaching methods, and then work to disseminate the findings and make them accessible to parents and teachers. In April 2000, after 2 years of work, the NRP issued its report: *Report of the National Reading Panel—Teaching Children to Read: An Evidence-Based Assessment of the Scientific Research Literature on Reading and Its Implications for Reading Instruction.* The major findings of the NRP report indicate that in order to read all children must be taught five essential elements:

1. Phonemic awareness
2. Phonics
3. Reading fluency
4. Vocabulary
5. Strategies for reading comprehension (National Institute of Child Health and Human Development, 2000)

And these must be taught by knowledgeable teachers.

In order to read all children must be taught five essential elements: phonemic awareness, phonics, reading fluency, vocabulary, and strategies for reading comprehension.

As we discuss below, these five critical components emerged from multiple scientific studies of reading and reading instruction; they also make sense in terms of what we know about the reading code.

READING REFLECTS LANGUAGE

Why do the lines and squiggles on a page have any meaning at all? There is now a strong consensus among investigators in the field that reading reflects language ability and that the central problem of struggling readers reflects a deficit within the language system. This evidence begins with the recognition, as noted above, that spoken language is instinctive, built into our genes and hardwired in our brains. For a person to read, the abstract lines and circles on the page that we call letters must link to something that already has inherent meaning—the sounds of spoken language.

For the object of the reader's attention (print) to gain entry into the language module, a truly extraordinary transformation must occur. The reader must somehow convert the print on the page into a linguistic code—the phonetic code, the only code recognized and accepted by the language system. . . . Unless the reader-to-be can convert the printed characters on the page into the phonetic code, these letters remain just a bunch of lines and circles totally devoid of meaning. . . . The written symbols have no meaning of their own but, rather, stand as surrogates for speech or, to be more exact, for the sounds of speech. (Shaywitz, 2003, p. 50)

To break the code, the first step a beginning reader must take involves spoken language—he must discover that spoken words have parts; he must appreciate that the word he hears comes apart into smaller pieces of sound. For example, a child becomes aware that the spoken word *man* is composed of three sounds—mmmm aaaa nnnn—or that if you take the *t* sound away from the spoken word *steak* the word remaining is *sake*. (These smallest sounds of language are called *phonemes*.)

To break the code, the first step a beginning reader must take involves spoken language—he must discover that spoken words have parts; he must appreciate that the word he hears comes apart into smaller pieces of sound.

The ability to notice, identify, and manipulate these bits of language is called *phonemic awareness* and represents one of the very first steps a child takes in learning to read. For example, in beginning reading children must acquire the ability to pull apart (segment) and to push together (blend) the individual sounds in a word. Thus, to read the word *bat* a child transforms each of the letters into the sound it represents—b aaaa t—and then blends the sounds together to pronounce the word *bat*.

There is now highly reliable, converging scientific evidence that problems in discriminating the sounds of spoken language are at the very heart of reading difficulties. Results from large and well-studied populations with reading disabilities confirm that there is an extremely strong correlation between a weakness in phonology (accessing the sounds of spoken language) and reading disability in young school-age children and adolescents. The knowledge that a spoken language skill, phonemic awareness, provides the foundation for reading is important for several reasons:

- It sheds light on the nature of the reading process
- It emphasizes the importance of assessing and teaching this critical skill
- It provides an approach to helping recognize incipient reading problems at the earliest time—perhaps even before a child is expected to read

Once a child is able to focus on the individual sounds in spoken language, she can relate the printed letters on the page to these sounds; in other words, she can now begin to link the abstract lines and circles to something that has inherent meaning, the sounds of spoken language. Learning how the different letters and letter combinations link to different sounds is called *phonics*—a critical and sometimes misunderstood element of learning to read. Given that there are 44 phonemes in the English language and only 26 letters, it is apparent that there are many permutations and combinations; learning the different letter-sound linkages is a complex and demanding process.

Knowledge of phonics is increasingly important as a child matures and comes to read more and more complicated texts with many new and unusual words. After third grade, a child may encounter as many as 10,000 new words a year and come across these words only rarely, less than 10 times during the year. How is a child to know how to pronounce these unfamiliar words? At this stage, simply memorizing words won't work—there are just too many words, and since many occur only occasionally, the child will be unlikely to remember them. Here's where knowledge of phonics is critical. Phonics provides the only strategy that allows a child to sound out and read words she has never before encountered. Analyses adhering to the strict criteria adopted by the NRP found evidence that systematic phonics instruction is more effective in helping children learn to read than approaches using either no phonics or nonsystematic phonics.

Phonics provides the only strategy that allows a child to sound out and read words she has never before encountered.

The evidence also showed that it is best to introduce phonics instruction early on—the earlier the better. And so the most effective beginning reading programs teach children

- about the sounds of spoken words;
- how to segment and blend these sounds;
- how to recognize the shapes of the letters of the alphabet;
- how individual letters and letter groups are linked to specific sounds; and
- how to use this letter-sound knowledge to spell words.

The Five S keys to unlock the doors to reading are

1. sounds of spoken words;
2. segmenting and blending spoken sounds;
3. shapes of letters of the alphabet;
4. sounds of letters; and
5. spelling according to the sounds of the letters.

In an effective reading program, children are provided with many opportunities to practice the letter-sound linkages they have learned; they do so by reading stories containing words with these same letter-sounds. This means that the components of a program are aligned with one another; for example, the provision of so-called decodable booklets for practice are aligned with the specific letter-sound linkages the child is being taught. In many programs, children are taught specific letter-sound correspondences in the first part of a lesson and then later in the period have an opportunity to practice reading stories. Children learn best when these stories contain words with the very same letter-sound linkages so that they can immediately apply the lessons they have just been taught. Surprisingly, and unfortunately, in many classrooms, stories read for practice have little or no relation to the phonics lessons just taught. The brain learns by practice, and the use of decodable booklets provides the repeated practice necessary to build the automatic systems in the word form region of the brain (see A New Level of Evidence on page 22) that are necessary for fluent reading.

Surprisingly, and unfortunately, in many classrooms, stories read for practice have little or no relation to the phonics lessons just taught.

In addition to *what* is taught, the NRP found that *how* reading is taught matters. According to the evidence, reading instruction is most effective when it is taught comprehensively, systematically, and explicitly.

It is inadequate to present the foundational skills of phonemic awareness and phonics incidentally, casually, or in fragments. Children do not learn how letters represent sounds by osmosis; it must be taught explicitly.

Children do not learn how letters represent sounds by osmosis; it must be taught explicitly.

Once a child has mastered these foundational skills, it is critical that he or she be taught how to read words fluently, that is, to read words accurately, rapidly, and with good expression. The NRP examined the evidence for two different methods for building reading fluency. In one, a teacher (or peer) models reading a passage aloud, and the student then reads the passage aloud, with the teacher (or peer) providing feedback and guidance to help correct any mispronunciations. This process is repeated as the student rereads the passage, corrects his oral reading, and progressively reads more and more words fluently. The other approach, based on the belief that reading is learned through reading, encourages the child to read silently by himself for various periods of time. Which approach is more effective? The NRP found good evidence that repeated oral reading with feedback and guidance results in significant improvements in reading fluency. In contrast, the NRP reported that there was insufficient evidence that simply telling a child to go off and read silently to himself results in improved fluency. While it is clear that there is a relationship between the amount of reading and reading skill, that is, the best readers read the most while poor readers read the least, this finding is based on a correlation. It is important to keep in mind that correlation does not imply causation. Thus, the question remains, Does more silent reading lead to better readers, or do better readers tend to choose to read more? Reading should always be encouraged; however, it is important to be aware that there is insufficient evidence that simply telling a child, particularly a struggling reader, to read more will result in a more fluent reader. At the same time, there is strong evidence that repeated oral reading with feedback and guidance improves reading fluency.

There was insufficient evidence that simply telling a child to go off and read silently to himself results in improved fluency.

An evidence-based, systematic phonics approach is in contrast to a so-called whole language approach, which is steeped in the belief, now disproven, that written language is natural and that surrounding a child with books will eventually lead that child to learn how to read those books. In the whole language approach, children are taught to guess what a word is—by looking at pictures or by using the context around a word—rather than first trying to sound it out. Phonics may be taught, but the letter-sound linkages are not taught in a preplanned or systematic way; often some, but not all, of these linkages are taught, and vowels are often overlooked. Children do not learn how to systematically analyze a word by transforming each letter or letter group into the sounds they represent and then blending the sounds together to pronounce the word. While the belief in the naturalness of reading is appealing, the evidence does not support it. Reading instruction based on this unscientific method fails to prepare a child to read the many new and complex words she will encounter as she progresses in school and in life.

WHAT CAN PARENTS DO?

Using evidence-based methods, it is possible to teach just about every child to read (see appendix A). As a parent, you can play an important role in ensuring that your child's reading program is based on scientifically supported methods that have proven efficacy. What can you do? Ask these questions: Is my child's reading program based on scientifically proven methods? Was this method reviewed and found to be effective by the

NRP and subsequent evaluations by the federal government (NIFL.gov)? Follow up by asking, Is there evidence of its effectiveness, for example, evidence reported in a scientific journal that is reviewed by scientific peers?

Note that stories in a magazine or newsletter or on the web do not meet the standard of scientific evidence.

Next, you can inquire about specific aspects of the reading program. Many programs now incorporate some phonics instruction; it is important to ensure that your child's reading instruction not only includes phonics instruction but also that it is taught using the most effective methods. And so you can inquire,

- Is phonics taught explicitly in a preplanned, systematic, comprehensive way rather than a more casual, "by the way" approach?
- How are the children taught to approach an unknown word? The most effective programs teach children how to analyze and sound out an unfamiliar word, in contrast to less effective ones where children are taught to guess from pictures or the surrounding context.
- Does the program include all the critical elements of an effective reading program that systematically and explicitly includes learning how to recognize the sounds of spoken words, figuring out how to segment and blend these sounds, learning to recognize the shapes of the letters of the alphabet, understanding how individual letters and letter groups are linked to specific sounds, and using this letter-sound knowledge to spell words?
- Is your child provided with opportunities to apply her newly learned skills to practice reading, to spell words, to learn new vocabulary words and concepts, to develop reading comprehension strategies, and to write her own stories?

To assure that reading instruction is matched to your child's individual needs, his reading skills should be assessed in an ongoing way throughout the academic year and not only at the end of the school year. An excellent resource that provides clear information to parents on these issues is *Parenting the Struggling Reader* by Susan L. Hall and Louisa C. Moats.

The new science of reading has not only provided highly reliable information about teaching reading, but has also debunked many myths about reading. One of the most dangerous and widely held of these misconceptions is the belief that reading problems are only transient, that they represent a developmental delay and will be outgrown.

One of the most dangerous and widely held of these misconceptions is the belief that reading problems are only transient, that they represent a developmental delay and will be outgrown.

Longitudinal studies such as the Connecticut Longitudinal Study of Learning, which has individually tested children and monitored their reading progress from kindergarten through high school, indicate that reading difficulties represent a persistent, chronic condition; they are not transient, nor are they a "developmental lag" (Figure 2.1). The Connecticut Longitudinal Study demonstrates that, over time, reading performance improves in both good readers (upper curve) and poor readers (lower curve). However, the gap

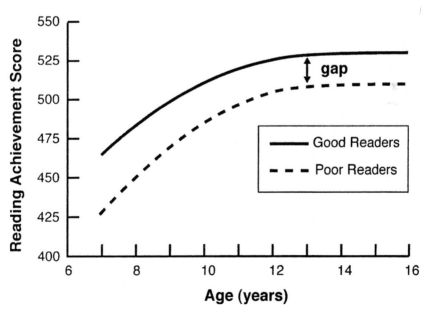

Figure 2.1.   Reading Achievement Scores (Francis, Shaywitz, Steubing, Shaywitz, & Fletcher, 1994).

between the two groups remains. While children do not outgrow reading difficulties, using the evidence-based interventions now available can result in improved reading in virtually all children.

A NEW LEVEL OF EVIDENCE: BRAIN SYSTEMS FOR READING

Parents and educators now look to the scientific evidence for guidance and direction in teaching reading. Today, exciting studies observing the brain as a child reads provide a new level of evidence. Although the work is relatively new, great progress has already been made in identifying the neural systems for reading in good readers and in identifying a functional disruption in these systems in struggling readers. We now have a greater understanding of the neural mechanisms associated with the development of skilled (fluent) reading. Perhaps most importantly, highly rigorous, well-designed scientific studies incorporating sophisticated brain imaging technology are now being used to help determine the most effective way to teach reading to beginning readers and which interventions are most effective in helping disabled readers not only learn to decode the printed word but to become fluent, skilled readers.

NEUROBIOLOGICAL INFLUENCES

Within the last decade or so, the dream of scientists, educators, and struggling readers has come true. It is now possible to "see" the brain at work. Even though the brain is protected by the hard skull, newer advances in technology make it possible to view the working brain as it attempts to read. Functional brain imaging, primarily functional magnetic resonance imaging (fMRI), uses the same scanner employed in MRI studies commonly used for assessing headaches or knee ligament injuries, but with the addition of more sophisticated software and hardware that make it possible to "see" which brain systems are activated as a child performs reading or reading-related tasks.

Using functional brain imaging, scientists around the world have discovered how the brain functions in reading and identified a glitch in the neural circuitry for reading in children and adults who struggle to read.

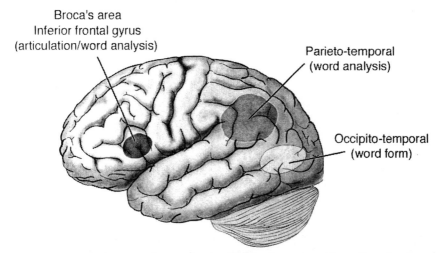

Figure 2.2.   Neural Systems for Reading in Children (Reproduced from Shaywitz, 2003, With Permission).

We, and other investigators, have localized three brain regions involved in reading; all are located on the left side of the brain: one area in front of the brain and two located in the back of the brain (see Figure 2.2).

Converging evidence indicates that in struggling readers there is underactivation of the two systems in the back of the brain, including the important area responsible for word formation (word form region) associated with skilled or fluent reading (see Figure 2.3). When asked to rhyme nonsense words, nonimpaired readers (left image) activate three neural systems for reading, one in the front of the brain and two in the back of the brain. In contrast, struggling readers underactivate the reading systems in the back of the brain and overactivate the system in the front of the brain. Importantly, the observation of this same pattern of underactivation, in both children and adults who are struggling readers, supports the view that reading difficulties and the neural disruption persist. They do not go away as children mature. Because both the neural deficit and its associated reading deficit persist, it is urgent that we identify reading difficulties as early as possible and begin to teach these children using effective reading programs to turn around a potentially serious and lasting reading and learning problem.

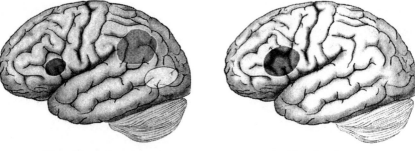

Nonimpaired   **Dyslexic**

Figure 2.3.   Disruption of Posterior Reading Systems (Reproduced from Shaywitz, 2003, With Permission).

Because both the neural deficit and its associated reading deficit persist, it is urgent that we identify reading difficulties as early as possible and begin to teach these children using effective reading programs to turn around a potentially serious and lasting reading and learning problem.

HOW CAN STRUGGLING READERS LEARN TO READ?

Now that we have this evidence of a disruption in the reading pathways, we have a neurobiological target for reading interventions. We examined the hypothesis that if we use an evidence-based, phonologically mediated reading intervention, we would improve reading accuracy and fluency and development of the fast-paced word form systems that are found in skilled readers. The experimental intervention provided struggling second- and third-grade readers with 50 minutes of daily, individual tutoring that was systematic and explicit, and that focused on helping children understand the alphabetic principle (how letters and combinations of letters represent the sounds of speech). Children received 8 months (105 hours) of this intervention over the school year. Immediately after the year-long intervention, children taught with the experimental intervention had made significant gains in reading fluency and demonstrated increased activation in left brain regions. One year after the experimental intervention had ended, these children were reading accurately and fluently and were activating all three left-sided brain regions used by good readers: one in the front and two in the back of the brain, including the word form region. This data indicates that the type of teaching matters and that use of an evidence-based reading intervention, as we have described, can facilitate the development of those fast-paced neural systems that underlie skilled reading. In summary, this data demonstrates that an intensive evidence-based (phonologic) reading intervention brings about significant and durable changes in brain organization resulting in brain activation patterns that resemble those of typical readers in the appearance of the left word form area and improvement in reading fluency.

This data has important implications for teaching children to read: The provision of an evidence-based reading intervention at an early age improves reading fluency and facilitates the development of those neural systems underlying skilled reading. Thus, there is for the first time a new level of evidence, based on functional imaging studies of the brain at work, that supports the findings of work conducted by the NRP.

PARENTS CAN HELP IDENTIFY READING PROBLEMS

Schools are not generally doing as good a job as they could to identify struggling readers. Currently, in the United States, most children with a reading problem are not identified until third grade—or later. To receive help, to gain the benefits of the effective, evidence-based reading interventions, children must first be identified as having a reading problem. Here, parents can play an active and important role in helping to identify reading problems early. Contemporary reading research, demonstrating the importance of language, and particularly, the difficulties struggling readers experience in discriminating (or perceiving) the differences in the sounds of spoken language, has now provided a new and powerful understanding of how such a weakness is expressed in a child's speaking and reading. An informed and observant parent, aware of these clues, can observe her child and help detect signs of a reading difficulty at an early stage.

See the tips for parents at the end of this chapter for a list of the most important clues to help detect a reading problem. As you will see, they involve both spoken and written language. If your child manifests these problems, the next step is for you to determine how many there are and how frequently they occur. If there are only a very few clues or if they occur only rarely, you need not be concerned. Clues are important if they form a persistent pattern—there are several of them and they occur over a period of time. If this characterizes your child, you must take steps to get help. As described in other chapters of this book, you can begin by speaking to your child's classroom teacher or school principal. Don't wait. Under no circumstances should you be talked into waiting.

> Change has been difficult to say the least. I would do this again. However, I would not wait until the end of second grade. Our son should have been screened in the 1st year of kindergarten. As an elementary education teacher, I should have known about phonological awareness. I should have understood about systematic phonics instruction. I didn't and neither did his teachers. I still hurt over Matt's struggle. So much failure could have been prevented.

Keep in mind that reading problems are not outgrown and that reading interventions are most effective when they are provided early on. Even if his teachers are unaware that your child is having a reading problem, often a child will know. Even a 6- or 7-year-old is capable of recognizing that reading is not going well.

Under no circumstances should you be talked into waiting. . . . Keep in mind that reading problems are not outgrown and that reading interventions are most effective when they are provided early on.

In summary, we are now in an era of evidence-based reading instruction. Objective scientific evidence has replaced reliance on philosophy or opinion. This evidence is supported by brain-imaging studies and by a rigorous scientific review of the literature by the NRP. Children enter school eager to learn to read. We cannot disappoint them by teaching them with unproven programs, because we now have the scientific knowledge to ensure that each child becomes a reader. Awareness of the new scientific knowledge of reading should empower both parents and educators to insist that reading programs used in their child's/student's schools reflect what is known about the science of reading and about effective reading instruction.

TIPS FOR PARENTS

Clues to a Reading Problem

Kindergarten and First Grade

- Failure to understand that words come apart; for example, that batboy can be pulled apart into bat and boy and, later on, that the word *bat* can be broken down still further and sounded out as: *b aaaa t*
- Inability to learn to associate letters with sounds; for example, being unable to connect the letter *b* with the *b* sound
- Reading errors that show no connection to the sounds of the letters; for example, the word *big* is read as *goat*
- The inability to read common, one-syllable words or to sound out even the simplest of words; for example, *dog*, *cat*, *hop*, *nap*
- Complaints about how hard reading is; running and hiding when it is time to read
- A history of reading problems in parents or siblings

From Second Grade On

Problems in Speaking
- Mispronunciation of long, unfamiliar, or complicated words; the fracturing of words—leaving out parts of words or confusing the order of the parts of words, for example, *aluminum* becomes *amulium*
- Speech that is not fluent—pausing or hesitating often when speaking, lots of um's during speech, no glibness
- The use of imprecise language—vague references to stuff or things instead of the proper name of an object
- Not being able to find the exact word—confusing words that sound alike, like saying *tornado* instead of *volcano*, substituting *lotion* for *ocean*, or *humanity* for *humidity*
- The need of time to summon an oral response; the inability to come up with a verbal response quickly when questioned
- Difficulty in remembering isolated pieces of verbal information—trouble remembering dates, names, telephone numbers, random lists; difficulty with rote memory, remembering concepts better than isolated facts

Problems in Reading
- Very slow progress in acquiring reading skills
- The lack of a strategy to read new words
- Trouble reading unknown (new, unfamiliar) words that must be sounded out; making wild stabs or guesses at reading a word; failure to systematically sound out words
- The inability to read small function words, for example, *that, an, in*
- Stumbling on reading multisyllable words; the failure to come close to sounding out the full word
- Omitting parts of words when reading; failure to decode parts within a word, as if someone had chewed a hole in the middle of the word, for example, *convertible* read as *conible*
- A terrific fear of reading out loud; the avoidance of oral reading
- Oral reading full of substitutions, omissions, and mispronunciations
- Oral reading that is choppy and labored, not smooth or fluent
- Oral reading that lacks inflection, and sounds like the reading of a foreign language
- A reliance on context to discern the meaning of what is read
- A better ability to understand words in context than to read isolated single words
- Disproportionately poor performance on multiple choice tests
- The inability to finish tests on time
- The substitution of words with the same meaning for words in the text he can't pronounce, for example, *car* for *automobile*
- Disastrous spelling; often spelled words don't resemble true spelling; strange spellings may be missed by spellcheck
- Trouble reading mathematics word problems
- Reading that is very slow and tiring
- Homework that never seems to end; parents who are often recruited as readers
- Messy handwriting despite what may be an excellent facility at word processing—nimble fingers
- Extreme difficulty learning foreign languages
- Lack of enjoyment in reading, the avoidance of reading books or even a sentence

- The avoidance of reading for pleasure, which seems too exhausting
- Reading whose accuracy improves over time, though it continues to lack fluency and is laborious
- Lowered self-esteem; pain that is not always visible to others
- A history of reading, spelling, and foreign language problems in family members (Shaywitz, 2003)

3

I Could Not Read Until I Was 30 Years Old

Diane Badgley Lyon

Diane Badgley Lyon is a national authority on parent involvement and helps families across the nation to advocate for their children's education. Ironically, she learned these skills the hard way—she has dyslexia and graduated from high school unable to read. When her son began to exhibit the same problem, she swung into action. This chapter describes Diane's struggles and how she learned to use parent power to change the education of her son and all children who are struggling to learn to read. The tips at the end of the chapter will help you do the same.

My name is Diane Badgley Lyon, and I have dyslexia. To those who might find the word *dyslexia* vague and confusing, it is very clear to me. As a young girl entering the fourth grade, I literally could not read even a simple children's book. I did not learn to read until I was 30 years old and only then with extensive and intensive scientifically based intervention. Even today at 45, I struggle when reading. I have difficulty with multisyllabic words, and my reading is slow and labored. My spelling is horrendous and has been a great embarrassment on many occasions.

Even today at 45, I struggle when reading. I have difficulty with multisyllabic words, and my reading is slow and labored.

While I was growing up, my reading difficulties made life miserable. However, it did not start out that way. I can recall how excited I was when entering the first grade. I had always envied my older brothers and sisters as they went off to school each day. When my time came to enter the first grade, I was excited, to say the least. The next morning I left my house, lunch pail at my side and a faded red backpack slung over my shoulder. I was ready for this new adventure, and I was determined to be the smartest student in the class.

Unfortunately, by the end of the first grade, something was not right. I recall watching and listening to my classmates as they read their books, sounding out each word when the teacher asked. In contrast, I had no idea what the sounds were, much less the ability to link sounds to the letters of the alphabet. In the second grade, I was in the same boat. My difficulties became much more noticeable to the teacher and to my fellow students. I had always thought I was pretty smart, but when I read, I felt stupid. My classmates seemed to think so, too. Am I really this dumb? I began to ask myself.

I had always thought I was pretty smart, but when I read, I felt stupid. My classmates seemed to think so, too. Am I really this dumb? I began to ask myself.

By the end of third grade, I gave up trying to read altogether. My teachers and my parents blamed my difficulties on not trying hard enough. And they were right. Three years of feeling stupid was enough for me, and I retreated into my own world. I hated school, and it affected everything in my life.

I entered high school—pretty amazing, considering I still could not read. At that time, I wanted so much to do what readers do. I wanted to sit under a tree and read a poem, to read the lyrics of songs I loved, to read the credits on the screen at the movie theater, and I wanted to write notes to my girlfriends without making horrible spelling errors. I wanted my parents to be proud of me. And I wanted this so much that I found the courage to ask my 10th-grade teachers and the school counselor to teach me to read. To be quite honest, I begged them.

My teachers were baffled. They had no idea how to teach me to read, and they said so. Therefore, I was placed in special education classes for the remainder of that year, all the next year, and the year after that. After four years, I graduated from high school illiterate.

I found the courage to ask my 10th-grade teachers and the school counselor to teach me to read. To be quite honest, I begged them.

So how did a complete nonreader graduate from high school? I can only guess that they felt sorry for me. But what was clear to my parents, high school diploma or not, was that my future was limited. They knew college was out of the question. They knew it would be a hard sell for me to apply for a job and not be able to fill out the application. But they did the best they could in advising me in what I should do: Get married to someone with a good job and a good future. And I followed their advice. Marriage did not require reading. I could cook, I could clean, and I could make our home comfortable. But with all that, I felt incomplete, stupid, and angry. My life, even outside the classroom, was painful.

What was clear to my parents, high school diploma or not, was that my future was limited. . . . But they did the best they could in advising me in what I should do: Get married to someone with a good job and a good future.

With marriage there came two wonderful children. My daughter Jodie learned to read very easily and flourished in school. But Kyle, my son, did not. In fact, at the end of the first grade Kyle was an emotional wreck and so was I, as I knew what lay ahead for him. Kyle has dyslexia. As Yogi Berra said, "Déjà vu all over again."

I knew Kyle was going to struggle with reading as early as preschool. He could not remember the names of letters in the alphabet; he could not get the nursery rhymes right. In kindergarten he literally had no idea that particular sounds went with particular letters, and he still could not name all the letters consistently. At the same time, he could engage in vibrant conversations with me and his father, his teacher, and his friends. He could solve any problem that he could get his hands on and loved to be read to as long as we could also talk about the stories.

But even knowing this, I still thought Kyle would be able to "catch on" to reading. I could not believe that my child would have to feel the pain that I did as a nonreader. Life was not that unfair.

But I was wrong. In the beginning of 1st grade, he literally hid under his desk when asked to read. By the end of the first grade, he was throwing the desk. His teachers said they had no idea how to teach Kyle to read. They said they had never seen a child who had so much difficulty with sounds and letters. But they also blamed his reading failure on his behavior and suggested another school.

I still thought Kyle would be able to "catch on" to reading. I could not believe that my child would have to feel the pain that I did as a nonreader. Life was not that unfair.

By the third grade, Kyle was a mess and so was I. Looking into the eyes of my 8-year-old and seeing such pain when he could not read crushed me. I watched him become frustrated and angry because of something he had no control over, and it devastated me. I also remembered my pain and anger growing up when people, schools, and teachers shunned me because I could not read. And once again in Kyle's case, I was told that nothing could be done. I was told that teachers had far too much to do than teach a third grader the simple reading basics. They said, you can't teach a child with such behavior problems.

Kyle's spirit and love for life crumbled before my eyes. I was furious and I knew that I had to do something. I decided to homeschool Kyle for his fourth-grade year. Let the blind lead the blind, I thought. I was mortified that I would not be able to teach him anything without reading myself. When so little could be done inside the school as well as inside the home, I stepped outside and looked to the community. I happened to strike up a conversation with another mom at a soccer game and learned that her son also struggled with reading. The good news was that she had found a reading specialist in town who was doing wonders for her son, and she gave me her number.

Getting that number changed Kyle's life and changed mine as well. I soon discovered that the reading specialist knew how kids learned to read and why some have severe difficulties doing so. Her teaching was based on the most recent scientific research on dyslexia and how to make written language clear to people like Kyle and me. She worked with Kyle 2 hours a day in her home for the entire year. At the end of his fourth-grade year, Kyle had made a complete turnaround. He had learned to read, although he certainly struggled with complicated words and text. But even these struggles were becoming less frequent.

As a Mom, my heart soared when I saw my young 9-year-old smile and feel good about himself for the first time in years. His confidence blossomed and his anger went by the wayside. He was on his way. This start, however, did not guarantee a grand finale. More work would be needed. I learned that any complex skill that is being developed must be nurtured through continued effective teaching. Reading skills must build upon one another, and a teacher must know how best to accomplish this. If newly developed skills are not reinforced and built upon, failure will set in.

When Kyle returned to school in the fifth grade, he could read well enough to keep up, although just barely. I knew it was critical to make sure his school understood his specific difficulties and made accommodations to address his needs. I quickly learned that his teachers needed up-to-date information about teaching students with dyslexia. Before long, I had piles of articles, lists of lectures, and contacts for professional development seminars and workshops.

I quickly learned that his teachers needed up-to-date information about teaching students with dyslexia. Before long, I had piles of articles, lists of lectures, and contacts for professional development seminars and workshops.

To be sure, helping Kyle's school and his teachers understand his difficulties and the need to modify teaching practices to ensure his progress met with strong resistance. I wanted Kyle's school to look at new ways of teaching; initially they refused to listen. But it had to be done, and I succeeded.

Kyle is now a sophomore at Indiana University, hoping one day to become an attorney. He continues to read slowly and with some errors. But he knows where to seek out help and he knows how to think. Most of all he knows himself and has realized he is one smart cookie who can work hard and achieve.

How about Mom? Watching Kyle grow from a nonreader to a student who could read his assignments and do quite well gave me hope and confidence. Because of Kyle's courage and progress, I asked for and received the same interventions from Kyle's tutor that had helped him so much. I was afraid of admitting that at my age I still could not read. I was also afraid of failing. But I was really motivated and pushed ahead. After 3 months reading began to make sense. I learned that our language is made up of individual sounds and that those sounds connect to letters. I learned how to apply what are called *decoding strategies* to words I did not know. I learned that I could use my strong vocabulary to understand what I was reading. I learned that the more I practiced reading, the faster I was able to read. I learned that reading can open up entirely new worlds.

And, most importantly, I came to realize that no one should have to live with the struggles Kyle and I shared. It dawned on me that other kids and parents need not experience our pain, frustration, and anger. I knew that I had to communicate to others about how it was possible to make sure all our kids can read.

You have heard our stories. Now let me share what worked to bring about changes as many in our state, school district, and schools began to listen and develop instructional programs based on the best science to help all kids learn to read. Hopefully you will find some of the lessons we learned and the strategies and recommendations that emerged to be useful to you.

TIPS FOR PARENTS

1. Learn how to mobilize your community
   - Identify local and county leaders. Know who they are and how to reach them. Organize and build relationships with them. Many of these leaders have someone in their families with a reading problem. Capture their interest this way.
   - Go to the Lions Club, other civic organizations, and churches and present your case. These are good training grounds for testifying at the state level.

- Learn the difference between those with real power and those who are surrogates for those in power. Don't settle for surrogates without power. Ask who has the ability to make decisions.
- Go to the wealthiest people in the community. Share your story and how it's affected you, your life, and your work. Ask for support and wisdom, not money.
- Don't assume leaders know the issue and how it affects them.

2. Stay focused
   - Consciously identify who you want to target, what you want to accomplish, and how you are going to achieve it. List important players—titles of people you need to know but don't.
   - Don't be emotional. Be thoughtful about what system can be built. Don't set out to destroy the current system.
   - Have a prepared list of questions—where do you find data about your school, state, and so forth?
   - Your actions will label you as wise, thoughtful, or irrational. Others will partner with you if they can predict your behavior.
   - Learn how to be personally effective.
   - Fight back resentment; act after you've had time to reflect.
   - Repeat like a mantra whatever gives you courage.
   - Be assertive, not aggressive and courageous, not angry.
   - Use a daily or weekly plan with specifics, and decide how you will measure success.
   - Ask questions, lots of questions.

3. Work with your school
   - Learn how to work with educators.
   - Know your school board, union leaders, and board attorney. Figure out who in the community can put pressure on the school board and ask, "If you just wrote this letter . . ."
   - Know the superintendent and curriculum developer. Ask them to teach you about the budget and where you can find data and articles.
   - Don't assume leaders know the issue and how it affects them.
   - Write to the school board and ask for a list of all the reading programs being used in the schools and how the programs were chosen. They should tell you they were based on scientific evidence about reading instruction. Ask how teachers are being trained to use these

materials and scientifically based reading instructional methods and if they are putting money in the budget for this purpose.

- Ask your child's teacher to give you the results of an evaluation of your child's reading ability in each of the five areas—phonemic awareness, phonics, fluency, vocabulary, and comprehension. Then ask how these results are being used to map out a program in areas where your child is having trouble.

- Listen to your child and note in a diary or journal what he or she is trying to tell you. This will be your barometer of what's happening in school. Generally, elementary school children love school and wake up in the morning and can't wait to learn and read. Kids who struggle in class struggle to get out of bed. That should be a red flag that something is wrong.

- Don't hesitate to schedule monthly visits to your child's classroom, but be sure to send the teacher a note that you are doing this. These visits will clarify what is going on, confirm that appropriate instruction is being used, and allow you to check on your child's progress.

- If these visits make your child feel uncomfortable, you might want to volunteer to help out in the classroom and recruit other mothers to do the same so you won't be the only one. Then everyone wins—the teacher gets help, you have a chance to see firsthand how your child is doing, and you can develop a relationship with the teacher so you can go to him or her with questions and suggestions.

4. Enlist the help of your family

- Include all family members in a family literacy plan. Create and share both short-term and long-term reading goals. Make everyone part of the solution, and celebrate when the goals have been reached.

- Order library cards, and give them as gifts. Order a subscription to a magazine your child is interested in, and create a reading hour. Turn that reading hour into a game with your child counting the number of pages she can read each day. Make a chart so they can check their own progress.

- Give your child a throwaway camera and suggest they make their own book with the pictures—their dog, best friend, what they want to be when they grow up, and so forth. They can dictate the story and you can write or type it for them. This could become a favorite book.

5. Take it personally
   - Picture yourself as a leader. Don't be a whining mother.
   - Reading failure is identified deep within a person. That's why it's so important.
   - If your employer gives you a hard time, explain that your child has a reading problem and how important a monthly visit to the school is. Make your boss part of the solution. Given how many children are having reading problems, employers may have people in their own families who are struggling to learn.
   - Fill yourself with love, take a deep breath, and with great enthusiasm tell your child that there is a lot of work to be done if they want to learn to read. Talk to your child about his or her struggles with reading. They know all is not well, and ignoring the problem makes it something too awful to talk about. This focuses on the problem and solution. The alternative is to have your child feel that they are dumb. Your child is part of his or her journey toward literacy.
   - Take your child to a coffee shop for a cup of hot chocolate, and take their journal with you. Tell them this is what you see regarding their reading struggle. Make it real because it is, and tell them it's not their fault. Tell him or her it's going to be like climbing a mountain. He or she is the climber, and you, his family and teachers, are walking sticks there for support during the the journey.

4

A Parent's Journey

Teresa Ankney

This chapter gives you the perspective of many parents who have worked hard to help change their children's schools. The mother of two dyslexic sons, Teresa founded and currently serves as the head of the Friendship School in Eldersburg, Maryland, a parent cooperative school to serve the needs of dyslexic children. Read on for specific advice about what a parent can do individually and how a group of parents can make a difference.

VOICES

The first thing a parent or guardian has to do on the journey toward getting the assistance a child needs to learn how to read is to find a way to sort through the voices. Anyone with a child who has struggled to learn to read knows the voices—those of the teachers and administrators who may be telling you that your child is doing fine and those of the teachers and administrators who are telling you that your child has a "problem." There will also be the voices of family and friends who offer countless suggestions and opinions based on personal experience with their children or their own educational experience. Authors of books and articles, website information, doctors, coworkers, neighbors—it seems that opinions are everywhere. And there are the voices of you and your spouse; perhaps you share a similar perspective, or perhaps you differ in opinion. No matter what the case, you will first have to navigate the waters of an endless sea

of voices when trying to make sense out of why your child is struggling
to learn to read. Some of the most common reasons for reading struggles
you often hear are,

What problem; there is no problem.
Wait until after the holidays; that is when reading just kicks in.
You must not be reading books to your child at night.
The problem is that you are divorced.
The problem is that you do not spend enough time with your child.
The problem is that you are poor.
The problem is an attention issue.
The problem must be a vision or hearing difficulty.
The problem is that your child is just developmentally delayed.
The problem is that your child is just distractible.
The problem is at home.
The problem is that you are not a good parent.

No matter what the voices say, at some point you have to stop the noise
and listen to your own inner voice of reason telling you that something
may be wrong here. But what could be sabotaging your child's learning?
How do you know what to do next to find a solution?

The first step to help your child learn to read is to stop denying and to
find facts. Is this a problem that your child has, or is it a problem caused
by the way he or she is being taught to read?

Let your first step forward be turning a deaf ear to the voices, discov-
ering the facts, and figuring out how to best help your child. Always remember that no matter what, regardless of whether you live in a large city
or a small town, if you are a single parent or have a supportive spouse, if
you are rich or poor, nearly all children can be taught to read.

Everyone told me I was being overprotective and that my son Jamie
would eventually learn. But I knew he was different, suffering and feeling
dumb. I couldn't let that continue.

This is hard work, and real accountability; it takes everyone looking,
asking, and adjusting. So if what you see is not working, go back and reassess the situation. Just realize that the school may not in truth have the
services and program you are looking for, so you will have to get creative.
It will be the knowledgeable consumers of education who will set the

trend. Remember, cars at one point did not have air bags. People used to be able to smoke on planes. Things change, and you can be there to help pave the way. Your child's future depends on it. The parents who think they can just drop their children off at the school door and go on to work are ill informed regarding the realties of educational practice today.

The experience of parenting your child through the school years is like driving a car. It is important to stay alert, be defensive, and stay out of the way once things are in place. But when you think things may be starting to slip, go back in for a tune-up.

CHANGE YOUR PLAN: FLEXIBILITY AND ACCOUNTABILITY

Remember that you have to give things time to work. Yet that does not mean waiting until the end of the year to look up and see if your child has made meaningful progress or not. Reassess the situation during every marking period. Ask to see any benchmark tests. You should not wait for three years to retest to see if progress is being made and to see if your child's achievement gap is closing. Have yearly assessments done. You will have to learn to take the bad with the good. Remember the average student will make 1 year's growth in a year. So just make sure that the school is not piling new information on a weak foundation. Think of the basics. Is there a sound foundation being systematically built in reading before the next skill is presented? If your child has poor phonemic awareness, for example, this is not the time to be worrying about poor vocabulary and comprehension.

It is important to build reading skills systematically and sequentially. First, get phonemic awareness intact, next phonics skills, then fluency and vocabulary, and then comprehension. Follow the guidelines of the National Institute of Child Health and Human Development (2000). Do not allow for educational programming that keeps putting the cart before the horse, like focusing on reading comprehension before phonemic awareness. Sound principles of teaching a child to read need to guide the reading program your child is utilizing. What you want to avoid at all costs is to wait and find a reading problem at the end of elementary school. We need to be tackling these issues early, by third grade, so that other subject areas are not compromised as well. Think early intervention, rather than remediation later. Get educationally empowered to make this happen for your child.

IMPORTANT THINGS TO REMEMBER

First, remember that there is great psychological discomfort when the way of doing business changes in any profession. In this case, there is uneasiness on the part of countless teachers who have been teaching reading the same way for years and who now have to change because we now have research-based reading instruction. Dedicated, hard-working teachers and school administrators have to retool and accept that what they were doing for years was leaving some children out of the educational loop. This is a hard realization after years of dedicating one's life to the service of children.

Further, it is difficult to go against the grain of one's education. Departments of education in colleges and universities have been teaching new teachers to use a whole language approach to reading instruction. It is a challenge to get individuals who spent years and countless dollars to achieve their educational degree to question the methods and practices they were taught to follow. Many who teach in colleges and universities that prepare teachers bring the education they learned in the field into their classrooms. Many professors bring their assumptions and worldviews into their teaching rather than scientific evidence of what works. It is equally as challenging for them to abandon some of their worldviews and assumptions about why some children failed to learn. In this way, education reinforces cultural cul-de-sacs of thinking, which reinforce outdated practices of teaching. The current science behind how the brain works is thereby abandoned to outdated, and sometimes harmful, philosophies of how children learn and what they require to stay motivated. In medicine, this is termed malpractice.

Parents also have to deal with their own discomfort. They now understand that their intuition was right and something is wrong. They now may feel frustrated and even guilty that they did not respond sooner to their child's struggles in school. For some parents this may be very painful because they too struggled in school when they were young.

Even when parents become informed, they could be up against an elaborate system that may try and say the parents are wrong and resist change.

The school system may even say it is doing everything in accordance with good research practices. Yet a parent needs to know what to look for, to see if there is truly a fit between what is being said and what is actually being taught. A parent needs to know if the reading materials used to teach really are in alignment with what we know about research in reading.

To move on, we must be willing to face the discomfort and the resistance that may come with change. It takes a great deal of openness and flexibility of thinking to allow for change in practice within education. It means that understanding, not blame, is required to get past the psychological discomfort associated with the retooling of how children are taught to read.

I was so worried that the school might see me as an interfering mother and make it hard for my son. But I learned that if I did my homework and offered to work with my school, the teachers and principal would do the right thing.

We have to understand and be prepared to face people in positions of authority who believe the status quo works and that your child is just not getting it. However, when parents have done their homework and are equipped with the facts about reading instruction, they can speak with equal authority. It is difficult for those who lead to have to change their thinking, because essentially they have to go back to ground zero and retool. Most of us are coming to realize that reading is a fiercely political issue, requiring a new form of educational leadership that is flexible and open to change.

We need to let our school administrators know that we, as parents, are of service. PTA fund-raising is not enough. We can bring the experience of our growing understanding and consumer demands regarding educational practice. We can also help to bring resources to school districts by voting for representatives who will support proven research-based practices and help to ensure the needed funding for their proper implementation. Let your local and state representatives know that we want our tax dollars to go to evidence-based teaching practices that will serve all children. This way, local school administrators will know that if they change with the times, parents will be there to support good practice. Equally, let those administrators know that parents are no longer willing to allow for outdated practices that leave children behind. Vote. It is the way to bring about systemic change.

Third, even if we all woke up one day and everybody was on board, and the teachers were retrained in their sleep, and school administrators realized that most children could be taught to read, a big problem would still exist. Our mentality is reflected in the things we produce and use. So, what about all the textbooks and materials that are not in alignment with sound research-based practices? Here again, parents can be the force behind the use of tax dollars to support the required shift in materials used to teach reading.

Parents hold a very important key to bringing about the necessary changes required to teach reading in ways that leave fewer children behind. By bringing understanding, not blame, into school systems actively attempting to retool, parents can be an important force for good. Parents who create the necessary consumer demand for research-based practices in education will send a clear message to their local, state, and national representatives to support, with tax dollars, the necessary changes.

Parents can further assist in quality control of materials used to teach reading by becoming aware of which materials are in keeping with sound evidence-based research practices. Parents can learn to read the "labels" of the books and materials used by their children to make sure they are in keeping with those on the approved lists often found on their state's department of education website. It is interesting to note that some states set higher standards for which texts are allowed on the approved list (a list of these websites for each state can be found in the resources section at the end of the book). This process of choosing texts and supplemental materials is very political. Let your school systems know you want what is best for all the children in your district. Do not allow "textbook leftovers" that are convenient to use because they are already there, or textbooks that are viewed as less structured, because the teachers won't know how to use them. Require that all teachers who use these materials be properly trained to use them effectively.

Anyone who has ever tried to master a computer, a digital camera, or a VCR without instruction knows how frustrating it can be when you don't know how to use the technology. Well, reading textbooks are no different. Teachers need to know how to explicitly work with them in accordance with the publishers' guidelines to use them optimally. Get out and see what is going on in your child's class. If it does not make sense, ask the teacher how reading is being taught in the classroom; ask the principal.

Let them know that you are looking and asking the hard questions. Don't settle for quick answers. Don't settle for a curriculum that is just on a sheet of paper. See if the textbooks truly support the kind of instruction that has been proven to work. (See the What Works Clearinghouse, listed in the resources section, for this information.)

Be professional and visit your child's classroom to determine if he or she is being taught appropriately. See if the following five critical skills for reading instruction are being taught:

1. Phonemic awareness
2. Phonics
3. Reading fluency
4. Vocabulary
5. Strategies for reading comprehension

Use a checklist and check them off when you see them. If you don't see them being taught, ask why they are not being used.

IF IT DOESN'T EXIST, CREATE A SOLUTION

There is a great deal a parent can do to help make effective change for a child and countless other children. Remember, not every child has a parent who is comfortable advocating, asking the hard questions, doing the consumer quality control on educational materials, and pushing local representatives to support educational reform measures. While it is true that, in the familiar words, "It takes a whole village to raise a child," we all can do only what we are comfortable doing. Not everyone is going to want or be able to push for systemwide reform.

I thought I couldn't make a real difference because I was one parent asking for change for one student. And then I realized how widespread this problem is and got together with other moms and joined forces. This really made a difference in convincing our school principal that we needed to make a change.

We just need to be able to do what we are able to do, at the time and in a manner appropriate for us as individuals. As the old saying goes, a few fleas biting strategically can make even a big dog uncomfortable. We must remember that a nation or world filled with illiteracy impacts us all. So if your school district is behind the times, and your state's reading scores are low, don't get discouraged; there is a great deal you can do.

TIPS FOR PARENTS

- Get your child's education stabilized. Make sure that your child is learning the sounds of language, how to combine them, and how to take them apart.
- If you can't get what your child needs in your local public school system, you may have to go for outside help. Recent federal legislation, No Child Left Behind, (see the resources section for information) requires schools to provide extra tutoring for some children, so ask for it.
- Organize with other parents. There is strength in numbers. By creating a grassroots group, you can help fellow parents navigate the school system and not feel so alone. Use the media (see chapter 8), and demand change in how children are taught to read. Parents' voices can give the momentum needed to those sitting on the fence to push them to the other side. Organize, organize, and organize for the future of children.
- Join local and state committees and task forces that focus on the achievement gap, testing, curriculum, special education, and any other areas impacting reading achievement. You will soon discover that almost every possible committee and issue a school system faces is linked to reading. And if it is not, you'll be there to help connect the dots.
- Find out more about the Reading First initiative in your state. If your school is receiving these funds, find out what they are doing different in a Reading First school. If your school is not receiving Reading First funds, find out why and what your school can do to emulate the successes of Reading First schools. See what reading program your child's school is using. Are the reading textbooks on the approved Reading First list? How were the teachers in your school trained to use the reading textbooks? Did the textbook publishers come in and provide the training?
- Let your local college and university systems know that you are watching. Check with your school board to see if teachers are being

recruited and hired who have had training in phonics-based reading methods. Let your local college and university know that you are watching to see that future teachers are being taught using a phonics-based approach.

- Run for the school board. Get parents in your support/advocacy group to run for local office. In some cases, you cannot do worse than what often already exists, so go for it. Participate; get involved in ways you never dreamed of. Put democracy into action in education by helping to open up closed systems that have run on public trust alone for years. Ask—no, demand—accountability at all levels. Get to know your community's leaders, and let them know that your support, and even your vote, depends on how well children in your area are learning to read. Keep it simple, be direct, have fun, and show your children what being involved and engaged in public education is all about.

- Don't give up. If you're frustrated and find the clock running down on the time for your child to learn to read, and you can't find a way to make it work currently in your local school system, create something new. Start a charter school with other parents struggling in your area. If your local school system is not set up for charter schools, push for legislative change. Set the model. Set the trend. Don't settle for your child's failure. Invent, create, and inspire reform. Go the distance. Create a teacher-training institute to teach best practice. The sky is the limit. Settle only for the best that the science of the brain and the craft of teaching can provide children.

- Adventure awaits those who are willing to be the pioneers of reading reform. The weary, downtrodden, and frequently abused parents who have tried to advocate for reform need to pull together. We have science and evidence-based practices on our side. Don't settle for any system that would leave countless children out of the literacy loop. In modern society, a child who cannot read will be an adult who cannot survive.

- Remember, widespread social change does not happen overnight. Be good to yourself and those you love. This type of effort can be hard on a family and an individual. Rest; enjoy the many gifts that surround you. Don't let your passions and desire to see change in your lifetime deny you the joys in the present. Stay centered, focused, and know you cannot do this alone.

- Trust yourself. Your knowledge of your child, and how he or she is doing in school, is often right on the mark. Be the lone voice of reason, telling it like it is, even if it makes the teachers or school administrators uncomfortable. In time, they will come to understand. A child gets only one childhood. Make sure your child's time in school results in measurable and clear educational growth.
- What we do together will have a ripple effect throughout time. What cause is better than helping countless children to be able to read and learn from history, so we do not come to repeat our past mistakes? A well-educated citizenry is our best protection against the perils of the future world. Think, learn, and question. Our children are depending on you!

5

A Parent's Pressure Cooker

Norma Garza

As parents, we all have dreams for our children. We want them to be happy and successful and enjoy good lives. But sometimes the road becomes rocky and these dreams are threatened by circumstances we didn't expect and are not sure how to handle. This was the case with Norma Garza and her son. This chapter guides you through Norma Garza's struggle to help her son Alec and her unrelenting search for the right kind of help for him. For every parent, this description of Norma's journey can point you in the right direction for becoming the most important advocate your child can have. See the tips at the end of the chapter for specific examples of how you can make sure that your child gets the best reading instruction from your school and state. Norma Garza's struggle to help her son led her to become a member of the National Reading Panel, chairperson of Brownsville Reads, and a member of the President's Commission on Educational Excellence for Hispanic Americans.

I knew very early in my life that I wanted to be an accountant. I never thought that choosing that career would help me advocate for my child later in life. When my three now grown, healthy sons were babies, my husband and I had visions of the perfect world where our boys would grow up to be well educated and successful, enjoying the wonderful things life would offer them. As young adults, we had done everything right. We went to college, came from good, loving families, and knew what we wanted in life.

As a mother, I felt fortunate to be involved in my children's school. I offered to help in any way needed, serving on advisory boards, volunteering as room mother, driving for field trips, or baking cupcakes for school parties. And, of course, my offers of help were readily accepted. While I wasn't involved in curriculum or instructional decisions, I now know that this was something I should have paid more attention to. But at the time, involvement at that level seemed unnecessary; my children were well taken care of, and they seemed to be doing "good" in school.

All this began to change with the birth of my youngest son. Alec's speech delay at 18 months went unnoticed by his pediatrician, and I naturally assumed nothing was wrong. Grandmothers, with their wisdom and experience in childrearing, often see things young mothers miss; Alec's grandmother alerted me to the developmental delay I had overlooked. My training as an accountant inclined me to view developmental milestones as kinds of deadlines—projects that needed to be completed—so off to speech therapy we went. With six months of therapy, my child developed speech and language appropriate for his age. We all relaxed, viewing this as a (small) bump in the road, and resumed our perfect lives. I later learned that this "small" bump in the road was a significant red flag for our son's future problems in learning to read.

Alec's first year of school would change my own personal and professional life in ways I could never have imagined. In kindergarten, Alec began acting out in school. Teachers increasingly reported his disruptive, attention-getting, and rambunctious behavior. His "class clowning," repeated interruption of classmates during instruction, and verbal outbursts attracted the attention of his teacher and classmates, and subsequently, his mom and dad. In retrospect, this was a blessing in disguise. We learned that these behavior problems are cries for help often misinterpreted by teachers and families. The significance of these warning signs is amplified when a child seems to be fine at home but a challenge at school. Without Alec's negative behavior, we might not have picked up the clues that something was very wrong. It became evident that Alec was struggling to learn the early skills of reading. Our son needed specialized interventions required to help him overcome his obstacles with reading, and it was going to be up to me to ensure that he got them.

Alec began acting out in school. Teachers increasingly reported his disruptive, attention-getting, and rambunctious behavior. . . . In retrospect, this was a blessing in disguise.

The realization that your child is now experiencing more bumps in the road than you bargained for can bring on a variety of emotions: guilt (I should have stayed home more and read to him!), shame (Is this genetic? Did we pass on a faulty gene?), anger (Why doesn't he try harder? He's just being lazy).

Some of the best advice on dealing with my emotions came from a book by Jill Bloom called *Help Me to Help My Child* (1990). Bloom tells us,

> The emotional process that you go through—the denial, the anger, the grief, and finally the acceptance . . . are the classic stages of mourning. . . . We were mourning the loss of the child we hoped would be: the child who breezed through life with no handicaps or traumas, who was able to conquer every goal he encountered and emerged feeling good about himself. (p. 5)

I experienced all the stages Bloom describes.

Denial tends to be the most common stage to get stuck on. Many parents experience denial when advocating for their children because it takes a lot of time and emotional energy to address difficult issues. For me, these included getting myself knowledgeable about all the areas (diagnosis, instruction/curriculum, legal rights, progress measurement), not finding the resources to help Alec, dealing with resistance from the education system, and facing the resistance from the child. It was important to allow myself to grieve and eventually to accept the reality of my son's situation. Only then was I prepared to take on the battle.

Denial tends to be the most common stage to get stuck on. Many parents experience denial when advocating for their children because it takes a lot of time and emotional energy to address difficult issues.

A key strategy for me was to read books on the subject of reading difficulties. I learned quickly not to believe everything I read. As a tax accountant, interpretation of the law is part of my profession. Interpretation separates good professionals from the not-so-good ones. The same applies to reading. The Texas Scottish Rite Hospital in Dallas, Texas, helped me look at reading difficulties through the eyes of the medical profession and the neurological sciences instead of through the eyes of a despairing mom. I learned that understanding definitions and technical jargon and knowing how to recognize dependable research were critical skills in discerning what advice to take.

While becoming knowledgeable about how children learn to read can be daunting, that knowledge is one of the most powerful tools parents can use in advocating for their children. Well-written books are available, including *Parenting a Struggling Reader* (2002) by Susan L. Hall and Louisa C. Moats and *Overcoming Dyslexia* (2003) by Dr. Sally Shaywitz, MD. Because I live in a geographically isolated community with limited resources about evidence-based reading research, for a long while books like these became my best friends. The Internet also offers a wealth of information for parents; many times this information is written in Spanish and other languages. Online resources include Learning Disabilities Online (www.ldonline.org), Schwab Learning (www.schwablearning.org), and International Dyslexia Association (www.interdys.org). (See the resources section for other books and sites.)

Typically, the central challenge for parents entails securing an effective educational setting for their child. Parents may well experience the school system as unresponsive to the needs of their child and resistant to their parental concerns about this. An adversarial relationship with the school can develop, fostering anger and resentment that are hard to overcome. "Why hasn't the teacher solved the problem?" the parent asks in frustration. "Why did I have to step in? Isn't it the teacher's job to teach my child? Don't they care? Why do they point the finger at the parents?" And yet, in my experience teachers do care and want to be successful with their students. Unfortunately, for the most part, neither schools nor teachers in the United States are professionally prepared to effectively teach reading.

Specifically, parents may have difficulty finding school settings — public or private — that incorporate scientifically based reading research (SBBR). SBRR refers to instructional practices that have been tested and proven effective for children with reading difficulties. Such practices include explicit and systematic instruction in all the essential reading components: phonemic awareness, phonics, fluency, vocabulary, and comprehension. (See appendix A.)

Even more fundamentally, university schools of education have not embraced research-based findings in preparing professional reading instructors. While this deficient preparation is not the fault of the teachers, when challenged by parents, they naturally become defensive. School leaders can react defensively as well, owing to their ignorance on the topic of reading instruction, their lack of resources and support to comprehensively retrain faculty, or both.

With these realities in mind, it is very important to shop around for the school that will provide the needed reading instruction for your child. I cried for 2 weeks when I made the decision to move my child from an elementary school that was tied to memories, family, and friends. It was a difficult decision to make but was one that I did not regret.

At times, you may experience real resistance from educators. In my experience I dealt with behavior ranging from intimidation to anger. I look back at my experiences and can't believe the struggle I went through for Alex. I was told, "If your son doesn't progress, it's because of your attitude." This attitude was the result of my holding the school accountable for the instruction that was given to Alec.

Some teachers and administrators become defensive when parents know more than school personnel about the nature of their child's difficulties and the instructional techniques required, or when parents have caught on to what educators wish the parents had not found out. Many times, educators hope a Band-Aid approach will take care of the problem or social promotion will mask the situation. Many other teachers are willing to make the necessary changes but are not supported by the leadership structure. Whatever the circumstances, the parent should not back down.

At times, you may experience real resistance from educators. In my experience I dealt with behavior ranging from intimidation to anger. I look back at my experiences and can't believe the struggle I went through for Alec.

Understandably, parents begin to feel helpless in the face of this apparent resistance from the education establishment. The thought of their child not learning to read creates a list of concerns. How will he keep up with his work? Will he be embarrassed in class? Will he drop out of school? How will he get a good job without a college degree? How will he help support a family without a good job? These worries sometimes overwhelm parents, fostering a kind of hysteria. In Jill Bloom's book *Help Me to Help My Child: A Sourcebook for Parents of Learning Disabled Children* (1990), she says that hysterical parents can be the strongest source of support a child can have:

> Hysteria . . . can be productive. The power of the hysterical mother, if used creatively and to its fullest extent, can be very effective in getting help. Parents do know when something is wrong with their child. No one should be able to convince them otherwise without overwhelming proof. (p. 95)

In accounting, one of the first concepts we learn has to do with "materiality," defined as the basis for the inclusion or omission of an item that would influence or change the judgment of a reasonable person. It's important to know the difference between those things that make a small change in your child's education and ones that are critical to his or her education. In other words, "pick your battles."

I recommend the following two tools for dealing with resistance in educators:

1. *Document everything.* As a trained accountant, I understand how essential it is to document all interactions with the school. Keep a journal and record time, date, and notes of all conversations with representatives of the school system. A single binder containing all testing results, notes from teachers, and other correspondence saves time when you need to refer to such information. I found that using a tape recorder in meetings provided useful documentation of discussion and decisions. At some of the meetings held for my child, I hired a court reporter for the same purpose.
2. *Copy correspondence.* When communicating with the school, send copies of all written information to people at different levels in the system, such as the teacher, principal, counselor, special education

department and superintendent's office. Faxing and e-mailing also provide proof of time and date of transmission.

In addition to resistance from educators, you might find that there is resistance also from your son or daughter, and it has many layers. The older the student is, the more resistance you will experience. Your child must deal with changes in instruction and changes in her classroom or school. She has to work harder than her friends and cope with the reality that other students aren't required to work as hard. She also must face the misunderstanding from peers, teachers, other family members, and perhaps even herself.

Alec's early elementary school years were filled with struggles at home and at school with behavior that got in the way of his learning. We were caught in a vicious cycle of frustration; the more negatively we reacted, the more negatively Alec behaved.

Your child has to work harder than her friends and cope with the reality that other students aren't required to work as hard. She also must face the misunderstanding from peers, teachers, other family members and perhaps even herself.

Among the reasons I sprang into action on Alec's behalf was an incident that revealed to me the pain my child was experiencing. One day when he was in third grade I found the following note he had written:

Mom, I know I am stupid and you hate me . . . tell me about my problem . . . you were getting so mad I could not understand and you had another mistake to have me born. This is how I feel.

Reading this note helped me understand that Alec's extreme emotions were the product of his daily struggle, feelings that would build up at school and were released only when he "let off steam" at home. Children experience our unconditional parental love as a safe haven in which to vent their emotions. Knowing why Alec was so unhappy made it easier in some ways for me to deal with the steam.

Had I not become knowledgeable about what Alec was dealing with in school, I would have reacted differently to his anger when he came home

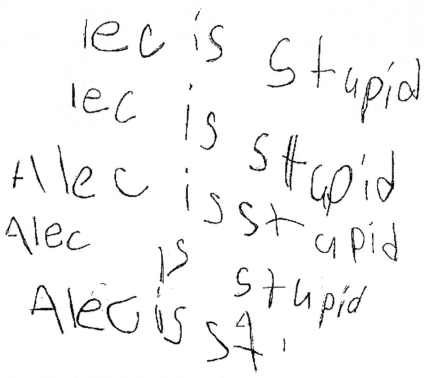

Figure 5.1.   Alec's Handwritten Note

after school. While I knew it was difficult for Alec and for me to change his educational setting, which included change in instruction, change in schools, working harder, and being honest about his lack of reading skills, I realized I had to for his own welfare. As hard as this was, I knew I was doing the right thing. There were many times when Alec was not happy with me, but I knew that I had to be strong and determined to get him to read on grade level. I had to remind myself that being his friend was not as important as being his parent at this stage of his life. I was confident that one day, he would thank me.

STATE ADVOCACY MODEL

In 1996, George W. Bush became the 46th governor of Texas. He announced the bad news about reading failures in the state in this statement: "Twenty-Five percent of Texas school children who took the state reading test in 1995 failed" (Walt, 1996). That meant there were 350,000 children lacking the most important basic skill—reading—to enable them to learn. Approximately 90,000 of them were third and fourth graders—an at-risk population in the making. With the help of the Governor's Business Council, the governor's office initiated the Texas Reading Initiative. His challenge to Texas educators, parents, and lawmakers was to use scientific research-based reading instruction to have all third graders reading on grade level or higher by the end of the third grade so that they would be successful in school and in life. The Texas Reading Initiative was a multifaceted approach to combating illiteracy.

By this time, I was well into a five-year fight to make sure my child learned to read. That fight had spurred me to step outside my community to look for answers to my questions at the state level, and I became involved with the Texas Reading Initiative and served on the Governor's Focus on Reading Task Force. I joined conscientious Texas business leaders who put together a statewide plan to improve Texas student reading levels. Strategies included statewide reading summits, a public awareness campaign, legislative changes, and others. It was through this model that I conceived of the idea of a local initiative for my community of Brownsville to include the key elements of the Texas Reading Initiative:

- Increase awareness of students' reading skills levels in kindergarten through the third grade.
- Target identified state funds to promote reading programs.
- Make reading programs a top legislative priority.
- Encourage the state's new Telecommunications Infrastructure Fund board to support innovative technologies to improve reading.
- Support excellence in teacher training.
- Motivate school districts to make proreading program decisions.
- Stimulate private sector initiatives.
- Encourage parents to share in their children's education.

However, by this time, Alec had been through five long years of frustration and failure.

LOCAL ADVOCACY MODEL

We face another challenge in Brownsville that is confronting many communities in the United States—how to teach a growing population of non-English-speaking children. According to August and Hakuta (1998), although the numbers of Latino students are increasing in the United States, their overall academic achievement is not. As a result, school districts like ours in Brownsville face an enormous challenge in educating language minority students. Nationally, over 60% of these students fail to learn to read and more often than not drop out of school in very large numbers. We have to figure out how to avoid the failure of these children to learn to read. I had the advantage of a good education, confidence and determination to take on a fight, and information to support me. What would these other parents do?

We have to figure out how to avoid the failure of [non-English speaking] children to learn to read. I had the advantage of a good education, confidence and determination to take on a fight, and information to support me. What would these other parents do?

BROWNSVILLE READS! A MODEL FOR COMMUNITY ACTION

It was then, in 1996, that I decided to join a highly qualified speech language pathologist, Elsa Cardenas Hagan, to form a nonprofit organization of community leaders and educators called Brownsville Reads! This was our answer to Governor George W. Bush's challenge to help promote research-based reading instruction in the public and private schools of Brownsville, Texas, with the overall goal of creating a more literate community. The Brownsville Reads! task force included representatives of our school district, our local college and university, and business leaders. Together, Brownsville Reads! developed a five-year action plan to be carried out by volunteers who gave up significant time and effort to improve reading scores in Brownsville, Texas. Brownsville Reads! goals were to

- develop public awareness of the critical role that research-based reading instruction plays in education;
- build the business community's support for research-based reading instruction;
- monitor schools' progress in reading through accountability measurements;
- promote Brownsville as a center for research and evaluation in the field of successful reading practices and biliteracy.

In fall 2001, Dr. Sharolyn Durodola, a reading researcher for the Center for the Achievement of Reading Skills (CARS) in Houston, Texas, wrote a paper on Brownsville Reads! Dr. Durodola wrote that from 1996 to 2001, Brownsville Reads! brought over 52 national reading experts to our community to present information at local symposiums. We trained all kindergarten through 2nd-grade teachers in scientific-based reading instruction, leveraged over $6 million for the training, and launched an intensive public awareness campaign. The most effective schools are those in which teaching and learning become central to the mission of the school.

Teacher training was done by the Neuhaus Education Center in Houston, Texas. Since Brownsville, Texas, is located on the Texas-Mexico border, 300 miles south of Houston, it was not economical for the teachers to travel to Houston, nor was there sufficient Neuhaus staff to send to Brownsville. Therefore, the solution to providing professional development to the teachers in Brownsville was Interactive Video Instruction (IVI). We developed a 30-hour course called Language Enrichment that helps teachers learn the explicit teaching of decoding and spelling skills designed for regular classroom settings.

Preliminary longitudinal studies show notable gains for the Brownsville Independent School District. According to the *Neuhaus News* (2002),

Standardized achievement test results from six randomly selected Brownsville elementary schools have been analyzed. Those results indicate that fifth-grade students who received Language Enrichment training during one or both semesters of second grade out-performed students who did not receive Language Enrichment training in second grade. . . . The results support the efficacy of Language Enrichment and suggest that

(1) Language Enrichment boosts longitudinal achievement for at least three years following instruction, and (2) the enhanced achievement extends beyond language arts to higher mathematics scores. (p. 1)

In a keynote address at a Brownsville Reads! dinner, Governor George W. Bush celebrated our success when he said,

The people of this community responded and I believe it's important to keep the initiative alive. I think Brownsville has responded more than any other town in Texas. I never believed . . . this community would pick up the ball and run with it.

THE LIGHT AT THE END OF THE TUNNEL

From the time Alec entered kindergarten at age 5 to the time he was in the fourth grade, my son struggled to learn to read. It was not until he was in fourth grade that I was able to successfully move the public school system to give him the reading instruction he needed. Finally, I could see a light at the end of the tunnel. Looking back at what we went through, at times it felt like an out-of-body experience. I couldn't believe that despite 20-plus years of scientific reading research, the type of research that is applied to the antibiotics prescribed by a medical professional, the education system I entrusted to educate my child had failed us.

It was hard to believe that the will of a parent to advocate for her child would be met with intimidation and resistance from a school system that was not willing or prepared to effectively teach children to read.

When Alec finally got the instruction he needed, I looked back on the battle we had fought and wondered what parents who were uneducated, not English speaking, and without the confidence or information to defend their children were going through.

HOW DOES THE STORY END?

While I still keep my CPA license current, I continue to do work in education. I am a coordinator for a United Way early childhood initiative called Success By 6. The focus for this initiative is improving the preliteracy and early literacy skills of children from birth to 6 years of age. The Brownsville Reads! experience taught us that many children entering kindergarten do not have the necessary early literacy skills to succeed. Successful literacy development must begin before the age of 5. Prevention is a key to thwarting future failure.

As a parent, I feel I gave my son the tools he needed to go on with his academic career. How and when he uses those tools will be his decision. As I talk to parents who are finding out that their children are struggling with reading, I emphasize the emotional pain these children go through. I suggest they talk to other parents in similar situations, know that the clock is ticking for their children, and realize that they will not outgrow their reading deficiencies but that they can learn to manage them and be successful readers and writers. A parent knows his or her child best. Go with your intuition. There are many battles to fight when raising children, and a child's struggle with reading is battle I think is worth fighting.

TIPS FOR PARENTS

For parents who find themselves in a similar situation, with a child who is not learning and a school that is unable to meet the needs of the local community, consider taking these steps.

- Let parents and other members of the community know what reading skills children at different ages should have and the importance of research-based instruction.
- Seek help at the state level. Every state has federal funds to improve reading. Find out how your school can qualify for these funds, and let other parents know there's an answer to the problem of reading failure.
- Make sure your school is using scientifically based reading instruction and that they help teachers learn how to use this research to teach children in their classrooms.
- Check your school's reading scores and compare them to those of other schools in your school district and state. If they are not up to par, ask hard questions and get answers about what changes will be made to ensure that reading achievement will improve.

- Seek help from your school board to make reading a priority.
- Enlist the help of your business community, places of worship, civic organizations, and parents' groups to motivate your school to make the right decisions about reading instruction.
- Encourage other parents to work with their children at home, before they enter kindergarten, and while they are in the first few grades, when learning to read prepares them to read to learn.
- Each journey will be unique. You'll have to create your own journey.
- Know that you'll give more than you take. You'll be transformed into a leader deep inside you.
- You will find that parents who take a stand can be change agents.
- Listen—everyone has a story and is invaluable.
- Create disciples who can add support to your story and your requests.
- You can get high off the power, but this is not a one-person show. Share the spotlight and prime other parents to shine in it.
- Audiotape your child's reading so you can demonstrate progress or lack of it.
- Use libraries as meeting places to acclimate people. They are universal, in every community, and have connections to others in all communities.
- Use indicators to know when you've accomplished things.
- Be aware that everything will impact your entire family. Include siblings in the effort.

II

CHANGING THE ODDS

6

When a Whole State Fails to Measure Up: One Grandmother's Fight for Phonics

Marion Joseph

This chapter gives you the inside story about how a large state, California, recognized that there was a problem teaching children to read and how Marion Joseph, a grandmother and member of the California Department of Education, used her conviction, knowledge, and perseverance to lead the way to changes in the system. Following is a description of the process of change from the time it was recognized to the moment of truth, when the problem was acknowledged and many people joined forces to fix it.

In the 1950s and 1960s, California had a model school system ranked among the best in the country. It enrolled one out of every eight public school students, or 6 million students in the nation. Today, California enrolls nearly 20% of our nation's schoolchildren. But since the mid-1990s, California has ranked near the bottom.

This didn't happen overnight. It happened because we were not watching closely enough. We were not paying attention to the continued failure of our students. We were not trying to figure out why and how this was happening. We should have seen the train coming but didn't until it was too late to get off the tracks.

Like most people, I have a work life and a personal life. It was on this issue that both converged. As a grandmother, I had been watching my grandson struggle to learn to read. As a member of the California Department of Education, I was responsible for helping develop policies for education in the state. I ended up being an advocate for a change in the way California's schools taught reading.

My story is the story of California. I realize that many think of California as a huge state and assume that it is an anomaly, and not applicable to their individual situation. With nearly 20% of the nation's citizens and a quarter of all K–12 students, California is a patchwork quilt of large cities, bustling suburbs, and small towns that serve students of virtually all races, religions, countries of origin, and languages. No, California isn't like most states. But if change can happen in California, it can happen anywhere. If we can overcome the bureaucracies and differences and sheer size of California, then you can make meaningful change anywhere.

I tell this story, not to seek commendation for what we were able to accomplish in California, but rather to serve as a blueprint for what any concerned parent or grandparent can accomplish. From time to time, we all become frustrated with what we see or hear in our schools. For most of these issues, we can simply go to our child's teacher or principal and come to a resolution. But for the remainder of the issues, there are times when we need to go further. When seeking to bring about change and improvement, how far do we need to go? Whom do we need to talk to? What do we need to ask for? When have we achieved victory? It is these questions that I hope to answer in this chapter.

In doing so, I have laid out a simple action plan that every concerned parent should know, as it can help you work through your state education bureaucracy to make an impact. Following these steps helped me in my quest to improve reading instruction in California and was essential in building the kind of instruction that is based on research and evidence that it works and, if used in all classrooms, would help 95% of all children to read well.

These steps include the following:

1. *Identify the problem.* What are you seeking to solve? By determining what the problem is and who is ultimately responsible for it (or responsible for its fix) you can begin your quest to make positive change.
2. *Identify the solution.* This could playfully be called "research is your friend." Once you know the problem, you need to do your home-

work. Understand the issues at hand. Who is for or against fixing the problem? What are their positions? Why? Explore possible solutions and what other schools or states have tried. Examine the data. Seek a research-proven solution.

3. *Use the power of information.* After you have identified and consumed the information and data available to you, you need to feed it to those who can make the decisions. This information is a powerful tool to support your request for change. Data shouldn't sit on a shelf; it should inform and guide policy and practical decision making.

4. *Insist on moving toward reform.* Don't accept no for an answer. There is always a way to keep the discussion going or to move your issue closer into the spotlight. By retaining focus on the change you seek, you help it slowly move toward becoming a reality. This is also the time to identify your allies and supporters and work with those organizations and individuals who can help you be successful.

5. *Overcome obstacles.* Change isn't easy. Trust me, I've lived it. But if you prepare for your opponents, for the naysayers and the protectors of the status quo, you can confront these obstacles and overcome them. That which is worth changing often isn't easy to change.

6. *Solve the problem.* Finally, we've reached a solution. After identifying the problem, digesting the research, determining the best fix, and pushing with all our might against all parties for its adoption, we have brought about reform and improved the situation.

Like anything else in life, these steps seem much easier in theory than they are in practice. But you need to trust me here. Change can happen, and you can achieve it. If this grandmother can shake the educational foundations of the nation's largest state and contribute to a real sea change in what and how we teach, so can you.

If this grandmother can shake the educational foundations of the nation's largest state and contribute to a real sea change in what and how we teach, so can you.

IDENTIFYING THE PROBLEM

One thing was clear in California in 1991—a lot of people knew that kids simply were not learning. The state had recently taken a big turn in how it taught children to read. Because a group of educators proclaimed that children could be taught to read using an approach that relied on children's supposedly innate ability to "pick up" reading skills by simply being immersed in literature (commonly known as whole language), the state decided that teaching fundamental skills like the alphabet, sounds of letters, and spelling was unnecessary. The year was 1990, and officials saw whole language as a new and wonderful reform, a reform that would do great things in the classroom. It was supposed to play out this way: Teachers were provided with a storybook anthology to use in the classroom. Students would learn to read almost magically. Teachers would read to students, kids would pretend to read along, and—shazam!—those kids would become good readers.

However, the magic didn't work for a very large percentage of students. Teachers, superintendents, and school boards knew this was a problem well before a national test called the National Assessment of Educational Progress (NAEP) released scores in 1994, clearly showing that California students were at the bottom of the pack on national reading tests.

At first, I thought the problem was implementation. Surely, the experts had vetted whole language and had witnessed its successes in other states around the country. The problem couldn't be the instructional program; maybe it was just the case that those at the local level didn't understand it yet and weren't using it effectively.

As a former staffer in the California State Department of Education, I was, of course, interested in understanding what was going wrong and in helping to identify how to fix it. But as the grandmother of a California student struggling to learn to read, I witnessed firsthand the misery of my grandchild and knew that thousands of other children were struggling as he was, and this caused me to intensify my scrutiny of the problem. So I began calling people throughout the state, asking them what had gone wrong in the implementation of this new program. I felt I had a moral obligation to do whatever was possible to get all our children reading again.

I was startled by the responses. Implementation wasn't the problem. Teachers throughout the state knew that kids were having trouble learning to read with whole language. They knew that this new approach was not working and was failing our children. You couldn't just read storybooks to kids and expect kids to learn through osmosis.

As I pushed further, I learned that the new curriculum had some disturbing aspects. Teachers were told never to teach spelling as children would learn to spell as they became familiar with literature. They were told not to teach kids phonics or how to sound out words. There was no mention of phonemic awareness or fluency or comprehension or the other components needed for students to become skilled readers. The idea was that children would gain reading comprehension from the context of the story and other clues, like pictures, whether or not the kids could read the words. How was this possible?

The idea was that children would gain reading comprehension from the context of the story and other clues, like pictures, whether or not the kids could read the words. How was this possible?

THE CALIFORNIA SHIFT

In California, we have something called state adoption of instructional materials. That means that the state decides what textbooks can be purchased by school districts with state money. Since textbooks are the foundation for what and how teachers teach, this is a critical decision. The state also creates the standards for what students should know and be able to do.

In 1989, we had no reading standards at all. No one did. Reading standards did not become an issue for most states until the mid-1990s. Because of this, there was nothing that laid out what, how, and when students should be taught reading skills and how we would know if they learned them. As a result, the framework adopted in 1989 by the state wasn't a framework at all—it was a philosophical position paper that was focused on higher/better/more-interesting literature. Foundational issues such as phonics instruction were barely mentioned, limited to two sentences calling for phonics to be taught quickly and early, completed by the second grade. When the state established its criteria for state adoption of textbooks, it created a point-award system for virtually everything you could think of. But it awarded zero points for phonics in the instructional program. *Zero!* The criteria rewarded great literature-based instruction, and sought to punish the "skill/drill/kill" instruction many associated with phonics.

IDENTIFYING THE SOLUTION—RESEARCH

What could I, as just one voice, do about this? I kept asking teachers and parents, "Are you having a problem with the implementation of the new language arts curriculum?" I kept seeking information about whether student reading performance was improving. I spent a whole year just asking questions and listening to answers.

In mid-1992, I was still searching for solutions. I was out driving on the freeway, listening to National Public Radio (NPR) as I normally do, when the answer finally came to me. NPR was airing a segment on people who were having difficulty learning to read. All the interviewees sounded like they understood the very issues I was struggling with. One of those interviewees, Reid Lyon, worked for the U.S. government and kept talking about what the research said. They talked about dyslexia and other learning disabilities and the skills needed to be a good reader that we never talked about in California. I was starting to get somewhere.

I seized the moment and did the one thing any concerned citizen or grandmother can do—I kept digging for more information. I called Dr. Lyon in Washington, DC, to ask for additional information. I started rummaging through research papers, finding presentations that had been given at the International Dyslexia Society and other conferences. I started finding other researchers who had spent years studying the most effective ways to teach reading. I spoke with individuals who had solutions to California's problems. I could finally declare, "Now I've got it!"

Armed with the research data, what was I to do next? Clearly, there was an issue here. California was doing it wrong, and we finally knew how to do it right. The state had made a big mistake, and there was an opportunity to correct it. But how do you get a state bureaucracy as large as California's to admit it made a mistake, and then spend the money necessary to fix it? This wouldn't be easy.

The state had made a big mistake, and there was an opportunity to correct it. But how do you get a state bureaucracy as large as California's to admit it made a mistake, and then spend the money necessary to fix it? This wouldn't be easy.

MOVING RESEARCH INTO THE CLASSROOM

Because of my experience in California government, I knew that I needed to do more than just push a few buttons. I not only needed to push the system for change, but I needed to push the system where it could and needed to be pushed. If I were going to move these research findings forward, I would need to be involved with those who had the power to change reading policy, including the following:

State legislature: These are our elected officials, responsible for establishing our state's policies and funding our state's programs. They may not be education experts, but they ultimately make the decisions on what programs our schools pursue. Like our U.S. Congress, most state legislatures are divided into two chambers.

State superintendent: Just as our local school districts have superintendents who oversee our local education, our states have state superintendents whose job is to safeguard our state education policies and ensure that the local districts are meeting state expectations.

State board of education: Again, just like our localities have boards of education that develop school district policy, the state board of education develops state policy and works with our state superintendent, legislators, and governor.

State director: Most states have directors for certain programs. With a growing emphasis on reading instruction, most states now have directors of reading programs, who are hired to know the latest research and ensure that it is being put to use in our classrooms.

But knowing whom to go to wasn't enough. Convincing these state policy makers and administrators that it was imperative to make changes in reading policy and instruction was the next hurdle. I needed to take the information and knowledge I had and actually put them to work for me.

It was fortunate that I knew many of those educational players in the state capital. I not only knew whom I should be talking to, but I was also able to actually get their attention. This would work with any large group of citizens who are trying to make change. They all told me that I needed to go to the very Curriculum Commission that recommended this whole language problem in the first place. So I went to the Curriculum Commission.

Originally, I thought that the Curriculum Commission simply left something out. I had a limited understanding of the reading research and had not originally seen that the state's whole language approach was contradictory and directly conflicted with that research. But I did know I was on very dangerous ground in taking this issue to the Curriculum Commission. Whole language instruction had infiltrated the state, and its advocates were stronger than ever. The Curriculum Commission was composed of many true believers. When California teachers said whole language wasn't working, they were told to simply keep trying.

Whole language instruction had infiltrated the state, and its advocates were stronger than ever. The Curriculum Commission was composed of many true believers. When California teachers said whole language wasn't working, they were told to simply keep trying.

As expected, the Curriculum Commission didn't like what I had to say. They were just not ready to hear it. I suggested that they consider a midterm correction to the reading curriculum. I asked them to look at all the research I had found. I asked about beefing up phonics and spelling in the curriculum. I would have thought my meeting was a complete waste of time if not for phone calls I received from Department of Education staff that evening. I learned they were aware there were real problems. I was on the right path. Kids were struggling. I needed to keep pushing.

During my time in state government, I was always a policy person. I wasn't a researcher, nor was I a writer. So I tapped a friend to help me move this to the next level. As we continued to push, the story became more and more clear. Then, on one fateful day, I suggested we develop a white paper, or research document, calling for increased phonics instruction in California schools. My life would never be the same.

At the time, I didn't realize what I was wading into. Because I thought the state had left out the explicit teaching of reading skills, I believed the answer was to call for balance—for literature plus essential skills. Since then, I have been deeply saddened because I started the phrase *balanced literacy* to advocate for the inclusion of basic skills—skills like phonemic awareness, phonics, fluency, vocabulary, and reading comprehension. Since the release of that paper, *Balanced Approach to Literacy*, the phrase has been used to mislead, misunderstand, and misinform. I was misguided. This wasn't an issue of balance. This was an issue of essential skills and the science behind them.

After finding the Curriculum Commission unhelpful, I decided to take this white paper to my friend, the state superintendent. The time had finally come to take this all the way to the top. While I hadn't spoken to Bill Honig in nearly 10 years, I knew he had to face the problem.

My conversation with Bill was a real eye-opener. He hadn't known the extent of the troubles this reading curriculum was causing. Those true believers who had so successfully pushed whole language instruction were jamming it into everything they could. Training groups. Schools. Preservice instruction. Professional development. Textbook adoption. And more. California had been transformed into a whole language world.

This discussion on reading had clearly caught Bill off guard. He was in the middle of planning a big state event rolling out a new "Elementary, Here I Come" campaign throughout the state. Building off the curriculum changes, this campaign had several key points. I'll never forget point 2— reduce time spent on basic skills. How can we reduce the time spend on these skills when there is already no time spent on them? We needed to change course. We needed to establish an approach to reading in California based on the enormous body of research.

MOVING TOWARD REFORM

If any time was the right time for this change in course, it was 1994. When I started my crusade in 1992, the state wasn't ready to listen. Everything was too new. Whole language was still full of hope. But in two short years, the entire educational landscape had changed in the state.

In 1994, the latest NAEP scores came out, and California had devastatingly low scores. Despite the "best" whole language curriculum available, California students were at almost the bottom of the pack when it came to reading scores. Our kids not only hadn't done better since phonics was removed, they had done worse. California's superintendent for public instruction had the tough job of telling all the state's residents that California had scored last on the national reading exam. Despite the billions of dollars we were spending, despite the massive curriculum overall, despite all the experts and true believers who had adopted a new system designed to take us to the "holy land" of reading, California's millions of kids were the worst readers in the country. We had no choice but to act. And we needed to act swiftly and dramatically before more children suffered the consequences of being poor readers.

Despite the "best" whole language curriculum available, California students were at almost the bottom of the pack when it came to reading scores. Our kids not only hadn't done better since phonics was removed, they had done worse.

For the past two years, I had been pushing everyone and anyone I could on the need to implement scientifically based reading instruction in the classroom. In 1994, we started bringing nationally recognized researchers to California. We had these experts talk to the state policy people, to the legislative committees in Sacramento, and to others who could bring about change. Now that Bill Honig had departed as state superintendent, I urged him to write about what he learned during his tenure—about noble intentions, misguided policies, and the failure to fix them. I urged him to set the record straight. He did just that, writing *Teaching Our Children To Read: The Role of Skills in a Comprehensive Reading Program* (1995), designed to provide educators with a better understanding of what the research says and how California's experience led to massive student failures.

I met with Bill Honig's successor, the current state superintendent of education, Delaine Eastin, to alert her to the problems with our reading curriculum. As a politician, she wasn't expected to have all the answers on this complicated subject. But she did have a responsibility to listen to the experts, to examine the data and research on the subject, and to look at how best to teach reading.

But I knew that my lone voice wouldn't carry the day. I needed more than my stack of papers and my advice. I needed to begin to identify and recruit supporters and allies, organizations that could help trigger success. To do so, I recognized that I should start tapping those who had a "dog in this fight"—the concerned parents, teachers, local officials, business leaders, and others who were directly affected by our precipitous drop in reading scores.

But I knew that my lone voice wouldn't carry the day. I needed more than my stack of papers and my advice. I needed to begin to identify and recruit supporters and allies, organizations that could help trigger success.

And the soapbox and information I had acquired were not going to carry the day, so I continued to read and talk to experts. I needed to stay one step ahead, knowing more each day. Eastin decided to appoint a state task force to examine the reading issues, and she asked me to serve on it. It would be yet another step down this long road.

SOLVING THE PROBLEM

After pushing and pushing and pushing and pushing, our final report was acceptable. But after this report was released, nothing happened. Frustrated parents and concerned policy makers started asking me, "What are you going to do now? What happens next? What's the plan? How do we fix this?" The time had come to act quickly and decisively.

How do we solve this problem? I knew everyone who was involved. I knew how to do this. Now we just needed to do it. The steps we took then are the steps that any group of concerned parents and grandparents can take to improve reading in their community or state. These were the steps we needed to take to move the research into practice.

Step 1: We need to set strong state standards. We can't settle for mushy standards or confusing standards designed not to offend anyone. This is too important an issue to try to stake out a mediocre middle. A state needs to come out strong, on both what is expected of our children and what is expected of our schools and teachers.

Step 2: We need to focus parents on the issues they can and want to deal with. Parents want to help their children first, and should. It is unreasonable to ask parents to make a priority of changing the world when their child is struggling. Parents first need to take care of their own children. They need to demand both proper testing and proper instruction. Once each child is taken care of, whether inside or outside the system, then parents can start thinking about how to make a difference in the district or the state. The first priority is making a difference in each family.

Step 3: Bring your friends close, and closer. When seeking to change the status quo, nothing is more important than rallying and using those individuals and organizations that share your concerns and your desire for reform. By growing your message and expanding your pool of concerned parties, you magnify your issue and your chances for success. These supporters often bring other layers of support, channels for communication, and leverage points for reaching decision makers.

Step 4: We all need to learn. Over the last decade, I have spent a lot of time talking with parents throughout the nation. There is no question that many of us are frustrated and angry about our child's education. The greatest impediment to changing the system is ignorance. Everyone is susceptible to falling into the "know nothing" category. It is appalling how many learned individuals and well-meaning true believers know so very little about the research and how to translate it into instructional practice. And they do not want to know it, fearing that it gets in the way of their ideology. So they reject it and then lay the burdens of failure on the children. But failure lies with inadequate instruction, not with the student. Ninety-five percent of children could learn to read if they were taught using research-based instruction. Without question, knowledge is our strongest weapon and ignorance our greatest enemy. (See appendix B.)

Step 5: Build bridges, not walls. Anyone who has looked at my background quickly knows that I am a liberal Democrat. I worked for many liberal Democrats while in California. But to make the reading changes necessary in California, I had to work with moderates and conservatives,

Republicans and Democrats. Because I was pushing for phonics instruction, I was often labeled as a right-winger. That was just ignorance. I didn't care what political label a person carried, as long as he or she was willing to listen to the research and make the right choice. Republican governor Pete Wilson, subsequent Democratic governor Gray Davis, and the entire state legislature all shared a common concern with reading. They were willing to listen, and willing to help.

Step 6: Prepare for the pushback. Change is not easy. As you advocate strongly for change, there will be equally passionate advocates seeking to protect the status quo. In California, I heard specific attacks from whole language advocates who believed that not everyone needed scientifically based reading instruction. While it seems ridiculous to me that we would be advocating to block proven instruction from our schools, these whole language supporters felt that not everyone needed systematic and explicit instruction on phonemic awareness and phonics and fluency. Some children will readily grasp phonemic awareness and phonics skills with minimal direct instruction, but most children need to be explicitly taught these skills and given plenty of opportunities for practice. These critics are flatly wrong. Using this argument to avoid using research-based instruction in our classrooms is an invitation to disaster, as we saw with our basement-level reading scores.

Some children will readily grasp phonemic awareness and phonics skills with minimal direct instruction, but most children need to be explicitly taught these skills and given plenty of opportunities for practice. These critics are flatly wrong. Using this argument to avoid using research-based instruction in our classrooms is an invitation to disaster, as we saw with our basement-level reading scores.

When the NAEP examination was administered in 1994, and revealed the same poor scores, I finally had the ears of those making the decisions. Instead of hearing *"No,"* I started hearing, *"Why?"* and *"How?"* The 1994 results were the objective proof that many decision makers needed. They had already wasted too much time on a failed policy. Now lawmakers were ready to listen. They accepted the research papers. They listened to my experts. And they unanimously passed the change we needed. California was finally headed back on the right track — the research-based proven track.

Today, California's NAEP scores show real improvement. The 2002 NAEP scores showed a significant rise in reading scores for California fourth graders since those 1994 tests. The scores of California students in all major reporting categories increased. Slowly but surely, California is recovering from its whole language experiment.

These latest scores provide Californians with a sign of hope. But they also reveal that there is still a great deal of work that needs to be done, both in California and in states throughout the country.

In California, we saw these low test scores as trouble signs and used them to enact effective reading instruction that is based on evidence that it produces results. The time has come for parents throughout the nation to do the same. As concerned parents, we owe it to our kids to look at their scores in our state and in our district and ask why they aren't doing better. We owe it to them to scrutinize the current reading curriculum and ask to see the research behind it. And we owe it to them to demand that proven instructional methods, like phonics, be used in our classrooms. If we don't, our children will continue to struggle and our schools will continue to fail them.

THIS WAS MORE THAN JUST READING

For those folks who have heard this story, it is often one of policy and of lobbying the state government and of rewriting the laws. But along the way, we also learned that this is more than policy and law, just as it is more than just K–3 instruction. This is also a story of our schools of education, a story of learning disabilities, a story of parents' responsibilities, and a story of possibilities for 95% of all children to be able to read if taught properly.

At the very heart of California's problems were the colleges of education. For decades, these schools have led our future teachers and our future policy makers astray, providing them with strong educational rhetoric while ignoring the research that should underlie all instruction. Had the research been used to teach teachers, the children they later taught would have succeeded, as they would have had the foundation skills that are the building blocks for reading.

Forget reading for a moment. If you want your child to become a great pianist, do you simply hand her tons of Mozart and Beethoven on CDs, and then point her to a piano to play? Of course not. You teach the child about notes and chords. You teach her to read music. You teach her the scales. She practices, practices, practices. You start with the foundational skills, and spend a great deal of time on them. One day, you'll get to Mozart. For now, it is "Chopsticks."

The need for a strong foundation is the same for virtually any skill. If you want your child to become a great tennis player, you teach him serves, volleys, drops, and the like. Success requires skill building, whether you are playing tennis, playing the piano, or reading. To become a great golfer, your child must learn to drive and chip and putt. And to become a strong reader, your child must learn phonemic awareness, phonics, fluency, vocabulary, and reading comprehension. Despite what many of our schools of education may have told us, you can't bypass the building blocks and move right into good literature. There is no way around it.

If our child doesn't take to the piano or golf, we can simply say it isn't their thing, and introduce them to new activities. Unfortunately, we can't do the same with reading. If a child is a struggling reader, we can't simply focus on math skills and hope that everything balances out in the end. We know it won't, and our child will remain at a serious disadvantage in learning everything else in school.

We know that 95% of students will learn to read if effectively taught these beginning skills. I am sad to think that so many struggling readers have been classified as learning disabled instead of being given the most effective instruction. Most of these children don't have a learning disability. They have an instructional problem. They just haven't been taught correctly. With what we know, there is no reason for a child not to learn to read.

I am sad to think that so many struggling readers have been classified as learning disabled instead of being given the most effective instruction. Most of these children don't have a learning disability. They have an instructional problem.

Reading is ultimately a code. In fact, the alphabetic code is probably the greatest invention of humankind. If you learn it, and understand that sounds of speech match the written squiggles—print—you can learn to read or write an infinite number of words. It is ultimate tool.

In California, we lost sight of this immensely powerful tool. Instead of going back to the alphabetic code to help those struggling to learn to read, we used our special education labels. We forgot that we have only two choices for reading. One is to memorize each and every word. The other is to have the tools to decode them. The whole language experiment relied on having children learn to read from context. If they knew some of the words, they could guess the remainder. But those experimenters never considered what one does if the child can't read any of the words. Despite the research calling for learning the foundation skills for reading, we simply labeled our struggling readers as having a learning disability. Today we see these problems as "curricular disabilities."

Instead, we should have been empowering our kids with systematic and direct instruction in phonemic awareness skills. We should have taught them how to decode the text including grammar, spelling, and comprehension. I should know. My grandson was one of these children. The teachers kept telling us, "He is so smart. He knows all of his letters. He'll come around." But they never asked if he was associating the sounds with corresponding letters. They never looked to see if he could string those sounds together to form words and those words together to build sentences. They labeled instead of solving the problem.

No parent should be satisfied if her child is struggling to learn to read. She should learn how he is being taught, how much time is being spent on reading, and what research supports this method of instruction and insist on appropriate changes—all the way up to the State Department of Education, the State Board of Education, and the legislature.

No parent should be satisfied if her child is struggling to learn to read. She should learn how he is being taught, how much time is being spent on reading, and what research supports this method of instruction and insist on appropriate changes—all the way up to the State Department of Education, the State Board of Education, and the legislature.

Dig into the research. Learn the difference between research you can trust and pseudo-educational research. This is critical because every reading program these days is advertised as "research based." There are several guides that can help in determining these differences, and they are free! I would suggest you obtain the document titled *Using Research and Reason in Education* by Paula and Keith Stanovich (2003) and review other sources in the resources section of this book. Don't take no for an answer. And do everything in your power to help your child. Teaching our children opens up a world of possibilities for us as parents. We need to seize those opportunities and confront the roadblocks. As caring parents or grandparents, we should never be satisfied if an educator tells us, "We'll work on it next year," or "That isn't the way it works," or "Don't worry. He'll outgrow it."

THE LESSONS LEARNED

Throughout this chapter, I've laid out a number of lessons for concerned families. I recognize that very few parents can enter this fight exactly the way that I did. But you can follow my example. Most of us don't know the policy makers in our state capitals, nor do we have the intimate familiarity with state policies and how to change them. Despite that, each and every one of us can make a real difference by remembering some simple lessons.

Knowledge is power. I was able to help argue for the essential elements of reading instruction because I knew I had research and facts on my side. It is easy for educators or policy makers to discount your opinions if these don't agree with theirs. But it is far more difficult to ignore or reject reams of data and information that prove your opinions. Research the issues. Know what they are teaching in your schools and why. Check out how effective those programs are. Analyze the results. The more you know, the stronger an advocate you become. Research is important, and a command of the research shapes the views and actions of others. Even if you are not in a position of power, an understanding of the trustworthy scientific research on reading and how it can be used gives you a leverage point.

Build bridges. Focus on potential supporters rather than those committed to a failed system. To me, not everyone was a potential supporter. If you are going to change reading policy, you need to win supporters and advocates. Even if you would never agree with them on another issue, if others are of like mind on reading, work with them and include them. It will take you far.

Truth isn't always simple to see. In California, it was clear that we were victimized by decades of misinformation, teaching from the perspective of ideology, not research, and bad advice. We all must recognize that the education industry does not operate on the basis of evidence, as does medicine. Instead, it relies on history and tradition. It can take a lot of work to get educators to look past that history and see the truth in the research. As Keith Stanovich, a well-known researcher, said, "Be sure you know the difference between romance and reality."

Our classrooms are not laboratories for experimentation on children. This whole language experiment was not based on findings from many studies of effective reading instruction, nor was it based on what was best for our kids. Parents need to know why changes are taking place and what results are expected. If California's parents had known that there were research-proven methods for teaching children to read, and whole language wasn't one of them, we could have avoided subjecting millions of California students to failed, ineffective instruction and the struggles that turned many of them off to school, increased our dropout rate, and caused misery for countless numbers of youngsters.

You are not alone. Walk through any school, any store, any community center, or any state capital, and you will find a great number of parents who are struggling with the same issues you face. Millions of kids today are having trouble learning to read, and their parents are out there looking for solutions. Work with each other, share your personal experiences, your research, and your solutions. Reach out to your fellow parents. Look for other children with similar problems. You will be far more powerful as a united voice.

Back in 1991, I recognized there was a problem. I could see that my grandson was not getting the reading instruction that he needed. I recognized that our schools were eliminating phonics and other reading building blocks from the curriculum. And I feared that an entire generation of young readers would be lost because of a failed experiment.

Today, I am frustrated because I see there is still a problem. I hear about it every day when I talk to parents throughout the United States. Despite the research, despite failing reading test scores, despite what we know about what works and what doesn't, many school districts still aren't doing it right. There's no excuse for that, not when we know what can make a difference for our children. I say our vision on the issue is in need of change. The time has come to shift this debate from the deficits of the child to the deficits of the system.

There is no simpler way to put it. Scientifically based instruction based on phonics works. The research proves it, and we've proven it in California. We just need to get that research and data into the hands of those who can demand it of their schools—parents.

TIPS FOR PARENTS

- Gather as much information as you can and put it to work for you. Learn about the reading research so you can explain it to others.
- Enlist the help of everyone who will work with you, even if that help comes from unlikely sources.
- Understand the motivation of your opposition and work around it.
- Be clear about what you can reasonably expect, and fight for those changes.
- Reach out to potential advocates and give them a reason to work with you.
- Understand that state agencies don't always get along. Learn the turf issues.
- When meeting with state leaders, bring data on key people in their home territory and about reading.
- Consider this work empowering and fun.

7

Pulling Back the Curtain:
Successfully Working With the Media

Patrick Riccards

In this chapter you will learn about the power of the media and ways to harness it to make changes in how your children and others learn to read. The media can be your best friend if used with skill, honesty, and determination. A seasoned communications expert, Riccards describes how to attract media attention to your cause. This chapter will help you learn those skills and give you some tools to help you get the results you want.

A Hollywood producer could not have provided a better scene. It was a beautiful April morning in Washington, DC. The sun was shining, the remnants of cherry blossoms still hung in the air, and a crowd was gathering on Capitol Hill. This same room under the Capitol dome had held discussions and debates on federal budgets, wars, and national policy. On this day, the room embraced a different, yet equally important issue. Today, the Capitol would house a discussion on reading research and the best ways to teach our children to read.

Such a topic is not usual fare for Washington. There was no celebrity spokesperson. There was no slick advertising campaign and no buckets full of free giveaways. And there were no promises of new federal funding or spending to bring back home. Instead, everyone gathered to begin understanding decades of research. After determining that "Johnny can't read" and that we were living in "a nation at risk," the discussion shifted from what was wrong to what could be done to fix it.

THE NATIONAL READING PANEL

When the National Reading Panel (NRP) began to summarize its two years of study and analysis of reading instruction research, it was no wonder that elected officials in the U.S. Senate and U.S. House took notice. However, what was remarkable was the media attention that the National Reading Panel faced as it gave the public a first glimpse into the research that promised to change the way children are taught to read.

There were multiple TV cameras there. Newspaper reporters waited in line to speak with members of the NRP. Media outlets from across the nation asked for copies of the NRP report. The Associated Press covered the report release, disseminating news articles in states and localities throughout the nation. It was editorialized in *USA Today*. And CNN ran stories announcing the findings every half hour. Finally, there was information getting out on proven methods to teach children to read.

What was so right about that day? The report was an analysis of more than 30 years of research, all of which had been out in the public domain. Yet the response to the release of the NRP's (2000) *Teaching Children to Read* report was enormous, particularly with the media.

The event succeeded because the NRP provided the media with information that could be easily relayed to citizens throughout the United States. Why is this unusual? The NRP knew that research findings are often difficult to discuss in a short newspaper article or radio story. But they were determined to get the information into the hands of parents and educators. It was about teaching children. It was about student achievement.

The event succeeded and the findings of the report got the attention of the media because the information was communicated in ways that reach many different audiences. Typically, similar reports are usually written only for other researchers, and these sometimes never see the light of day in classrooms and around kitchen tables. But while the NRP wrote a comprehensive report for researchers, complete with all the data, it also wrote a summary report written for practitioners in the field. And more importantly, the NRP produced a video version of the report, so parents and teachers could see how its findings work in real classrooms—like those your children attend.

The media was attracted to the report because what it says affects virtually everyone—parents and teachers, elected officials and community leaders, colleges and businesses. All are touched in some way by the reading skills of today's students. Knowing how to read is the single most important education issue. The ability to read and comprehend allows children to learn about science or history or any other subject in school. It provides the tools needed to succeed in middle school or high school. It equips students to perform at a college level. And it empowers them to succeed in their lives.

Yes, because of its far-reaching consequences, learning to read is a powerful issue. But its power as an issue depends on the ability to communicate how to teach it effectively, understand the research that supports the kind of instruction that works, and get support and understanding from lots of people in different roles. Reading is more than another subject learned in school. It is the foundation for all learning. To help your child, you need to ensure that everyone understands the issue and its impact, and there is no better way to get this attention than by harnessing the full power and influence of the media.

> The first time I talked to a reporter, I was really scared. I didn't want to blow this opportunity. I put my points together, rehearsed what I wanted to say, and was surprised that it wasn't as bad as I thought it was going to be.

To many, communicating with the media is a scary prospect. We fear that we will be misquoted. We worry that it is a job only for the professionals we see on television, those official, hired "spokespeople." We wonder whether we can make a difference, as one single voice.

Yes, one person can make a difference. And one person can work with the media. All it takes is some preparation, some background knowledge, and a great deal of passion.

WE'RE OFF TO SEE THE WIZARD

Virtually everyone is familiar with *The Wizard of Oz*. As concerned parents, we assume the role of Dorothy. We want to reach our ultimate goal but don't necessarily understand the best and fastest way to get there. We face a great number of obstacles. People who distract us from our path.

Secondary battles. Individuals with less-than-honorable intentions. And, yes, we are intimidated by that wizard, the media, whose reach extends to all that we come in contact with, but which is never completely understood or appreciated.

No matter who Dorothy spoke with, it seemed everyone was in awe of the all-powerful wizard. Communities were all too aware of his reach into their neighborhoods. Very few understood how he did what he did, but nary an individual was prepared to challenge him. Yet all relied on him to dispense information and direction to the public.

When Dorothy and Toto pulled back the curtain, revealing just an ordinary man, the wizard became far less feared, but no less respected and appreciated. The same can be said of the media. None of us questions the media's powerful reach or impact on policies and behavior. We should respect the media. But we need not fear them nor misunderstand them.

This chapter is an attempt to pull back that curtain and help you better understand who the media are, what the media do, and how to best work with them to accomplish your goals of making change in the way schools teach reading. With a keen understanding of the media, we can all reach a successful end to our journey of bringing research-based reading instruction to our children. And we will all learn that we've had the power to do so all along.

KNOWLEDGE IS POWER:
THE WHO, WHAT, AND WHY OF THE MEDIA

It is a harsh reality, but changing the reading failure rate of so many students will never happen if we don't scream it from the rooftops, and from the streetcorners, and out the windows, and from our cars, and have our family and friends scream it right alongside us. Very few of us have the luxury of printing our own newspapers or broadcasting our own news shows. So we need to know what we can do. What venues are available to us? With whom at those media outlets do we work? How do we communicate with them? And how can we ensure that communication is truly effective and that we reach the people we want to reach?

First, we need to have a clear understanding of available media outlets. Dorothy's original problem was that Oz was a foreign land for her. She didn't know a good witch from a bad one. She didn't know where the power lay. Heck, she didn't know a lollipop kid from a flying monkey.

Even the highest-paid media relations pros sometimes lack understanding of how the wonderful world of the media truly works. Too often, they believe that the job is done if only the *New York Times* covers it. Nothing could be further from the truth. As nice as a *Times* piece is, true media success is measured by its reach on Main Street, USA. After all, news of the Wicked Witch of the East's death didn't originate in the Emerald City; it all started right there in Munchkinland.

Media outreach, particularly on an issue like reading, is not a trickle-down approach. We can't expect one major national media article to result in a groundswell of change in our community and in other communities across the county. Those publications are great for the Sunday morning news shows, but let's face it—they aren't our primary source of information about what's happening at home. And they aren't what our family and friends rely on for events in our hometowns, either.

BUILD UP MOMENTUM

The release of the NRP report worked as a media event because of all the media work that went into it for nearly two years before. That Capitol Hill press conference was the final media event the NRP conducted, not its first. Prior to arriving in Washington, the NRP had conducted a series of meetings and public events throughout the nation. The members met with parents, teachers, and reporters in a wide range of communities. And they used everything they heard and saw on Main Street, USA, to send a compelling message to Washington, DC.

All this translates to a simple rule: You succeed by building up. You prove to those national publications and radio and television shows that reading is important because local communities around the nation care about the fact that their children are not learning to read and are in danger of failing in school. Reading is discussed in small-town newspapers and city dailies. It is buzzing on local radio. It is spotlighted in community newsletters and organizational publications. And it is featured on the local news. It is that buzz you saw in Munchkinland, as soon as the world turned to color. From house to house, neighborhood to neighborhood, all

> We held meetings with our local reporters—the ones who cover school
> board meetings. We found reporters whose kids were having problems in
> schools because they weren't learning to read. And we told them our story.

in the community soon realized that they were in for a change—for the
better.

THE SCARECROW: GETTING TO KNOW THE MEDIA

As that buzz was starting up in Muchkinland, Dorothy soon turned to her
first of many allies in her journey—the Scarecrow. Think of the Scarecrow as our knowledge base; he is the information we need to navigate
through our journey. He understood the forest. He knew about Oz. He
even understood how to get what he wanted from the heartless trees. At
his very core, the Scarecrow served as the guide for Dorothy's journey.
Without his assistance, Dorothy would still be standing at the fork in the
road. But with his support, she had the information she needed to move
forward. He led her from those first steps on the yellow brick road straight
through to the wizard's castle. We have a Scarecrow of sorts. Only for us,
our guide is knowledge and information—specific information about the
media outlets with whom we can work.

Believe it or not, the media can truly be our best friends. By knowing
the local reporters and media, and using them to lead us through the
process, we can build up our success. Reporters can be our best friends
and guides, if we allow them to be. You can work through all the media
outlets in your community, including

- Daily newspapers: These are the publications we are used to receiving on our doorstep. Most cities and towns have one newspaper of
  record, the one paper that everyone reads with their coffee in the
  morning. This newspaper usually has a large circulation, an online
  edition, and a very structured staff. To identify the best ways to reach
  these publications, just read them. When the NRP met in Mississippi,
  it received enormous support from the *Clarion-Ledger*. And that support translated into hundreds of parents and teachers attending an

NRP town hall meeting in Jackson in the middle of July. You'll start to notice the same reporter covering education issues or issues related specifically to your community. That person will be your first point of contact and will be able to guide you through the staff structure once you've built a relationship. Just remember that these reporters are often juggling multiple stories and are on multiple deadlines. Their time is at a premium, so use their time wisely.

> Before I called a reporter, I had done my homework and it was right in front of me. I gave him facts about the best ways to teach reading, numbers of kids who were failing, and our test scores compared to other schools'. I really tried to help him write his story.

- Weekly/nondaily newspapers: While weekly newspapers aren't as popular as they once were, they still play a valuable communications role in our community. Working with a very small staff (if there is even more than one person), weekly newspapers have the time to explore a story and spend time fleshing out the details.
- Radio: Radio is more than the national call-in shows with which we are familiar. Virtually every radio station in the country covers news and community events in some form. There are local talk shows to discuss issues at length. There are news reporters who attend local events. There are on-air announcements of gatherings. We often underestimate the amount of time we listen to the radio, but think about the time during the day when you listen—when you're driving, awakening in the morning, and so on. To better understand the stations and programs in the community, just ask your friends, family, and coworkers what they listen to. The wide range of their responses will surprise you.
- Television: Just like newspapers and radio, there is more to television than prime-time entertainment programs and the national nightly news. Each major network (ABC, CBS, NBC) should have a local affiliate in your community that covers local issues and broadcasts local news. Additionally, the number of cable networks and shows continues to grow. When the NRP met in New York City, it wasn't NBC or CBS that covered the meeting. It was Channel 1. And its reach was

significant because New York parents watched that channel. Don't forget that local issues also appear on programs like CNN, Fox News Channel, and MSNBC. You have a good story to tell, as education and reading issues remain popular. Just watch the news programs you usually watch, and ask yourself if you could see an airing of a reading story focused on your school.

- Internet: The Internet is a fantastic repository for information and news. Not only do we have a wealth of online news sites, but there are also chat rooms, special interest pages, and websites. And if you don't see the information on reading that should be out there, you can create your own website and serve as your own news source.

WHOM DO YOU CONTACT?

Knowing what media outlets are available is just the beginning of effective media outreach. Many stations run news stories 24 hours a day, so even the smallest media outlet is busy. It is vital to know whom to go to, and calling the main number of a newspaper isn't enough. Review past articles and staff lists to help you target your approach. Just remember to follow a few simple rules.

To generate media coverage of an event or meeting, be sure to contact both the assignment editor and the reporter who handles similar activities. And if you will have a particularly compelling visual (such as a march or event with signs), be sure to ask if they can send a photographer as well.

If you think there is an untold story out there or have a great idea for a follow-up story, contact the reporter who originally covered the story.

If you are unhappy with current coverage of reading issues in your community, contact the reporter first. If you are not satisfied with her response, contact her editor (newspapers) or producer (radio and television).

You should never shy away from contacting a columnist. If you have a great idea for a future column, lay it out for him. If you enjoyed a particular piece he wrote, tell him. You'll find a particular columnist will focus on a few key themes. Watch for them to figure out which local columnists cover education issues.

In addition to providing news coverage that is objective reporting of facts and events, newspapers also take an official stance on an issue on their editorial pages. These editorials are read by local officials, and they often influence them to take action. If there is a particular issue that you believe has been neglected by the community, try to meet with the editorial board of your newspaper. These meetings could lead to an official editorial and could make a real difference.

We all recognize the importance of teaching vocabulary to our children. Working with the media, we will need to learn a few new vocabulary words of our own. Reporters often seem to speak their own language, so it is important to be up on the current lingo. Using the language they use and adding a few more words to our vocabulary goes a long way.

We often hear a reporter is on deadline. That means she's trying to finish another story. To avoid hearing this disappointing response, just understand a reporter's work cycle. Most print reporters go on deadline in the mid-afternoon, as they get ready for the next day's publications. So be sure to contact them during the late morning or soon after lunch. With radio and television reporters and producers, just be sure not to call them right before their shows go on the air.

We've all heard of Deep Throat of Watergate fame. And we've all seen the television newsmagazine shows where sources are behind a screen, talking with an altered voice. So most of us have heard terms like *on the record*, *on background*, and *off the record*. These words mean different things to different people. So just follow a simple rule. Don't say anything to the media you don't want on the front page the next day. When talking to a reporter, always believe everything is on the record. That will keep you away from any trouble.

For the media, reading instruction is not a new issue. And many reporters have been bombarded over the years with education stories. They have reported on "The Reading Wars," telling tales of the skirmishes between phonics and whole language. So a reporter's first question will be, what is the news hook? What is the pitch? A news hook is the particular angle you are selling. The start of the school year, the purchase of a new text book series, or new test scores are all news hooks. That news hook becomes part of your pitch. The pitch lays out what the story is, why it is important, and how it ties into the news of the day. It is your executive summary of the article you'd like to see. It's your opportunity to sell your story.

THE LION: THE ARSENAL AVAILABLE TO YOU

With the Scarecrow by our side, we can now move our journey forward. We have found that knowledge to guide us is useful, but we are also in need of strength. Working with the media is a tool to help us in our fight to help our children get the best reading instruction possible, and it requires us to use every available tool. We need to stand guard, take advantage of every opportunity to get our message out. And we need the courage to stand up for what we believe in, push forward on what we know to be correct, and ensure that our schools are doing the right thing. We need our Lion.

For Dorothy, it took some time to discover exactly what the lion had inside him. For us, it takes a similar amount of time to truly appreciate the wide arsenal of informational tools available to us.

Very few of us are elected officials, with a media relations office and a press secretary to set up meetings. We're not a company, with a large advertising budget and a significant economic impact on the region. Most of us are concerned parents, seeking the best education possible for our children and our neighbors' children.

This sincerity and desire for the right thing give us a powerful voice. And with a powerful voice, we have a full arsenal of tools available, specific actions that can help reach and influence the different corners of the media. Many of these tools are simple. And all can be successfully used with a little effort and a lot of enthusiasm.

Media relations have been around a lot longer than we think, and their early activities were carried out by individuals who just wanted to make a difference. Paul's missives in the New Testament were the world's first "letters to the editor" campaign. Paul Revere's ride was likely the first editorial board tour. Franklin Roosevelt's fireside chats were simply a radio distribution of his op-eds. Woodstock was nothing more than a lengthy community meeting set to music. And those postcards you receive today, announcing real estate open houses in your neighborhood, are merely a hybrid of a media advisory. Anyone can get the media's attention if he understands how to do it.

When we want to tell a friend or family member something, what do we do? We pick up the phone, shoot out an e-mail, or have a face-to-face conversation. The same goes for reporters. If we want to talk to a reporter, we just give her a phone call. If we want to provide information, mail it to her or send her an e-mail. Phone calls and e-mail are the most successful ways to reach the media. We may not get an immediate response, but with some follow-up and perseverance, we can have an impact.

The most read section of newspapers remains the Letters to the Editor section. This is our opportunity to respond directly to what appears in the newspaper or happens in the community. By writing a short letter (usually around 100 words) we have an excellent chance of getting our message printed in the newspaper. (See the sample letter to the editor in appendix D.)

If a 100-word letter is not enough space to fully communicate our argument, we can submit an op-ed article to our local or regional newspaper. Op-eds actually are opposition editorials. They were originally designed to allow outside voices to respond to the newspaper's official editorial. Now, op-eds are opinion columns written by a wide collection of individuals. They allow us 700 words to express our opinion, in our words, and under our signature.

MAKE A SPLASH

The media are often drawn to a public event—a community meeting, a student march, a school-based activity, or a presentation by a respected official. If we decide to use an event to draw attention to our children's reading instruction, there are a number of things we need to do. First, ask the local media to publicize the event beforehand in their calendar. Be sure to provide the media with a short media advisory, which provides key details of the event (location, time and date, participants, purpose) as well as a contact name and number they can reach with any questions. Then be sure to follow up with a phone call to reporters, reminding them of the event. (See the sample media advisory in appendix D.)

Following the event, we should provide the media with a press release. Just think of it as a summary of our event. Simply lay out what the event was, who attended, and what was accomplished. Include a short quote from a participant, stating how he was affected by the event and the issue. Then send it to the media, along with a contact person they can talk to for more information.

If you aren't planning a specific event, you can still reach the media. If you want to discuss a particular issue or concern with a reporter, ask for a desk-side briefing. This briefing gives you the opportunity to talk to the reporter about reading issues, telling your story and providing any relevant information and statistics. Or you can seek a meeting with the editorial board, presenting the same case to the newspaper's editors and editorial writers.

These may all seem like simple tactics. But put together, they make us as savvy as any press secretary and as skilled as any corporate spokesperson. Using these activities, we behave in a manner familiar to a reporter. Coupled with the passion for really making a difference in how reading is taught in our schools, we are now an unbeatable presence. We are the kings of the education jungle. (See the sample news release in appendix D.)

THE TIN MAN: BUILDING THE BRIGADES

Knowledge and strength are valuable tools. But there is more that we need on our journey. True success comes from using that knowledge and strength to display our heart and passion for improving reading instruction to give our children a good start. Just as the Tin Man wanted to show the world he had feelings, so too must we put our heart and soul into this important issue. Unless we feel the passion for it, we won't be able to get others to join us.

Why is this support important? Yes, one dedicated parent voicing concerns about classroom instruction is important. You can convince a reporter to write a story. You can make an appearance on a local radio program to discuss the issue. You can begin to move the issue forward. But imagine the impact if 10 parents are all doing the same thing with the same reporter. Imagine 100 parents. Imagine 1,000 parents, along with

> I never realized how much other mothers felt the way I did until I shared how I felt when my son came home telling me he thought he was dumb. That pain got me to raise my voice, and I couldn't believe how much of a difference it made to talk about real kids, not just numbers.

their kids, buzzing throughout the community about the need for proven reading instruction. That is how change is made, and that is how the media begin to take real notice.

The heart of the Tin Man is your rallying cry. Reading instruction is important to us because we have kids, relatives, and neighbors who are directly affected by it. It is important because if our kids don't read, they can't learn. It's important because if they can't read they won't get jobs and be successful members of our community. Don't underestimate the number of people who have an interest in the problem, who are already very upset about this issue, or who are trying to figure out what they can do about it. We can use their help to reach out to the media to gain even more supporters. Even Dorothy had an army of three to help her along her journey.

Don't despair. You are not alone on this trek. If anything was learned during the release of the NRP report or by the increased discussion of reading instruction since then, it is that reading is an issue that is important to the vast majority of Americans. There is strength in numbers, and finding supporters of scientifically based reading instruction only helps us make a real difference in the classroom.

Where do you find support? Family is a good start. Even the smallest school children can stuff envelopes and lick stamps. Look to friends. Those with children are probably equally concerned with the quality of instruction in the classroom. Get them involved. Reach out to the organizations you belong to—the PTA, your place of worship, and the youth soccer league. Those organizations and their members can be powerful voices. Talk with colleagues at work, strangers in the grocery store, tellers at the bank, and anyone with whom you happen to spend time. You'll be surprised how your passion can generate concern in others.

Once you have built a cadre of supporters, you need to know what to ask of them. Whether someone wants to be involved a little or a lot, there are a great number of things you can ask them to do. They can attend a meeting. They can send a letter to the editor. They can call a reporter. They can enlist the help of their friends. They can talk to friends they might have in the media. They can sign a petition to get the attention and enlist the support of an elected official or community leader. Just don't take your supporters for granted; be sure to effectively use them to accomplish the ultimate mission—improving reading instruction in your schools and boosting reading skills in your kids.

An army without supplies can never win. So you must equip your supporters with information. Provide them the same arsenal you rely on. As you speak with the media, you need to develop a series of talking points that you want to communicate. These messages should be short and simple. They should be important to you, and attract the attention of others. Share these messages with your supporters, making sure that all of them are also using them in their discussions, their letters, and their advocacy.

That groundswell described earlier, of a thousand parents showing their concern for reading instruction, is a powerful one. But imagine how powerful it is if all of those parents are speaking with the same voice. They express the same concerns. They use the same vocabulary. That is the power of messaging.

MESSAGING: SPEAKING CLEARLY AND WITH ONE VOICE

Messaging need not be difficult, nor need it be complicated. What are we trying to say? Why are we concerned? And what change do we want to see? That is the core of messaging. As we begin to work with our local media to improve reading instruction, our messaging can include points such as the following.

We know how to teach reading. We know what works, and we know what doesn't.

Reading is a skill that must be taught and must be practiced. And just like teaching a child to play the piano or hit a curve ball, learning requires explicit and systematic instruction.

Strong reading skills are the key to future successes. If we don't teach our children correctly through proven methods from the start, they will be forced to play catch-up in other subjects later in school.

Our kids are too important to experiment on in the classroom. Classroom instruction should be based on proven facts. Lessons should be built on the strongest research that shows that reading skills must be taught systematically and explicitly.

Most people who work with the media are doing so because they are paid to or because it is part of their job. That is what sets us apart. We are doing this because we truly care enough to make a difference. We are doing this because, in the deepest crevices of our hearts, we know it is the right thing to do. Our payoff is better classroom instruction for our kids. Our profit is improved achievement for our kids. And nothing should keep us from that ultimate payday.

AND DON'T FORGET LITTLE TOTO: THE POWER OF RESEARCH

Along the way, we may have forgotten that we had Toto along with us. Before she had even eyeballed a yellow brick, Dorothy had come to trust and depend on her beloved dog. Toto spoke up for her, he defended her unconditionally, and he gave her the strength to face everything from a tornado to a wicked witch.

We have an equally strong and dependable friend—reading research. Is my child learning to read? Why not? What can I do? What should the school do? Why isn't it being done? Underneath the answers to all of these questions is the research that answers the questions—a friend that has been with us since before the journey started.

Dorothy more closely embraced Toto as they continued through their journey thought Oz. We must do the same with the wealth of reading research that we can trust in and depend on. It is the ammunition for the arsenal we are ready to deploy. It is this research that ultimately helps the media see the story move from the concerns of one parent to a systematic shift in how we teach our children to read.

No one expects us to be research experts. We aren't expected to conduct experimental or quasi-experimental studies, nor are we asked to develop meta-analyses. We don't need to go back to school to get our PhDs to improve reading instruction in our local schools. Just knowing where the research is, and the highlights of what it says, and how it applies to our classrooms are valuable weapons. And they are weapons that virtually no one can defend against.

Over the past few years, we have seen a wealth of information surface on reading research and the proven and successful ways to teach reading. But it is important to know that not all educational research is equal in quality. There are a number of sources that can assist parents in making a distinction between research that can be trusted and research that cannot.

These online resources or print materials can loyally stand by your side.
Some of these include

National Reading Panel (www.nationalreadingpanel.org)
Partnership for Reading (www.nifl.gov/partnershipforreading)
No Child Left Behind (www.nclb.gov)

(See the resources section for more.)

Simply having the research in our basket isn't enough, though. The
Scouts told us to "be prepared." It is important for life, and very important for media relations. Any time you ask someone to change, you are
bound to receive resistance. Ask your son or daughter to change clothes
before leaving for school, and you'll face dozens of questions as to why.
Ask our schools and communities to change how they teach reading, and
you are in for a far less civil exchange.

If we ask children to do something they are not willing or ready to do,
they are likely to go to another grown-up to get a second opinion. In the
field of reading, people who resist change are likely to tell their story to
the same reporters you are talking to. Just as we talk about what should be
done to improve reading skills, those negative critics are telling reporters
why it won't work. We cannot shrink from such resistance. Instead, we
must rise up and confront it directly.

To do this, we need to know our opposition. Identify who is opposed to
our issue, and why they are opposed. Pull together our research, get our
facts in order, and get ready to go on the attack. Remember, we have
decades of proven research on our side. That is our strongest argument.
Toto stood up to seizure, fire, and flying monkeys. The reading research
we have equally stands up to all that the witches of the East and West can
throw at it.

I couldn't believe the people who were just waiting to prove us wrong.
They argued that we didn't know what we were talking about, it was too
complicated. They said that we didn't understand what we were asking
for—it would cost too much. But they couldn't say that the way they were
teaching was successful for all kids. We knew they didn't have a leg to
stand on.

Just remember, too often, people tear down ideas without offering substitutes. It is important to keep our messages and our work with reporters positive. Above all, we are seeking to fix the problem. We are offering solutions. We are trying to make a difference. Let the critics stay negative and wring their hands over the solutions. While they are doing so, we are helping the media better understand that there is a right way to teach reading. And that we should be using it, *today*, in our classrooms.

CLICKING THE HEELS OF THOSE RUBY SLIPPERS: REACHING OUR GOALS

It has been a long journey. When we first started, we had a simple goal. We wanted to make sure our children were learning how to read. We wanted to build strong readers. And we recognized that using the power of the local media was an effective way of bringing about change and reform in our local community.

As we started down the path, it looked like a daunting challenge. After all, the realm of the media is for professionals, for those wizards who know how to manipulate words and ideas. For those witches who know how to shade the facts and shout down new ideas. It is not a place for regular parents just trying to make a difference.

But we've learned that nothing could be further from the truth. Accompanied by a number of friends along the way, we can make a difference through the media. We just needed to know where to start, with the following:

- Knowledge, both of the media outlets in our community and the reporters, editors, and producers who work there
- Strength, displayed through the use of and appreciation for all of the tactics and activities that are effective in reaching the media
- Heart, demonstrated through our passion for this issue and for our ability to build community support for our goals

Now, we know we had the power to change all along. All we needed to do was click our heels together, and share our passion and dedication with the media.

TIPS FOR PARENTS

Tricks of Trade: What You Should Know When Working With the Media

Developing Your Message

- Know your goal. Be clear what you want to communicate in your conversation.
- Know your audience. Use terms and experiences they can relate to.
- Modify your message to reflect current situations, but always remember your underlying theme(s).

Understanding the Media

- Understand the culture and goals of the news media, how the business operates, and who reporters compete with and report to concerning their stories. You not only need to sell your story, you also need to show how it fits with the goals of the media outlet, the interest of their readers, and the reporter. Remember, you're giving the reporter an opportunity to tell a story that has yet to be told.
- Know the variety of media outlets available in your area. There is more than the local newspaper. Look to radio stations, TV, cable, and even community newsletters.
- Target the appropriate editor or reporter at each outlet. You want to know who covers your neighborhood, education in your community, or local politics.
- Remember that there are different methods for delivering your messages. You can provide the facts and figures. You can tell a personal story. You can do whatever is necessary to relate to your audience.
- Know your rights in an interview. You don't have to answer every question. You don't have to talk about issues with which you are unfamiliar or uncomfortable.
- Realize that different types of media are interested in different types of stories.

Delivering Your Message

- Prepare, prepare, prepare. You can never be too prepared.
- Use succinct and quotable talking points to summarize and communicate your messages.
- Prepare talking points in advance so you know exactly what you are going to say. Stick to these points. Doing so ensures that your message will come across in the final product.
- State points simply and briefly. Be honest and stop when you have answered the question.
- Make your points relevant. Use colorful language and offer useful analogies, personal experience, and common sense.
- Use data wisely, and highlight disparities and imbalances. Don't be afraid to state the statistics. They validate your point.
- Offer the big picture, stress the bottom line, state your agenda, and make a pitch for the help you need.
- If you don't know an answer to a question, say you don't know and tell the questioner you'll find out and get back to her. Say only what you know to be true. Don't guess.
- Don't answer questions not related to the topic at hand. The interview is your time. You should talk about your issues.
- Bridge back to your message. Take the question you've been asked and link it to an answer you want to provide.
- Don't fill in dead air if you feel you have already answered a question.
- Get to know your local newspaper editor.
- Don't get angry with reporters. They have their jobs, you have yours.
- Repeat your basic message as often as possible!

8

You Can Do It! How to Change Laws to Better Educate Children

Richard Long

You may find that you have tried working for change at your school, in your school district, and with your state, and there are still problems causing children to struggle. Despite Reading First, the federal law that funds schools to use research-based reading instruction, educate teachers, and use appropriate materials, you may find that there are some unresolved issues getting in the way. Perhaps it's the requirement for students to be tested and diagnosed for possible reading problems. Maybe your school finds the funding is not enough to do the job. This chapter tells you the secrets of lobbying like a pro and walks you through the steps so you can get the results you want. Richard Long is an experienced Washington insider who has successfully worked on children's education issues for several decades.

Every day almost 54 million children go to school. Some walk, some take the bus, some are driven. All arrive with a vast array of hopes, problems, challenges, assets, and potential, and as they move into their classrooms they change from being individuals to being part of a group. They are instructed as a group, yet it is as individuals that each learns. Unfortunately, the system of teaching in groups leaves many people behind. When the instruction is poor, or based on outmoded thinking, the entire class suffers. Even when the instruction is effective for many children, others are lost.

When a parent walks into a school and wants to help the school meet the needs of his or her child, there can be a set of problems that never were anticipated. Frequently, the school can't change, there are rules, there is a lack of resources and a lack of options. While there are many things a person can do, often it requires some type of government intervention. This chapter is a discussion about what you can do. However, before you take the steps needed to advocate for your child with the federal government, see if you can talk with people in your local school system. Ask the principal if something can be done to help your child, ask the superintendent, and communicate with your school board members. Many problems can be solved at the local level.

Schools often see parents as volunteers, helpers, or members of the PTA rather than child advocates. Rarely are they welcomed as equals. So how do you go from worried parent to advocate? This chapter zeros in on how you can make a difference.

BACKGROUND

The federal involvement in education is an important part of our complex multilayered system. It has traditionally been the advocate for children of poverty, those who have special needs, who speak different languages. Government is also part of our national conscience when it comes to large-scale change. Too frequently state and local levels of government don't want to or are unable to raise taxes so that all children have access to a good basic education. Or they are limited by tradition about how they teach, govern schools, and keep everybody accountable. The federal government has stepped in when individuals are ignored by some parts of the education system.

The basis for this intervention lies in the 14th amendment to the U.S. Constitution that says that all Americans are entitled to equal protection under law and that they have property rights. There are numerous examples of how the federal government stepped in to fill a gap in the education of groups of children, and in each one, parents played a very important part. In 1964, Congress decided that children who lived in states with few resources were being put at an unfair disadvantage when compared to children who lived in wealthier states. Congress found that students who lived in these states were not being taught how to read and that this was resulting in their inability to learn in other academic areas. This in turn meant that other students were getting an unfair advantage in getting jobs, higher education, and the fruits of those endeavors. The result was the landmark Elementary and Secondary Education Act. This act has been redrafted nine times since it was first enacted. In each of these rewritings, the role of parents has been changed.

In the recently passed version, the No Child Left Behind Act that includes Reading First, parents have moved from an occasional advisory role to having many alternatives and much authority. Among these alternatives is the right to be advised as to whether or not their child's school is failing to make adequate yearly progress, called AYP. Another is the ability to choose whether or not their child needs to have after school tutoring help and to be able to use public funds to secure that help. Parent advocates for this program were focused on the need to push schools to change faster, to affect more students more effectively, and to do it now.

In 1976 Congress found that children who had disabilities were being disenfranchised from the public schools. These children were kept out of general education classrooms and as a result were not learning what they needed to know to be full members of society. Congress responded with the Education for All Handicapped Children's Act. Now known as the Individuals with Disabilities Education Act (IDEA), this legislation was a result of the determined efforts of parents who had a strong need. They wanted their children with disabilities to be educated. The research was clear. These students would be better educated and more likely to become active members of their communities if they were part of general education classrooms. The key was that parents started talking to their legislators.

Congress also passed the Magnet School Act to assist in school desegregation. In this act Congress decided that children who were of a specific ethnic or cultural group couldn't be effectively educated if they were in classrooms limited only to children who were of the same background. Children, Congress found, learn better when there is a mix of students from different cultural groups who have a wide range of learning goals.

Recently several parents whose children were enrolled in bilingual education classes were upset. They believed that their children were getting an inferior education. They wanted their kids to speak and read in English. They wrote letters to Congress and were eventually invited to testify. As a result, in recent years, Congress has acted to change the laws governing bilingual education, which for many years had students placed in special classes in which they used their native language to help them learn. This resulted in children taking a very long time to learn to speak and write English before they could enter English-speaking classrooms to learn academic subjects.

For each one of these groups Congress acted, but members did not do so out of the blue. They acted because somebody brought the problem to the attention of key members, found others who thought like they did, told more people about it, and pushed. Those people were parents.

How do they push? Developing an advocacy program is demanding work. Simply standing up at a public meeting and making a statement that something isn't right usually isn't the total formula for success. It is, however, the beginning. Effective advocacy requires having several critical elements. These elements include the idea—fixing something that is wrong; the champion—the legislator who will take up the issue as his own; the process—managing the legislative process; and the organization—building the support team.

THE IDEA

The first phase of an advocacy program is to develop an idea of what needs to be done. With a clear idea a champion can be found to push the concept through a legislature. It also is the first step in finding allies who will help your champion to win more attention and win votes.

The idea is critically important. The idea is the actual fix of the problem. Usually it is some wrong that you want to have righted. What will make or break an advocacy program is whether or not the idea is appealing to more than one person. This means that if some problem is so highly defined that it is about just a very few people, it will be very hard to rally others to your cause. Others may care, but they will not help you get

---

The first time I stood up to speak at a public meeting, I felt sick. My hands were sweaty, my stomach was in knots, and I was trembling. But what drove me forward was the thought that if I didn't stand up for my son and the other kids, who was going to do it?

something done. The issue needs to be defined so that others can develop a stake in the problem and become willing to help fix it. The best idea needs to be simply stated or it won't gather any others to promote it. Frequently the fix is simply stated like this: Schools should be able to teach children who aren't learning to read using the best methods possible. What makes it gather strength is when others see their own children as having the same problem. The clarity of the idea is important because it moves people from the problem to the solution.

It is important to take the idea for change and see what research has been done on the subject to determine how many children may be suffering from a similar problem and what happens to these children as a result. Seeking a legislative remedy will collapse if someone says, "Didn't we try to do something like this a few years ago?" or "Didn't we look into this a few years ago and find out that only a few people really have this problem?" Checking to see what data may be available is critically important. How can you get this done?

First, an Internet search is a good start. Second, find out if any legislation has been introduced that has tried to deal with this problem, what was done as a result, and who were the organizers of the effort. Your members of Congress or their staff can help you locate this information. In addition, you can also get help locally from teachers or administrators who would like to jump on your bandwagon because they would like to see a change made.

FINDING A CHAMPION

Finding the champion is more than just finding a friend who will listen and give advice. It means finding a legislator or a columnist who will take on the issue—the problem and the solution—as theirs. There are several ways to find a champion. One way is to meet with all the legislators who work on education and see if there is any interest among this group.

It was so hard for me to fight back against the resentment I felt. Why did I have to take this action? I had a job, a family, and other things, and there were not enough hours in the day to do what I had to do without taking on another job.

Another idea is to look into the backgrounds of all the legislators and see who has children or grandchildren in school, and see if you can learn any information about how they are doing in school. All parents, whether your next door neighbor or a member of Congress, want their children to do well in school and will get very frustrated when they aren't getting the information or help that they need for their children to be successful.

Now that the background information is in hand, ask the appropriate members for an appointment to see them. Do bring information about your child—the problem, how many others it affects, and what needs to be done. Avoid raising the subject of a legislator's child, as this may feel like an intrusion of her privacy. She knows about her child, and she has already made a decision as to how public she wants to go with her child's problem.

Sometimes a legislator is looking for an issue that will make him a leader in the eyes of his colleagues and the wider community, even if he doesn't have a personal stake in the issue. Finding a champion based on what idea may be appealing to him or her requires a little work. You can find out which members have already taken up similar "causes." This is important as rarely can a member of Congress be seen as the champion of too many causes. So they may "specialize" in some aspect of education. Frequently, some of the best champions are fairly new to the legislative arena and have served for only one or two terms, but they have learned that fellow legislators hold knowledgeable colleagues in high regard, and they want to build their reputations.

However having a champion isn't enough. You need to help your champion build allies. Sometimes the allies come before choosing the champion. To find allies, you need to talk to others—start with other parents, and then talk to other community leaders and elected leaders. Don't be afraid to ask if they will help you. If a leader doesn't want to be your key leader or champion, she will say so. When this happens, she will sometimes say, "I will help, but I have a lot of other things on my plate," and offer a different way of helping you. Ask if the bill comes up, can you count on her to vote for it? Ask who she thinks is important in the legislative process for you to talk with. It is important to find out what the "natural" network is for your idea.

THE FORMAL PROCESS

In civics class you learned about how the government works. Unfortunately, for most teenagers this wasn't their greatest hour. However, it is important to understand how the formal process operates and the best time to intervene in it. Voters elect representatives who vote in bodies—legislatures at the state level and Congress at the federal level. The sequence of events is as follows. Ideas are introduced in a bill, then they are studied by a committee of the legislature, voted out of committee, and then voted on by one chamber of a legislature. The next step is to work through the same sequence in the second chamber. After each chamber finishes a bill, the differences between the chambers then have to be resolved in what is called a conference committee. Finally, the bill is signed by the executive—the governor in a state or the president at the federal level. Simple.

One of the key links in this process is the agenda-setting role of the committee chairperson. The committee chairperson becomes the first filter in the formal legislative process. Once an idea is introduced and it becomes a bill, the committee chairperson must decide if it will go forward. This decision is made based on the support the bill may have, as reflected by the members of the committee. You can help to get this crucial support by spending some time briefing committee members to win their votes. This is done by setting up appointments and taking a copy of the draft legislation, some examples of how the problem affects the committee member's district, or any other information that will help connect the committee member to your issue. Remember—you can more easily get support if people are attracted to the issue.

Your goal is to have them cosponsor the legislation. This will send a signal to other members that there is strong support for the proposed bill, as the more members sign on as cosponsors, the more strength and importance it has. One of the keys to seeking support and cosponsorship is having members of both of the major political parties signed on as cosponsors. Having bipartisan cosponsors is one way of telling a committee chairperson that the proposal/idea/bill has the attention of the members.

Another way to get the chairperson's support is to ask for it directly. When a chairperson cosponsors a bill, this is a powerful signal that he or

This is how a bill becomes a law:
1. Bill is introduced
2. Committee hearing
3. Floor action
4. Other chamber—bill introduced
5. Committee hearing
6. Floor action
7. Conference committee
8. Signed into law

she is in favor of it. To do this effectively, you need to find the support of others in the chairperson's home district.

THE INFORMAL PROCESS

The informal process of taking an idea and making it a law includes all the elements of the formal process with one addition—by mustering the energy, compassion, or attention of lawmakers at each level of government, you can kick the formal process into gear. Sometimes the informal system pushes the formal system through compelling testimony by a parent at a committee hearing.

> The first time I testified, I was so intimidated. I wondered if I could convince these legislators that I had a critical problem they should deal with. I felt they were probably too busy with bigger, more important people and issues. But I was so surprised when a couple of legislators told me later that they could really relate to what I was saying because it was clear it came from my heart.

Members of the legislature are frequently captivated not only by the information in the presentation but also by the pain with which parents talk about the needs of their children. This personal testimony that takes the issue to a human level makes a very powerful impression and argument and one that members will sometimes quote during formal consideration of a measure.

VISIT YOUR LAWMAKER'S OFFICE

Visits to a member's office also make a strong impression. Most legislators maintain offices in their home district and in the capital. To find out about them check your telephone directory in the government section, or check online. Call them and ask for an appointment. Once the appointment is made, keep it, come on time, and bring any information that is helpful to clarify your point. After saying hello, get quickly to the point and make it as clear as possible without making disparaging remarks. Let the facts speak for themselves. After you have presented these facts, ask for questions and don't be surprised by the questions you get. Remember, you have been living this issue, but the legislator is just finding out about it. Always be polite, but ask for a commitment or suggestion for what can be done.

> My trick to help me gain courage was to picture myself as a leader. I thought about what I would say, how I would look standing at a podium giving testimony. It was like—soon I began to believe I could do this.

Frequently, legislators will respond by saying that the first step will be a letter they will send asking for clarification of the issue from the responsible agency or individual. If you have come to ask for help with a problem that affects only your child, this may well make a difference. But if many children share the problem, then another solution is needed. Ask for it.

CALL YOUR LAWMAKER

Phone calls are another important tool to communicate with legislators. And the rules for communicating effectively hold here as well. Stay on task. Write down the points you want to make. You will be surprised that you can forget to ask for help or get caught up talking about some hurt or person who has treated you badly rather than staying focused on the problem at hand. Make sure you are polite and listen, but don't forget you are asking for their help.

> I knew I had one shot at convincing my legislator that I had a problem he needed to do something about. I made notes, practiced saying the important points, and made it clear what I wanted him to do. I didn't want to appear to be an angry, aggressive parent who was frothing at the mouth. That would make it too easy to ignore me and my issue.

WRITE LETTERS TO YOUR LAWMAKER

You may be unable to make a visit to speak to your legislator, but you can send a letter. Here are some guidelines. Letters to members of a legislature have to have several critical points. First they need to be clear, state the problem, and make your request for action. Don't send a letter with more than one issue in it. Don't threaten—anyone. Threats rarely invite people to solve problems, and once you make a threat, any hope of discussion is over. Find the address of your legislators on the web or in the phone book. Address them and any elected official as The Honorable (George Smith, for example). State who you are and why you are writing. Be specific as to what you want done. Letters can also be a great way to communicate with more than one member of the legislature. They can provide individual lawmakers with background information about what the problem is and why your proposed solution makes sense. (See the sample letter to your legislator in appendix D.)

LETTERS TO THE EDITOR

In most political offices there are staff members who are responsible for reviewing letters to the editor that appear in the lawmaker's hometown newspapers to get an advance warning of problems his or her constituents are facing. If you want to raise attention about the issue you're dealing with, consider writing a letter to the editor that responds to an article that appeared in the paper. The letter should be brief, to the point, and either refute or agree with the points in the original article. Send your letter no more than two or three days after the original article, as it becomes old news after that time. (See chapter 8 for more information about working with the media and the sample letter to the editor in appendix D.)

DON'T BE AFRAID TO COMPETE

The legislative process is competitive. For every person who wants money spent one way, there are others who want it spent another way. And for each person who wants to change the status quo, there are others who want to keep things exactly as they are. So it is important to learn who may be in opposition to your idea and why.

In the education field there is a wide range of interest groups. Teachers, administrators, publishers, politicians, computer vendors—all have their own special interests. President Eisenhower, one of the nation's most respected presidents, had an interesting perspective on this. He never subscribed to the notion that those in opposition to his ideas were motivated by anything other than doing good. He avoided a lot of anger and focused on getting what he thought was the right thing done. He also did not give his adversaries any fuel that could be used to complicate arguments to support his primary purpose. He talked about what needed to be done.

But it's important to understand the perspective of your opposition. For teachers it might mean that the change you want will add to the demands of their day, or they don't have the training or the textbooks to teach a new way. They don't want to fail, either. For administrators a new requirement might mean that funds are going in a direction they can't control and that they already have to cut back on things. For others, it may mean that a book series that they worked on for 10 years could become out of date. While it is important to understand what the barriers are, it is not a reason to stop pushing for change.

To be successful in advocating for your child and others, you need to understand that the legislative process involves people. Just like you, they had to start at the beginning to learn the process, and just like you, they have many pressures on them. It is hard not to take every setback as a slap in the face, but the reality is that the process is designed to be complex. The reason for this is simple: Our founding fathers did not want the government to pass laws too easily. They didn't trust government, so they wanted to make sure that it required a lot of agreement by many people to make a law. It is also a reason why it is important to always be polite. You never know when the person saying no to you today might be able to help in a small way later on in the process—remembering you as polite, yet forceful, may pay off down the road.

TAKING THE FIRST STEP

Several years ago a mother begged her fourth-grade son's teacher, "Please just teach him to read." The teacher didn't know what to do. The mother asked the principal of the school why her children and others were not learning to read. The principal said it was complicated. At that point the mother went from pleading mother to advocate. This scene is played out in schools each day. When a parent is unable to get change made in her child's school, she has two choices—to accept the limitations of the school and therefore sacrifice her child's future, or to seek a remedy elsewhere. And at this point, a parent steps into the role of being a state or federal advocate.

Taking this step requires courage and conviction. It also requires persistence. It doesn't require lots of money, lots of high-priced talent, or legions of movie stars standing in your corner. They are just tools. But you can use your voice, your determination to provide your children the best possible education, and groups of other parents to help move mountains. Others have done so over the last 30 years, and the result has been federal laws that require all schools to provide a quality education in the No Child Left Behind Act; to allow children with disabilities to get a free, appropriate public education in the Education for All Handicapped Children Act; and to help struggling children of poor families to gain special help through the Title I program. These parents took their problem and turned it into an idea, found and recruited champions and allies by writing letters and making visits. They told their story and in doing so helped not only their own children but also millions of other children.

Just as women have redirected our medical research to address heart problems and breast cancer, and concerned parents have made a tremendous impact on drinking and driving laws, parents can also improve the education that their children receive and in so doing help many others. If not parents, then who will speak for the children?

TIPS FOR PARENTS

- Do your homework. Learn about your legislators and the issues they are concerned with.
- Move from worrying about the problem to coming up with a solution and figure out who may have a stake in the problem and be willing to work on the solution. Organize others who share your concern.
- Find some data to support your argument that this is a problem that affects lots of children.

- Learn how the process operates and when you have the best chance at influencing it.
- Learn how to clearly communicate your issue and convince others to take action. Propose solutions rather than simply discuss complaints.
- Use the media to help influence legislators.
- Use visits and calls to your legislators to ask for their help. Follow up and thank them when they provide it.

9

Team Up With Teachers

Sara M. Porter

Sometimes we take for granted that a teacher knows the best way to get your child over a hurdle. But many times, the teacher is experiencing a similar challenge himself or herself. He or she may not have been taught to teach reading using the latest research and does not know how to get "caught up." This chapter was written by a now retired and very experienced teacher who gives her perspective about why we are facing an epidemic in reading failure, how your child's teacher can help you, and ideas for other teachers who are struggling to help their students learn to read. The first part will help you create an alliance with your child's teacher. Part II will help teachers rethink their reading instruction. Consider sharing both with your child's teacher.

TEACHERS CAN BE YOUR ALLIES

Your teacher can become a very important partner in helping you to get the best and most valid reading instruction for your child. As you learned from earlier chapters, scientifically based comprehensive reading instruction that integrates the systematic teaching of phonics with explicit strategies to develop fluency, vocabulary, and reading comprehension has not always been used in schools. It's important that you know how this problem evolved, as this will help you determine your starting point with your child's school and exactly what you have to overcome to make changes in reading instruction.

The reading programs that reflect what we know from research about how children learn to read include systematic and direct instruction in phonemic awareness, phonics, reading fluency, vocabulary, and reading comprehension strategies and provide opportunities to practice them as they are taught. For many, many years they have been hard to find. Ask elementary school administrators why they don't provide such programs, and more than likely they reply that they *are* already doing so. They honestly believe this.

How did we get into this situation? How did learning how to read, which is without question the very foundation of an adequate education, come to be so badly misunderstood? Part of the answer is found in the reasons that we want children to learn to read in the first place.

Being able to read means a child has a wonderful ability to share ideas, to communicate, to learn what others have thought and done across ages. Because we read, we are able to learn things we might never have known. We grow mentally, we see more. Reading can make us laugh, give us knowledge, even help us cook, build things, and more. Reading is like nothing else we do. But it is a learned skill rather than one that comes naturally like learning to walk and talk.

Reading can make us laugh, give us knowledge, even help us cook, build things, and more. Reading is like nothing else we do. But it is a learned skill rather than one that comes naturally like learning to walk and talk.

The biggest hurdle in teaching children to read used to be that no one really understood what reading was. The brain was like a black box. Teachers put something in, and sometimes what they wanted came out. Sometimes it didn't. Why one child learned to read easily and the next one not at all was a mystery whose solution was elusive. Every time educators thought they had found a way to solve this problem, schools were asked to retool and retrain teachers, but still the group of children who did not learn to read persisted. To everyone's mystification, these children included some of the most intelligent students in our schools.

I couldn't understand how Josh, who seemed to learn everything so quickly, had such a hard time learning to read. I couldn't get answers from his teacher—everyone seemed to be as surprised as I was.

At long last science has given us answers, but schools are wary. Educators cannot see how these answers are any different from the other approaches that were previously purported to be magic bullets but that failed to succeed with all children. Teachers are immediately suspicious of claims that one approach will work for all children because our experience tells us that no one method works equally well for every child. Consequently, the science and evidence that now tell teachers that they must teach children to read using instruction that is systematic, structured, and comprehensive, and that this is necessary for all children, are viewed with suspicion. They do not understand that this is not simply an "approach." They do not understand that scientifically based reading instruction is not a "one-size-fits-all" solution. On the contrary, scientifically based instruction is built upon our knowledge of how children learn to read and why some children have difficulty learning. It asks that teachers understand this knowledge in depth so they can adjust instruction to meet every child's needs—needs that differ from child to child.

HOW WE GOT WHERE WE ARE TODAY

Educators have always been stymied by that stubborn group of children who simply don't learn to read as well or as quickly as their classmates. These children fall behind and give up. In times past that did not seem so important. They grew up to be farmers or artists, laborers or inventors, or frontiersman. Kentucky's Daniel Boone and Simon Kenton were both illiterate. But the world has changed, and not being able to read affects people in the most fundamental ways.

Reading texts have changed mightily over the years. Early in the 20th century educators discovered that most children could remember whole words, contrary to what was believed previously. They devised the concept of the "basal" reader. Children memorized a few words, and then used these to read simple stories. Lessons were standardized with a day-to-day plan for teaching a story. This method sidestepped an emphasis on learning the alphabet, which was seen as an arduous, dull job that got in the way of reading for meaning. While basal readers did include teaching phonics skills, the skills were not taught comprehensively and systematically. Therefore, many children who did not bring a wealth of early literacy and language experiences with them to the classroom were stymied when new words that they had not seen before were introduced in the texts. Their reading difficulties were heightened in the fourth and fifth grades when at least 10,000 new words were introduced in the reading materials. If the student could not use phonics skills to unlock the pronunciation of these new words, all was lost.

The basal reader approach to reading is in direct contrast to a comprehensive phonics program based on current research. This research tells us that phonics must be taught systematically and directly as part of a reading program that also focuses on the development of phonemic awareness, reading fluency, vocabulary, and reading comprehension strategies.

As students learned to analyze words for phonetic similarities and differences, they gradually increased their vocabularies. By controlling vocabulary load and readability levels (determined by various formulas that count the number of syllables in the words and the length of the sentences), the texts gradually became more difficult. Publishers assigned grade levels to represent different degrees of difficulty, but these designations tended to vary somewhat by each publisher's standards. Therefore, a second-grade book from one publisher might be considered more difficult than a second-grade book from another publisher.

Educators stayed with the basal readers for a long time. Teachers chose which to use according to what they felt their class needed. Their choices depended, of course, on what the school system allowed and could afford, and the amount of freedom granted to the teacher. He might have two or three reading groups in his class using various readers for various reasons. Some emphasized phonics more—some less.

Teachers were attracted to some supposed advantages of teaching with a basal reader: the controlled vocabulary that systematically taught new words accompanied by guides that became more and more elaborate as time went on. They provided daily lessons, practice exercises, and suggestions for interesting activities related to the story.

However, there were also significant drawbacks to teaching from a basal reader. First, there were no universal generalizations for teaching phonics and phonetic principles. For example, rules for segmenting a word into sounds were arbitrary. A child could be taught one method in third grade that differed from the one that had been taught in second grade. Another drawback was that good literature was rewritten to accommodate the reading levels. This could make excellent stories vapid and dull. A third criticism was that the use of basal readers meant dividing children into groups, and this practice harmed the self-esteem of those in the lowest groups.

The bottom line was that the group of children who didn't learn to read was growing. Using basal texts had not changed that.

The bottom line was that the group of children who didn't learn to read was growing. Using basal texts had not changed that.

WHOLE LANGUAGE ENTERS THE PICTURE

Educators decided that the faults of the basal readers outweighed their advantages. They said that if so many children failed to learn to read, then the problem must be that what they were asked to read had no relevance. The use of boring, watered-down basal stories must stop. Promoters of whole language asked teachers to believe that children would learn to read in time if they were exposed to "rich literature" and were given opportunities to write meaningfully. They called this unproven process "emergent language," and it sounded good. The practices that stemmed from it were easier to carry out if the teacher convinced herself that reading would, in fact, emerge. If it didn't emerge in her class it would emerge later on. She no longer had to work with groups.

She read aloud to the whole class from a big book while they followed along. Whole language expected teachers to teach phonics on an as-needed basis, and since ability grouping was discouraged and the use of prepared materials was also discouraged, the conscientious teacher found it much harder to make sure that her class mastered phonics skills. No doubt many teachers continued to group children according to their needs, but emergent language practice does not encourage structured, sequential, and explicit methods, and consequently an even larger number of children joined the group of nonlearners.

Promoters of whole language asked teachers to believe that children would learn to read in time if they were exposed to "rich literature" and were given opportunities to write meaningfully. They called this unproven process "emergent language," and it sounded good.

Ideas in the field of education tend to live in a closed system. Research from other fields is often excluded. Frank Smith, a strong whole language proponent, published an article in the *Phi Delta Kappan* in February of 1992, which closed with these words:

The great debate may never end, but perhaps it never should. The most productive way to deal with fundamental education controversies might be to take them into every school and every community where they can be dissected, discussed and honestly argued. The endless debate over teaching reading could serve to keep teachers and the public at large conscious of the profound importance and delicacy of the noble art of teaching. (p. 441)

This is a sad commentary on the teaching profession. The debate itself has become more important than successful outcomes for children. Should we allow children to fail for an "art" when we have scientific proof that failure isn't necessary?

Should we allow children to fail for an "art" when we have scientific proof that failure isn't necessary?

However, while education research focused on reading material and the goals of reading, other research, from other fields, looked at the process of learning how to read.

RESEARCH THAT TEACHERS NEED TO LEARN

Needless to say, the field of education isn't entirely devoid of people who are willing to listen to fresh thinking. If new ideas were totally excluded, the findings of such researchers and thinkers as Jeanne Chall, Marilyn Jager Adams, and Joseph Torgesen, who are psychologists, would never have found their way into educational thought. It is unfortunate, though, that views from other fields are not as readily accepted and incorporated into teacher education as theories that come from the education profession itself.

Jeanne Chall was a psychologist who taught at Columbia Teacher's College. None of her degrees were in education. Her influential *Learning to Read: The Great Debate* (1966) came almost 20 years after Flesch's *Why Johnny Can't Read* (1986) and restarted a discussion about the need to teach phonics. She studied a confusing set of basal readers and showed that those that emphasized learning a "code" were more effective than those that emphasized memorizing whole words. Her research showed that knowledge of the alphabet and the sounds of spoken words was the most reliable predictor of success in learning how to read, but to everyone's disappointment, teaching children the alphabet did not automatically make them better readers. Why not was the next question to be tackled.

In 1990 *Beginning to Read: Thinking and Learning about Print*, by Marilyn Jager Adams, created a sea change in the thinking of some educators. She, too, is a PhD psychologist who studied cognitive and developmental psychology. Her book introduced the term *phonological awareness*, a totally new concept. Teachers had to learn its meaning, and its meaning rested on an understanding of the alphabetic principle. Without at least a rudimentary understanding of linguistics, *phonological awareness* became little more than a buzzword. (See appendix C.)

A FLAWED PHILOSOPHY TAKES HOLD

Whole language is a philosophy, not a science, and was a reaction against the lock step methods and diluted content of the basal reader. The difference, of course, is that a philosophy doesn't have to stand up to scientific scrutiny. Proponents told teachers that the brain searches for "wholes" and that this tendency would cause children to learn to read. One advocate for whole language demonstrated this by covering a line of type on an overhead projector so that only the tops of the letters showed. An audience of teachers was asked to read the line, and slowly and laboriously they did. That demonstration was offered as proof that the brain filled in the blanks to make sense of what it saw. However, every adult there was already thoroughly familiar with the alphabet, and no difference was drawn between reading skills of those who know the alphabet and those who don't and how that affects their ability to become a capable reader.

Whole language is a philosophy, not a science, and was a reaction against the lock step methods and diluted content of the basal reader. The difference, of course, is that a philosophy doesn't have to stand up to scientific scrutiny.

Whole language paid little attention to the alphabet. It lost sight of the importance of breaking the code. The children who became successful readers through whole language were those who entered school with phonemic awareness skills and good memories.

To the detriment of children and their teachers, teaching strategies and exercises based on this method were vigorously promoted, and though the majority of schools today no longer claim to use whole language as a method for teaching reading, they continue to use the materials and the methods that came from the whole language movement. It was a big enough movement to change the way entire school systems across the country taught reading. It wasn't discredited until after many, many children failed. Test scores attested to its lack of efficacy.

But it had become ingrained in education. Many teachers still have affection for whole language instruction, and many are still strongly influenced by this philosophy. Colleges of teacher education have trained teachers to use whole language methods, and in large part, that training

---

When I learned that it wasn't just Luis who was having trouble but that a lot of kids in his class couldn't read, I knew I had to do something!

has not been supplanted by scientifically proven methods of teaching reading.

Many schools now tell parents that they use a balanced approach. Newer materials—for example, Open Court, a research-based instructional program —may now be in the schools; however, if teachers don't understand or believe that reading has to be taught systematically and explicitly, they may continue using whole language practices. In doing so, they fail to pinpoint the reasons that some students cannot keep the pace, or if they do recognize a problem, they don't change instructional methods. Their students continue to fail. Teachers blame the reading series or they blame the child. A teacher who understands the reading process will behave very differently.

LEARNING HOW CHILDREN LEARN TO READ

As educators looked to the reading material itself to provide the answer to why some don't learn, and as neurologists used technology to get a look into the "black box" to learn what actually goes on in a reader's brain, others were actually working with hard-to-teach students. In the process, they developed methods and materials to undo the damage done by ineffective and harmful teaching.

At first it seemed as if everyone had a different program, and no one really knew whom to listen to or how to judge the reliability of their claims. One teacher might use VAKT (visual, auditory, kinesthetic, tactile) a la Fernald, another might use it according to Orton and Gillingham. Over the course of years, many teachers and researchers collected, collaborated, distilled, and disseminated their findings, and in doing this they shaped a body of knowledge. While there could be disagreement in the details (for example, whether to have children pronounce sounds or to say letter names as they spell), every effective program adhered to the same principles:

- The program is highly structured.
- Skills are presented systematically, sequentially, and taught explicitly.
- Opportunities are provided to practice new skills and knowledge.
- Phonics skills are taught both synthetically (putting speech sounds together) and analytically (breaking words into individual sounds and syllables.

These researchers established the content for effective reading programs:

- Phonology and phonemic awareness skills that are firmly grounded
- Sound-symbol association that includes a minimum of 43 pairings
- Uniform instruction about dividing words into syllables
- Direct instruction of syntax provided in later stages of teaching reading

> I went into Matt's school with a checklist of the parts of a good reading program. And then I sat down with his teacher and asked him to explain how he was teaching those things.

This description is a very cursory look at a complex system. Understanding the structure of language takes time and study, and for those who would like to learn more, I recommend *Speech to Print: Language Essentials for Teachers* by Louisa C. Moats. This book contains exercises and explanations that give breadth and depth to teachers' understanding of why they do what they do.

Though these principles and content were developed for the hard-to-teach, the success of these methods has helped us understand the causes of reading problems. The education system itself creates these hard-to-teach learners. More than home life, more than inadequate brain power, more than emotional problems, it is uninformed teachers forced to follow the directives of their education system that are the unwitting cause of children's reading problems.

The education system itself creates these hard-to-teach learners. More than home life, more than inadequate brain power, more than emotional problems, it is uninformed teachers forced to follow the directives of their educational system that are the unwitting cause of children's reading problems.

Remedial programs plug in holes. If little Johnny isn't taught that *r* does not stand for /ar/ he will try to decode and encode using a faulty tool. He won't be successful, and he will add to his repertoire of misconceptions. As these problems accumulate, his faith in the code diminishes. He can't count on any letter linking to a specific sound or "saying." In a few months he sees himself as a nonlearner, and unless help comes fast, Johnny begins a downhill journey.

While there may be some children who despite appropriate instruction may still have difficulty learning to read, fewer than 5% of children would continue to have problems if teachers used the research to guide their classroom instruction. As it stands now, many children wind up in special education classrooms because they can't seem to learn to read.

> When I finally figured out that Debbie didn't have to be in special ed, I was furious. All this misery could have been avoided if she had been taught using proven methods. I felt she was the victim of a grand experiment in reading instruction. So I went to the school board and superintendent with this new understanding and insisted that they work with some experts to change reading methods in our schools. I never thought I'd have the courage to do this, but I knew Deb's future was at stake.

Regardless of which publisher writes the book they use, teachers need to understand the structure of language. They need to know the concepts children must have before they can move through increasingly complex reading levels without getting stalled. Teachers need to understand what occurs in the brain as students learn to read. (See chapter 7 for more about this.)

Just as important, teachers and students need access to materials that dovetail with what is known about learning to read. It isn't enough to teach students the sound-symbol relationships; they need to know and believe that this knowledge is important. They need to practice what they learn. Teaching children a sound-symbol correspondence then showing them one word in a book or story where this particular relationship is used is defeating. Early learners especially need to use what they are taught. They need to understand that knowing that letters stand for sounds unlocks the mystery of learning to read. English is 87% phonetic, but the 13% that is not can cause big problems. Learning to ride a bicycle without learning how to balance is impossible. Learning to read without phonemic awareness is equally impossible.

If we are to avoid "creating" learning-disabled children, we need to provide direct, explicit, comprehensive reading instruction for all children.

Those who understand quickly will move along quickly. Those who need more practice to master the principles will take a little longer, but all children must master the same sequence of skills to become good readers.

Learning to ride a bicycle without learning how to balance is impossible. Learning to read without phonemic awareness is equally impossible. If we are to avoid "creating" learning-disabled children, we need to provide direct, explicit, comprehensive reading instruction for all children.

UNDERSTANDING THE DILEMMAS TEACHERS FACE

Teachers want to see children succeed. However, they have been and continue to be faced with numerous challenges. Many colleges of teacher education have left gaps in teachers' educations. They do not emphasize learning how to find reliable research and translate it into classroom practice, and they spend very little time on the teaching of reading. But many supervisors in schools do read the research, and when ideas on the best way to teach beginning reading change, they want to see this change reflected in classrooms.

Change is also forced on teachers by their lack of control of materials they must use in their classrooms. Books they come to depend on may disappear from approved lists and from the book room; however, good, experienced teachers moderate this swing. They accept new thinking but keep the old practices that worked. School boards and superintendents may require that teachers use a particular method of instruction that they believe works. Teachers say that in these instances, they may simply have to close their doors and teach the way they know will best help students.

Recent graduates from teachers colleges have learned to teach reading —even beginning reading—with an emphasis on content without an equal emphasis on skills. Whole language techniques were devised by educators, and undergraduate college courses reflect their bias. Some teachers may never have heard of the most current techniques, and if they have, because they are completely opposed to what they were taught in their college class, they reject them.

It was pretty clear to me that my journey was going to have to take me to the state department of education. They really couldn't accept the fact that teachers were not being taught to use research in their college training programs. I figured out that if I could convince them to add this to tests for teacher licenses, we could change the system. It took many conversations with people in the know to get me there.

First-grade teachers are aware that historically there has been a group of children in every school who do not learn to read. They have been taught to place the blame for this on changes in our culture, the child's family, the child's emotional state, or the child's own lack of ability. A thick college text from the 1960s lists personality maladjustment, neurophysiologic factors centering on brain pathology, and cultural factors as reasons that children do not learn to read. The chapter on cultural disadvantage mentions language, but primarily gives teachers advice about their teaching styles, telling them to respect their students and to become "performers." Is it any wonder that after so many years of looking for the culprit for illiteracy outside the education system, these reasons for not learning are so firmly ingrained in teachers' psyches? Teachers who give home life, "faulty" brains, and emotional problems as reasons for not learning to read are still failing to accept responsibility for how well a child learns.

However, when a child doesn't learn, most teachers know it, are distressed by this, and are willing to admit that they don't have the expertise to deal with the problem. They first look for someone within the school for help—a reading specialist or the special education teacher. Unfortunately, whole language inserted itself into remedial programs. When it was learned that many children were not learning to read in classrooms, whole language proponents devised a "remedial" method. School systems gave special education teachers extensive training in diagnosis—but did not change the materials that they used to teach reading. Therefore, sometimes teachers not only cannot help their students, but find there is no one in the school who can share effective methods with them.

Another reality contributes to teachers being unable to effectively teach reading. Many children today are less able to concentrate than they were in years past. Video games and stimulating movies have made reading less entertaining. Learning how to read can be a slow process, and children who have become accustomed to instant rewards find it hard to concentrate on a task whose rewards are not immediate and accompanied by bells and whistles.

Further, teachers have been asked to help solve society's ills. A social problem is identified, and someone somewhere decides that teaching about it in elementary school will solve it. Smoking, drugs, the environment, nutrition, how to behave in a disaster like a tornado or a fire all become "units" to be taught along with reading, math, and social studies. This is a heavy load that takes a big bite out of the time teachers are allowed to teach children how to read.

> I couldn't believe my ears when I realized that they were blaming Darren's reading problem on the fact that his dad didn't live with us. Like that had anything to do with it. I pulled out the list of things they should be teaching according to the research I found and asked them to tick things off. I think this was the first time anyone had ever done this and the last time they blamed single moms.

Teachers who want to see changes may frequently know one another and sometimes work together. A reading specialist will sometimes work with a classroom teacher to try to improve instruction for a group of struggling readers. Friends share ideas. No one wants to see children fail. Success stories from similar schools that have tried new methods and found that they work will often inspire a school to try the approach used successfully.

Somewhere in your school there is a teacher who is as concerned as you are about the school's reading program. He is your ally. How will you know who he is? Read below to figure this out.

TIPS FOR PARENTS: FINDING ALLIES AT YOUR SCHOOL

A teacher ally will

- be able to tell you that new reading science has brought us an understanding of the reading process that we have never had before;

- know that children must have a basic understanding of the sounds of spoken language before they are asked to master individual sound-symbol relationships;
- agree with you that most children's reading problems are a result of their confusion, their inability to make sense of the structure of language;
- discuss early intervention, not just as a way to recognize children who are at risk for failure, but also as sign that their reading instruction must be scientifically based;
- care about literacy—for the teacher, learning how to communicate through reading and writing will be the most important part of education;
- be familiar with the research work of leaders in the field, including, among others, those mentioned in the references section at the end of this book;
- know about the work of the National Reading Panel and be able to talk with you about the difference between research that is science based and research that is not;
- know and believe that there is such a thing as "friendly phonics." She will agree with you that when youngsters are first learning to read, they find decoding exciting and that educators must act on this "teachable moment";
- be aware that we always read for meaning, but understand that the prime task of one just learning to read is mastery of phonetic principles;
- believe that 87% of the English words are phonetic, and use this fact in the selection of beginning reading materials;
- have looked for answers for children's failure, and even though conventional wisdom blames failure on the child and the parents, accept the blame and continue to look for ways to help the hard-to-teach.

Find this teacher if you can, but if you find he doesn't quite reach your ideal, remember the roadblocks he faces. His classroom program is dictated by curriculum designed by someone else. The materials he is given have been purchased in previous years by someone who may or may not be aware of his specific needs. Her training may or may not have included information about the actual process of learning how to read. She attends workshops and conferences that are suggested by other educators, but she is not encouraged to look outside her field for answers to her questions. He tells his supervisors of his problems, but his supervisors think differently and are unable to give him the kind of assistance he needs.

10

Johnson Elementary School: A Transformed School

Benjamin T. Sayeski

It's difficult for you as a parent to communicate the kinds of things that could be done to improve your child's school. How would you know the technical aspects of running a school? How would you begin to set priorities for what should be done? And it's simply not your job. This chapter and the following one can help you help your school principal or superintendent. They describe two schools in which most children were not learning on grade level, and how their failure to learn was turned around. Here you'll find a description of how these schools changed, what was done and why, and the role that parents played in making these changes. When a teacher or principal says it isn't possible or he or she doesn't know where to start to implement reading programs that are based on research evidence, and there seems to be no hope, you can take these two examples to the principal of your child's school to show (1) it can be done, (2) it has been done, and (3) here's how to do it. Benjamin Sayeski made sea change in the way reading was taught and students learned as the principal in an elementary school in North Carolina. He shares his sometimes painful experience in going through this process of change.

This is the story of Johnson Elementary School—a story that I hope will encourage all educators, children, and parents who are struggling to boost students' learning. We were able to create new opportunities for children to learn and succeed by rejecting a culture of failure and resignation that formerly held them back. All worked hard to produce this change despite the fact that we were dealing with poor students who started school with the kinds of educational and environmental challenges that caused their older brothers and sisters to fail to learn and eventually drop out of school.

Perhaps it was because it was my first year as a principal that I didn't succumb to the "can't do" attitude in the school. I saw the positives and was determined to put them to work immediately. My initial year was spent getting to know the ins and outs of the school community. I quickly learned that the 330 students at Johnson Elementary School were expected to fail. Their lack of achievement became a consistent fact of life, and much of it was attributed to the demographics of the student body as about 70% of the students were poor and qualified for free lunch. In addition, 75% of our students came from single-mother households, and approximately 80% were African American. There were many myths that circulated in the school about students living in poverty and their ability to learn. And these beliefs caused staff to accept the children's underachievement and prevented them from looking at alternatives such as the instructional methods and structure of the program as a means to bring about change.

While the 1st year of my tenure was spent analyzing data and getting to know the community, I also focused on setting clear expectations beginning with the first faculty meeting. During our first meeting I pointed to the past 3 years of student achievement data in reading. It was a sad story, as during those years only 40%, 34%, and 49% of the students passed the third-grade level on the Virginia state reading assessment called the Standards of Learning (SOLs). As in many schools across the state, the percentage of White students who passed the third-grade reading SOL was twice as high as the percentage of our minority students on this assessment.

Adding to this terrible failure rate was the realization that while we had much going for us, we were still unable to respond to the learning needs of so many of our students. Our district was well funded—the average per pupil expenditure was around $10,000 a year. We had small class sizes with ample instructional and personnel support. Our resources were about as ideal as they were ever going to be. If success was not possible under these conditions, then the students and staff deserved a better school, better principal, and new teachers. Most importantly, these kids deserved a better shot at life, and we knew that time was running out for them. We had to help our students become proficient readers at an early age to avoid their future school failure. The majority of Johnson's students had several liabilities, and we didn't want to further jeopardize their learning potential and contribute to their eventual dropping out of school. The next 3 years would give us a chance to change the outcome for these students, and improved reading success was priority one.

At face value, many of the instructional practices at Johnson appeared to be sound. All children received instruction at their reading level, and numerous interventions were in place for children who were behind. Reading time was sacred; blocks of morning time across the school were free from interruptions. Staff development was provided both in-house and in coordination with the local university. Finally, an in-house reading specialist provided ongoing and intense follow-up support on a small-group and individualized basis. However, the irony was that these very practices had produced a tradition of underachievement among our students.

> Lessons learned from the 1st year had a tremendous impact on the way we began to think about effective reading on a schoolwide basis. These can be powerful guideposts for parents. If students are not making measurable progress, the single most important question a parent must ask is, why?

As we began to dig deeper into the reasons why our children were not learning to read, we began by looking at the structural aspects of our program: How much time was devoted to reading instruction and how prepared were our teachers to teach effectively?

WAS THERE ENOUGH TIME DEVOTED TO READING?

I encourage all parents to ask their child's teacher and administrator how the instructional day is broken up by time. This will give you a concrete idea about the priorities of the school. I noted that kindergarten students had an inordinate amount of unstructured time during their day; in fact, it was double or triple the amount of time devoted to reading instruction.

Recess alone accounted for more time than did reading. This was hard to justify given that only 18% of entering kindergarten students knew the letters of the alphabet and only 40% had attended any form of organized preschool. Because our children came to school without having the prerequisite skills and experiences to learn to read, we needed to make significant changes in time devoted to reading instruction. Kindergarten students spent one hour on direct reading instruction, and 1st-, 2nd-, 3rd-, and 4th-grade students spent 90 minutes. We began by examining how staff was assigned during this 90-minute block.

> If reading is going to be a school priority, then time allocation needs to reflect that priority. How we spend our time speaks volumes about our priorities.

GROUPING OF STUDENTS

Children were placed in small groups with others who were reading at the same level, rather than being grouped according to grade level. This helped us to create the lowest student-to-teacher ratios for reading instruction. But to have these small groups, the school employed an all-hands-on-deck approach to delivering instruction, using teacher aides, special education teachers, the gifted education specialist, Title I reading teachers, and regular classroom teachers. Using a variety of reading assessments, all 2nd-, 3rd-, and 4th-grade students were tested and then placed in a reading group with one of these staff members. Like many of the practices at Johnson, this approach had strong face validity; we were able to teach students at their instructional level in the smallest group setting possible. The implementation of this plan at Johnson, however, was flawed due to some unintended consequences and lack of focus.

In general, parents were happy when told their child was receiving instruction at their reading level. However, most parents did not ask the most important questions that would have revealed the soft spot in this arrangement: What is the plan for accelerating my child's learning because he or she is already one or two years behind grade level in reading? If my child makes one year's growth as planned, won't he still be a year behind? The answers to these questions can reveal serious problems for schools that do not have a plan for kids who are significantly below grade level. The structural model at Johnson practically ensured that children would not make the needed gains to be grade level readers.

> Without any plan for acceleration, students are doomed to their current pace and achievement gap and perhaps to becoming high school dropouts years down the road.

Another major flaw of the structural plan was the fact that all students were in groups with the same teacher-student ratio, regardless of how severe their reading problems were. Staffing was not differentiated to meet the needs of children who were most behind in reading. Therefore, if parents of a struggling reader asked if their child was in a smaller reading group, the answer was no. The additional reading teachers were used to lower reading group sizes across the board without consideration for children who were struggling the most.

Further complicating these group assignments was the fact that some groups were taught by certified teachers and others were taught by instructional assistants. Regardless of how far behind they were, the needs of students did not drive the assignment of staff members. In addition, children were moved from one group to another as their achievement levels changed, causing them to have a number of different reading teachers throughout the year. The result—no single teacher had responsibility for any one child. Without a doubt, at first glance, low student-teacher ratios and instructing children at their appropriate reading level sounds good. However, parents need to find out exactly what that means and how it is going to be implemented in their child's classroom.

STAFF DEVELOPMENT WAS UNCOORDINATED

Johnson's reading program relied heavily on staff development to help teachers learn about effective reading approaches and develop the expertise to use them in their classrooms. This view was deeply rooted in the community, and our small university town boasted a bright and dedicated teaching force. Working hand in hand with the university, staff development focused on preparing teachers to both understand reading research and develop the tools necessary to teach reading. Staff development was organized according to the six components of effective reading resulting from the research results from the work of the National Reading Panel—phonemic awareness, phonics, reading fluency, vocabulary, and strategies for reading comprehension. However, staff development emphasized only one of these components each year.

But that meant a teacher would be fully prepared to teach these five components of reading only after receiving the full five years of staff development, and it created a lag time for teachers to incorporate it into the curriculum, and we would have lost the opportunity to teach these critical skills to an entire group of students from kindergarten through fourth grade. Simply stated, this model did not recognize the urgency of providing high-quality instruction in all core components from the beginning. A school does not have five years to wait for a teacher to receive staff development in reading. Most importantly, a child does not have five years to wait for the teacher to receive this instruction.

In addition, the success of this staff development model was dependent upon a low turnover of teachers. We had no way of helping a teacher catch up when arriving at Johnson after the staff development cycle had already begun.

Another major shortcoming in the staff development plan resulted from the variety of teaching strategies teachers used. Our premise was that teachers would receive intense and ongoing staff development that would allow them to create their own reading program under some broad parameters. However, there was no guarantee that the research about what makes for effective reading instruction was consistently and effectively incorporated into each classroom. And predictably, the instruction from room to room looked vastly different due to teachers' different experiences, preferences, and knowledge.

RESULTS AFTER YEAR 1

My 1st year at Johnson ended like many of the previous years. Student achievement was devastatingly low—among the worst in the school district. The spring SOL scores in reading showed that a little more than one third (37%) of the third graders passed. This was a far cry from the 70% needed for state accreditation of our school. The achievement gap remained the same. Sixty-seven percent (67%) of White third graders had passed the test, while only 33% of our African American students passed the test.

The collective angst felt by the staff took many forms. Some teachers showed their frustration with tears, while others left the school year with a blank expression. Others blamed the usual culprits—poverty and transience. Another year had gone by, and most staff were sick with disappointment knowing we had failed to eliminate failure for our students.

> One of the most dedicated veteran members of the staff was most upset. While crying she said, "I just can't do this another year. I work so hard and get the same bad results. I just can't do this another year." I replied by saying, "Me neither."

But our parents seemed to stoically accept the results. We heard few criticisms, as parents were intimidated and fearful that if they were critical of the school it might result in future problems for their children.

We knew that we could not do the same thing over and over again and expect different results. Because our school could not be fully accredited, I was asked by the school board to present Johnson's school improvement plan. I had no intention of going before the board and telling them we were going to stay the course. I was also not going to use poverty, transience, and single parenthood as an excuse for low performance. Factors outside our control were not going to change student achievement; only we were capable of doing that. We needed to face the fact that a change in the structure of our school and the type of instruction we used were the only things that were going to get us out of the mess we were in.

And we were dedicated to doing it right by targeting our neediest readers rather than the "bubble students" who were scoring just below the benchmarks on assessments. Targeting these "bubble students" was viewed as the best and quickest way of boosting student achievement. But past years had made it crystal clear that our struggling readers were not getting what they needed and they should be our focus.

YEAR 2

We swung into gear and created a kind of academic triage. First, we abandoned the practice of having all students receive the same type and length of instruction. Now students with differing needs were going to get instruction geared to their needs. As in an emergency room, our most needy readers would now receive our most intense treatment. But to offer such treatment we would have to change the way we structured reading instruction. We changed our reading schedule to dedicate two-hour blocks of time to reading in second, third, and fourth grades in a setting that averaged six students for every teacher. Those children who were hurting the most were now getting our best medicine.

But this initial step in our triage approach had challenges. The first challenge we had to deal with was the time of day we provided reading instruction. The second was opposition to increasing the size of our groups for some students. All reading instruction had taken place in the morning, but our new model rotated reading times for grade levels so that some grades had reading right before lunch or in the afternoon. This caused great consternation at first. Teachers felt students would not be available for learning at any hour other than the first thing in the morning. I politely reminded them that we had been instructing all of our students in the morning for as long as anyone could remember with very poor results. This reminder would prove to be my response for other resistance to changes.

Teachers were also concerned about the increased size of the reading groups for all but the struggling readers from seven to nine children in a group. Teachers would now have nine to 12 students in a group, and this increase seemed dramatic and took time to adjust to. I reminded our teachers that research indicated that class size of 15 or below was related to higher student achievement. Even parents of above grade level students complained of the increased group size for their students. Eventually, the resistance from teachers and parents diminished as they saw the results teachers were getting. Regular classroom teachers saw improved reading carry over into their classroom, and their resistance disappeared as they were able to have more meaningful instruction in the other core subject areas because their neediest students were improving their reading skills and could handle it.

Our reading instruction was revamped to include instructional techniques that were based on research. Our children were taught using systematic and explicit instruction in the most important core areas of reading instruction, and we used comprehensive and ongoing assessment to measure student progress and change direction if needed. The program taught each component of reading and systematically moved in small steps to ensure student success. We worked hard to help students who were behind to make up the ground they had lost and to begin to keep up with their peers who were reading on grade level. Our program was designed to make up lost ground in the shortest amount of time.

Our decision to use this approach was not embraced by all three Title I teachers. One teacher had used a similar program many years earlier and was excited to get going again as she had been forbidden to use this approach by the previous administration. Another teacher was very open to trying something new as she realized she was not getting the results she wanted with her students. The third teacher was quite skeptical and rather hesitant about using a program that was so structured and changed the way she was used to teaching. But to their credit, these teachers dove in headfirst and never gave the program and their students anything less than their best.

The teacher who was the most skeptical would later tell me she woke up every morning for months and said to herself, "I hate my principal, I hate my principal." By November, she had gotten over these feelings, as her students were really learning. Like the rest of the staff, effectiveness and student achievement were foremost in her mind. She quit cursing the ground I walked on and became a champion of the program and the reading instruction her students were responding to.

Our program gradually gained favor as it produced results. Classroom teachers, parents, administrators, and the students themselves were seeing undeniable progress over the year. At the end of the year, the number of students identified for intervention by a statewide reading assessment called the Phonological Awareness Literacy Screening (PALS) was at an all-time low. Roughly half of the students passed the reading portion of the SOL test. The bottom quartile of children was reading for the first time. And the major structural and instructional changes we made had paid off. We made certain that students would have the same reading teacher for the entire year, and this had many benefits.

Accountability was much higher because each teacher was working with the same group of students for a prolonged period of time. Students benefited from having one reading teacher as teachers knew the students better and students knew the teachers better. Communication with parents became much easier because parents had one contact person to answer their questions and address their concerns. Across the board, the Johnson community seemed enthusiastic and happy with this structural change.

My 2nd year as principal of Johnson was quickly coming to an end, and I anxiously awaited end-of-year reading assessments to see if our practice of academic triage was working. As student data rolled in, the answer to that question was quickly being answered. Across the board, student achievement in reading was markedly better. Our school community saw more children with higher achievement in fluency, accuracy, and comprehension and fewer students who needed intervention. We waited anxiously for our SOL scores as these scores would determine the school's accreditation ranking.

Our work was rewarded this year. Whereas only 37% of students passed the SOL in prior years, 71% of students, almost twice as many, passed this year. And we were closing the gap. The scores of African American children rose from 33% to 62%, while Caucasian children's scores rose from 67% to 92%. For the first time in recent history, Johnson students were breaking through the barrier of learning failure. Students would be welcomed back to school the following year with a large banner stating, "Welcome to YOUR Fully Accredited School."

YEAR 3

Changes in Instructional Materials

Our district administrators were willing to financially support a pilot of a well-known reading program called Open Court because it systematically and explicitly teaches the skills necessary for students to become proficient readers. Open Court also provides applications in spelling, vocabulary, grammar usage and mechanics, penmanship, listening, and speaking skills that allow the students to connect all areas of reading and writing under one program. We felt that the comprehensive nature of the program would provide the systematic and connected instruction we were looking for, and we could avoid the problem of lack of continuity of teaching from one grade level to the next. We also appreciated the program's ongoing assessments that would allow our parents, teachers, and students to identify the end-of-year goals and monitor progress toward those goals.

We, of course, faced some challenges that come along with the implementation of any new program. First, we had to structure staff development so that teachers were ready to begin using it in their classrooms on the first day of school after summer break. So we had our teachers take the materials home early in the summer to help relieve their anxiety over implementing a new program, and we backed this up by providing intense and ongoing staff development from a trained consultant that would allow teachers to feel comfortable with the nuts and bolts of the program.

> Implementation without staff development would have doomed the program from the beginning. Systematic and explicit instruction relies on a qualified, skilled, talented, and competent teacher.

The most challenging rough spot resulted from a few teachers who had philosophical differences regarding the use of the program, as they felt that the children might not be developmentally ready to learn. This was coupled with the inevitable resistance to a new and unfamiliar way of teaching.

Looking back, the root of our problem was a failure to change teaching practices to reflect today's high expectations for all students. These veteran teachers were still living in a world of years gone by in which many students were simply not expected to meet current standards. They were not bad people; they had simply failed to adjust to the times. However, the children they were educating would have to compete, perform, and interact with a world that was fixed to current, not past, expectations.

Our students and teachers had never seen such high expectations for students and felt they were unattainable. But to their credit, teachers stayed the course, and the overwhelming majority of students did reach these higher achievement goals.

> At the heart of making change in a school is the need for parents to see educators as good people who are working hard even though they might not be getting the desired results.

As the 3rd year came to an end, the Johnson staff anxiously awaited end-of-year reading assessments to see if our modifications to academic triage had improved student achievement. Our efforts were rewarded. For the 2nd year in a row, our students' reading levels had risen to heights never before achieved. Our students' scores were the best we had ever seen, and the number of students identified as needing remedial instruction was now at an all-time low. Three years before, the PALS test identified 46 children in need of substantial reading intervention. This year, we decreased that number to only 18 students. Reading fluency also dramatically improved. Instead of students struggling to read each word, they could read quickly, with ease, accuracy, and comprehension.

When the SOL results came in, Johnson Elementary School was once again a fully accredited school. The Johnson staff were finally able to welcome the new school year with confidence that the coherent, sustainable, and successful model of reading instruction they implemented was doing the job.

There was no one thing that caused our students to be successful. Curriculum changes can be implemented only by a competent and hardworking staff. A competent and hard-working staff can't implement a curriculum unless time is structured efficiently. The leadership of the school can make or break success. Ultimately, the principal needs to orchestrate all efforts to ensure that all students can achieve. Parents played an integral part in changing the culture of Johnson. The overwhelming majority of parents responded to the needs of the school by helping their children come to school well behaved and ready to learn, but many were single working mothers living in poverty, and they needed the help of the entire community. We had to pull together, and we did.

HOW PARENTS CAN HELP

As parents, there are a number of ways your involvement can support a similar change in your children's school. (See the checklist for effective reading instruction in appendix D.) It simply isn't possible to make such a major change without you. Parents need stamina to stay involved with this issue until children's achievement improves. You need to be outspoken until things get markedly better, as your presence and voice speak volumes. Those parents who stand up to be counted are the ones who change things for children.

TIPS FOR PARENTS

- Never attack the teacher. Attacking a teacher will galvanize others to resist you and your message. The more nonthreatening you are, the more information and help you will get.
- Ask a lot of questions. Teachers are a great source of information. Ask them, Who decides how you teach reading? How much time do you spend on reading instruction? Who is responsible for monitoring the progress of students? How is progress monitored? What should my child be able to read now? What should she be able to read at the end of the year? How many words per minute should he be reading now and at the end of the year? Percentagewise, how accurate should her reading be? What happens to my child if he is not reaching benchmarks? How is my child performing in relation to grade level expectations right now? How do you know? How do you know if interventions are working? What, specifically, should I be doing at home to help my child?
- Check things out with the principal. Ask the principal of the school the same questions to find out if there is congruence with teacher responses. This will tell you whether a teacher is choosing her own methods or if there is a schoolwide effort to make research-based changes in instruction.
- Question the district staff. Ask the same questions of the person in the school district who is in charge of reading. He should be able to explain how decisions regarding reading instruction are made and what research supports their decisions.
- Take advantage of existing structures. Use the PTA or PTO, parent advisory groups, teacher unions, school board members, volunteer groups, school-business partners, and the local media to discuss reading. Many

times, a PTA or PTO can ask questions about the curriculum and data related to results that teachers feel uncomfortable asking.

- Go to the top. Don't be afraid to speak to the school board concerning poor results in your child's school. A school board is the ultimate level of oversight for any school division. It is the school board's job to ensure the best education for all children. Keep going back and persevere until your questions have been addressed. Keep the issue alive by attending school board meetings and asking for updates.
- Arm yourself with the facts. Know your facts when talking to school officials, and do not deviate from them. All discussions will go much more smoothly if you use accurate data provided by the school system. More than likely, the data alone can generate a discussion.
- Be informed. Do your homework before you meet with the principal or district personnel. Every state department of education has a website that allows you to access school-level data for your school. This information shows how students as a whole are doing and how subgroups of children (broken down by race, socioeconomic status, gender, special education status, and English as a second language status) are performing. Pay particular attention to the participation rate of these students in annual testing. Almost all of these students should be participating every year. Being perceived as an informed stakeholder wanting to affect positive change for kids is powerful.
- The bottom line must be results. Have faith in the fact that any school can be turned around. Kids are never lost causes.

11

Hartsfield Elementary School: The Story of a Turnaround

Ray King and Joseph Torgeson

This chapter describes the second school in which most children were not learning on grade level. Fortunately, these "before" and "after" stories demonstrate that change is possible for most children if approached with strong leadership and knowledge of research. Joseph Torgeson, a nationally known researcher from Florida State University, teamed up with Ray King, principal of Hartsfield Elementary School, to describe what was done and why. This can be a helpful blueprint for change in your child's school.

This chapter provides a description of a six-year project at Hartsfield Elementary School in Tallahassee, Florida, to improve reading instruction and achievement for the whole school. While many variables contributed to the success of the reading program, only a few of them are described here. Those that are not detailed here, but were also instrumental in accomplishing the gains we experienced in student achievement, include (1) changes in teacher and parent attitudes contributing to significant changes in school culture; (2) increased parent and teacher expectations for behavior and academic performance; (3) substantive changes in personnel and the roles of certain staff; (4) expansion of prekindergarten programs; and (5) the district's commitment to site-based decision making at the school level.

We will describe the six key elements that we consider critical to the gains in reading achievement experienced over a five-year period:

1. Committing to meeting individual student needs at all levels
2. Adopting and implementing a research-based reading curriculum
3. Using objective assessment to evaluate student progress and the effectiveness of reading programs
4. Designing and implementing an effective instructional delivery system
5. Maximizing available instructional time
6. Monitoring student progress and program implementation

The period of time covered by this chapter is from the school year 1993–1994 through the year 1998–1999. Although there have been some improvements in assessment technology and curriculum materials since that time, the basic principles of effective instruction and assessment described in this chapter have not changed since then.

DESCRIPTION OF THE SCHOOL
BEFORE THE CHANGE PROCESS BEGAN

Dramatic Change in Demographics

In the 10 years before we worked with Hartsfield Elementary School, it changed from a school that was predominantly White and middle class to a school with many poor children, 67% of whom qualified for a free/reduced lunch, and a 60% minority (predominantly African American) student body. The middle-class neighborhoods in the school district were aging, and fewer families were moving into these areas. At the same time, the size and number of families in the public housing neighborhoods located in the district continued to increase. Teachers accustomed to teaching middle-class children were not prepared for the increasing instructional demands associated with the changing characteristics of our students.

Teachers accustomed to teaching middle-class children were not prepared for the increasing instructional demands associated with the changing characteristics of our students.

School Culture Regarding Reading

The overall attitude among staff was one of providing the content and letting students who could learn do so while others continued to fall academically further behind. There was a wide range of academic abilities in the classrooms. For example, some kindergarten students entered school able to read many familiar words and also able to "sound out" simple unknown words, while others did not know one letter of the alphabet and could not distinguish letters from numbers. Our situation precisely reflected the difficulties noted in Olson's (1998) observation that a central problem in reading instruction arises not from the absolute level of children's preparation for learning to read, but from the diversity in their levels of preparation.

A central problem in reading instruction arises not from the absolute level of children's preparation for learning to read, but from the diversity in their levels of preparation.

In our school at this time, there was little variation in the curriculum to address the different reading needs of students. Students academically behind did not receive the focused, intensive instruction necessary for their success. Instead, teachers developed a culture of acceptance of failure for these students, blaming their homes and lack of parental support.

Students falling behind were referred to special education or Title I programs and sent to "pull-out" resource classrooms. The resource teachers in these classrooms were expected to address the needs of these students. As a result, there was no sense of ownership by the regular classroom teachers for these students' achievement. Little was done, except in a few classrooms, to address reading deficits within the regular classroom reading curriculum. In addition, more academically able students were not challenged in the regular classroom since teachers taught "to the middle." As a result, neither the middle-class nor the less advantaged students received effective instruction geared to their reading levels.

Teachers developed a culture of acceptance of failure for these students, blaming their homes and lack of parental support.

Curriculum Disorganization

At this point in time, curriculum and textbooks in reading were adopted at the district level. Kindergarten through fifth-grade teachers were expected to teach the traditional curriculum areas of language arts, math, social studies, science, art, music, and physical education. Schools generally went along with the adopted texts with some degree of flexibility at the school level. But although the district had adopted texts, their use varied within a school and even within grade levels at a school. Hartsfield Elementary was an excellent example of how curriculum varied both within a school and among teachers in the same grade level.

Hartsfield Elementary was an excellent example of how curriculum varied both within a school and among teachers in the same grade level.

There was little curriculum coordination among teachers at a grade level except in a few instances where teachers adopted a common "theme." These instructional themes could involve dinosaurs, sea life, or some other topic. However, this same theme could appear the next year with the next grade level's teacher. In some instances, students received the same theme for 3 consecutive years. Also, some teachers used the adopted language arts text to teach reading, while others used no textbook at all and simply pulled instruction from "a variety of resources." Hence, there was no reading program except the adopted reading series that was sporadically used in the school. Students at a certain grade level were exposed to whatever skills or content a teacher chose to use in her or his class. At the end of the year, with the exception of districtwide achievement testing, there was no assessment of reading skills to provide information to next year's teacher. Additionally, there was no ongoing reading assessment in the classrooms.

Uncoordinated Instructional Delivery

Instructional delivery was very "departmentalized" at the school. The "departments" consisted of learning disabilities, speech/language, and Title 1 services. Coordination was rare among the teachers in grade levels, Title I, and special education.

Pull-out programs were the sole instructional delivery system for students with learning disabilities and speech and language deficits and those who qualified for Title 1 services. There was little communication about reading strategies and curriculum approaches since there was not a schoolwide curriculum for reading at Hartsfield. This meant a classroom teacher might use a context-based approach (whole language), while a resource teacher might use an approach emphasizing explicit instruction in phonics. Since there was no assessment or coordination of instruction, accountability for student learning was nonexistent. Students receiving these pull-out services experienced what Slavin and Madden (1989) term *cognitive confusion* created by multiple instructional approaches to reading.

Since there was no assessment or coordination of instruction, accountability for student learning was nonexistent.

The problem was made worse by the fact that students needing additional learning time spent much of their day in "transition," walking the corridors from their classrooms to speech therapy, to the Title I teacher, and finally returning to their classrooms. A great deal of instructional time was lost in travel as well as at transitional points among classrooms. Regular classroom teachers were concerned that they rarely had the whole class intact, due to constant pull-out time for certain students. Also, due to the departmentalized approach, there was not a focus on the most pressing needs of an individual student. Instead, each classroom teacher and resource teacher was operating independently and was unable to consider individual student priorities. The primary need for most of these students was learning to read. Despite this need, many spent extra instructional time in mathematics and continued to fall further behind in reading.

Each classroom teacher and resource teacher was operating independently and was unable to consider individual student priorities.

Special area services for art, music, and physical education were scheduled so they did not occur at the same time every day for all classes at the same grade level. This meant that one 1st-grade class would have physical education on Tuesday at 9:00 while another had music at 9:30. The blocks of time for special area services were also varied during the week from 30 to 60 minutes per day. Although there were some days with common special area times for a specific grade level, it did not occur on a daily basis. This scheduling arrangement created frequent noise in the corridors and no constant planning times for grade-level teachers.

Poor Student Achievement

The California Achievement Test (CATV) was the standardized test that was administered to groups of students in our district to assess their progress. The CATV was administered to third through fifth grades in the spring of 1993 and 1994. The average median percentile scores for children in third, fourth, and fifth grades for the 1993 and 1994 school years were 50, 52, and 48. Although these figures placed our children close to the national average in terms of overall performance, far too many of our students were performing from one and a half to two grade levels below their current grade placement. Poor reading skills were interfering with many children's progress through the curriculum in third, fourth, and fifth grades, and these children were also not prepared to move into the middle school curriculum after leaving Hartsfield.

Poor reading skills were interfering with many children's progress through the curriculum in third, fourth, and fifth grades, and these children were also not prepared to move into the middle school curriculum after leaving Hartsfield.

Preparation for Change—Admitting We Had Problems and Deciding the Direction

During the 1993–1994 school year, there were a series of meetings among parents, teachers, and the administration. The School Advisory Council, comprising parents and teachers, and the Parent Teacher Organization

(PTO) met together to discuss concerns about student discipline and academic achievement. We worked collaboratively on a series of belief statements and a school vision, which emphasized student responsibility and student achievement. Parents unanimously adopted it. The faculty and administration met together—sometimes with parents, sometimes without—to discuss the vision and belief statements and identify strategies to begin moving in a desired direction.

> I finally felt that my son's problems would be taken care of. Working together with our school kept me involved, and I understood for the first time what was being done and what I could expect for Jimmy.

The faculty, after much discussion and two inservice sessions discussing reading research, identified our two primary problems. First, students were not prepared to enter kindergarten, and second, we had no consistent reading program at Hartsfield. The first problem was addressed by expanding the prekindergarten program through constructing an infant-toddler wing on the school (supported by a $470,000 grant) and doubling the size of our early childhood program. The second area, lack of a consistent reading program, was our core problem. Admitting that this was a problem was the first step to solving it.

THE CHANGE PROCESS: SCHOOL YEAR 1993–1994

Tackling the Instructional Delivery System

In 1993–1994, teachers expressed the concern that they had little time to plan together to ensure more consistent content and instructional strategies at each grade level. Also, they expressed frustration at our "helter skelter" schedule of pulling students out of their classes for resource assistance. Some teachers had their entire class together for less than one hour per day. We decided that one of the solutions to these problems involved block scheduling for special area (art, music, physical education, and media) programs.

[Teachers] expressed frustration at our "helter skelter" schedule of pulling students out of their classes for resource assistance. Some teachers had their entire class together for less than one hour per day.

This block scheduling allowed, for instance, all of the second-grade classes to attend a special area for the same 45-minute period every day, enabling teachers to share common planning times. In addition, we moved all our primary class special area times to after lunch. This allowed these classes large blocks of instructional time during the mornings, a prime learning time for younger children. Third through fifth grades had 75 to 90 minutes of uninterrupted periods in the morning and the same in the afternoons, while primary grades had 180 uninterrupted instructional minutes in the mornings and 45 in the afternoons.

To address the concern regarding the constant pulling of students from their regular classrooms, we began a team-teaching approach piloted the year before in a fifth- and fourth-grade classroom. The team-teaching approach meant the resource teacher came to the classroom instead of groups of students leaving their class to go to the resource teacher. While the rest of the children were receiving reading instruction in groups from the classroom teacher or working at centers, the children with reading difficulties received small-group instruction from the resource teacher. We adopted this service delivery system for students with learning disabilities (LDs) in grades one through five in our school.

This practice required us to "cluster" our LD and language-impaired students in certain classrooms, but it had several important benefits. It eliminated student travel time to resource rooms, reduced the number of transitions between classrooms, and saved instructional time. This increased the total amount of instructional time during the day for our academically needy students. We also noticed another significant benefit associated with this service delivery system. It created interaction between the regular and resource teachers and fostered consistent instructional approaches for all students. Also, students who did not quite qualify for special programs and who traditionally "fell through the cracks" began receiving the individualized small-group instruction necessary for their academic progress. Since they were frequently included with the special needs students because their curricular needs were similar, this resulted in regular and special education students receiving instruction at their academic level.

Using a Research-Based Reading Curriculum

After reviewing research on reading and reading instruction with our faculty, we focused on two commercially available reading programs. One was *Collections for Young Scholars* (Open Court Reading, 1995), and the other was Science Research Associates' (SRA) Reading Mastery Rainbow Edition (Englemann & Bruner, 1995) program. At this time, our special education resource and Title I teachers were using the SRA Reading Mastery program with our students with learning disabilities and some Title I students at all grade levels, and they strongly supported this approach. Our K–2 teachers were sent to observe these programs, and we reviewed research and materials and invited representatives from the two publishers as well as teachers who had used these programs to speak with us about their success.

The Open Court curriculum provided guidelines and materials to support explicit and systematic instruction in essential early skills like phonemic awareness and phonics, while at the same time it provided support for meaningful and interesting reading activities. The program supported teaching of phonics using sound-spelling cards, alliterative stories, and controlled vocabulary texts that practiced the rules just taught. We used Big Books story-sharing activities to promote oral language comprehension and love of literature as a parallel strand. We had studied the summary of *Beginning to Read: Thinking and Learning About Print* (Stahl, Osborn, & Lehr, 1990) and were pleased to note that Marilyn Adams, the author of the work from which this summary was made (Adams, 1990), was a senior author on the Open Court reading curriculum.

THE CHANGE PROCESS: SCHOOL YEAR 1994–1995

We Changed the Basic Reading Curriculum

For the 1994–1995 school year, we included the adoption of Open Court's *Collections for Young Scholars* in our school improvement plan for kindergarten through second grades. We also decided to continue the SRA Reading Mastery curriculum with our third-, fourth-, and fifth-grade students with learning disabilities and some Title I students in second grade.

Kindergarten through second-grade and resource teachers attended a three-day summer inservice training program to help them learn to use Open Court, and Open Court's consultant came to the school to help us begin the program in our kindergarten through second-grade classrooms. The consultant returned every three to four weeks during the first semester and met with the grade level teachers. One problem with the initial inservice was that it should have been more explicit regarding the importance of addressing the key components of the Open Court lesson on a daily basis. Teachers thought, and justifiably so, they could select some components of the lesson and not use others. In addition, there was some resistance from several teachers, who claimed that they were being "forced" to teach in a way that was inconsistent with their "philosophy" of reading, while others simply were not able to provide adequate instruction. For these reasons, the implementation was "uneven" within grade levels, with some teachers fully implementing the program and others inconsistently using parts of the program.

THE CHANGE PROCESS: 1995–1996

For the 1995–1996 year, we continued our special area block scheduling and committed ourselves to significant changes through the school improvement plan process. These included

- requiring the use of the Open Court curriculum in kindergarten through second grades, and reinforcing it by written memos and discussion in team meetings as well as frequent administrative observations in the classroom;
- eliminating all pull-out resource times except speech articulation;
- completing the adoption of the SRA Reading Mastery program in third, fourth, and fifth grades for all students;
- initiating small-group reading instruction for all students in all grades;
- suspending the social studies and some math curriculum in first and second grade; and

- using reading subtests from the Woodcock-Johnson Psycho-Educational Battery-Revised (Woodcock & Johnson, 1989) to individually evaluate the reading level of all 1st- and 2nd-grade students.

All of these changes were addressed directly or indirectly in our school improvement plan for 1995–1996. We used a small writing team and frequent meetings among teachers and administrators in grade level groups to discuss the research and proposed curriculum changes. A parent from our School Advisory Council was on the school improvement plan writing team.

We used a small writing team and frequent meetings among teachers and administrators in grade level groups to discuss the research and proposed curriculum changes. A parent from our School Advisory Council was on the school improvement plan writing team.

We got buy-in from administrators and changed the curriculum. Once the curriculum was discussed and written in the plan, all staff understood that it was the administration's responsibility to ensure that the plan was effectively implemented at the school. There was a faculty meeting and a series of grade level team meetings that continued throughout the year. We outlined in detail expectations of changes we were making in curriculum and instructional delivery and involved teachers at every step in the scheduling, assessment, and implementation of programs. Teacher performance evaluations now included how well they implemented the program.

The adoption of the SRA Reading Mastery program for all 3rd- through 5th-grade students meant a commitment to teacher inservice and expenditure of school dollars to purchase materials and supplies to run the program.

The adoption of the SRA Reading Mastery program for all 3rd- through 5th-grade students meant a commitment to teacher inservice and expenditure of school dollars to purchase materials and supplies to run the program.

This step ensured extra help for students below grade level and advanced instruction for more academically able students. Once the program began, we saw the need for periodic monitoring of the program to ensure that students were instructed at the correct reading levels. We also found that some teachers, on the basis of philosophical differences, resisted grouping students for instruction. This was similar to what occurred when Open Court began in the lower grades and was a factor throughout the 1st year of using SRA in all the upper grades. We knew that this made the program less effective.

At the midyear point, we noticed that a substantial number of our second graders were still struggling with beginning reading skills in the area of phonetic decoding (being able to sound out novel words in text). For these children, we began using SRA Fast Cycle (a combination of Reading Mastery I and II) in their small-group instruction. By the end of the year, we noticed a marked change in their word-attack skills, although some students learned at a much slower rate and required more repetition.

We Made Major Changes in Instructional Delivery

Eliminating all pull-out programs except speech articulation required a great deal of preparation and teacher cooperation. We began the previous spring by loading classes with approximately the same number of students at each academic level. In other words, in every class we attempted to have equal numbers of students with high, average, and below-average reading skills.

We did not at this point have reliable assessment results and were using the CATV for grades three through five, Marie Clay's (1985) Concepts About Print test (found in *The Early Detection of Reading Difficulties*) for kindergarten, and teacher judgments to make these decisions. Our purpose in using the assessment information for class loading was to ensure that enough students at a given academic level were assigned to each class to form an instructional group for that class. We did assign all of our language-impaired and LD students in two classes per grade level. The other class or classes received "borderline" students with similar academic needs who did not quite qualify for a special program. We continued to form self-contained classes for students with moderate to severe mental handicaps and behavioral disabilities.

To initiate small-group instruction, we clustered small groups of three to six students according to reading levels in each 1st- through 5th-grade class. We then scheduled each resource teacher to be in a classroom for 75 to 90 minutes per day. This meant the resource teachers were seeing three to four classrooms per day and teaching two to three reading groups per class. Some classes received a trained paraprofessional to run reading groups. Paraprofessionals, as long as they received periodic inservice training and were monitored, were as effective as teachers using the SRA program. Decisions about when to move students among reading groups resided with the resource and classroom teachers The resource positions were funded from special education and Title I funds.

The regular teachers saw two to three reading groups while the resource teachers were in the room. The other students not in a group were assigned to work at independent centers and rotated into a reading group during the resource teacher's time in their class. This captured a great deal of instructional time since it eliminated student movement outside the classrooms.

Teachers were concerned about the large amount of instructional time used in kindergarten through second grades to implement the Open Court program. We agreed to eliminate classroom science and social studies and some math for the year. This enabled our primary teachers to focus on the reading and writing curriculum for their students. We assessed all children's reading skills to determine if the changes were effective.

At the beginning of the 1995–1996 school year, we began assessing children's reading levels using the Word Attack and Word Identification subtests from the Woodcock-Johnson Psycho-Educational Battery-Revised. These assessments were administered to all first- and second-grade students within the first three weeks of school by our resource teachers and guidance counselor, whom we trained to administer the assessment. To eliminate any bias, we also decided that the resource teachers would not administer the test to students they would be teaching during the year, and classroom teachers were not involved in the test administration other than providing blocks of times for the resource teachers to test students. This testing arrangement increased the reliability of our results. The resource teachers and guidance teacher used this same procedure at the end of the year. We used the results to assess individual student progress for the year and the aggregate data to evaluate the effectiveness of our reading program in 1st and 2nd grades. We continued the individual assessment of kindergarten students but changed from the Concepts of Print assessment to the Bracken Basic Concept Scale (Bracken, 1984).

The usefulness of our individual reading assessments for documenting the effectiveness of the changes we made to our reading curriculum is illustrated in Figure 11.1. In this graph, we have plotted the number of children in first and second grade who had word-reading skills below the 25th percentile at different points in time. Among children in first grade, the percent of children with word-reading skills below the 25th percentile

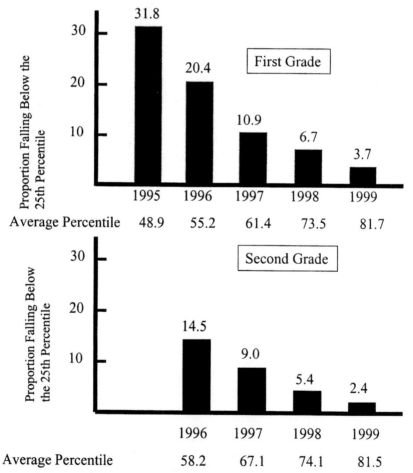

Figure 11.1.   Changes in Year-End Reading Performance of Children During Period of Rapid Curriculum Changes in Reading

decreased from 31.8 at beginning of the 1995–1995 school year to 3.7 at the end of the 1998–1999 year. During the same three-year period, the average percentile scores of 1st-grade children rose from 48.9 to 82. Children in 2nd grade were not tested at the end of the beginning of the 1995–1996 school year, but achievement was generally stronger as children had been in the program longer. During this same period of time, the median percentile in reading achievement for our 3rd-grade children on the CATV jumped from 49 at the end of 1994 to 73 at the end of 1999.

THE CHANGE PROCESS: 1996–1997

Encouraged by these increases in student achievement, we continued to use the school improvement plan process to plot our course of action. For the 1996–1997 school year we focused on the following:

- Continuing our direction begun the previous year, including clear expectations regarding implementation of curriculum; scheduling to increase instructional time, team-teaching approach in all classrooms, small-group instruction, and objective assessment of student progress
- Emphasizing changes at the kindergarten level to include assessment and programmatic changes for language and phonemic awareness to intervene with our youngest students
- Initiating a six-week summer program for our "at-risk" four-year-olds preparing to enter kindergarten
- Initiating a pre-/posttest (Bracken Basic Concept Scale) for pre-K students
- Implementing Accelerated Reader, a reading and computer-assisted instruction and assessment program, as a supplement to our basic reading curriculum
- Initiating a "home reading" program for kindergarten through third grades

Administrative Support

The commitment to the previous year's changes and the will to continue those improvements needed to be continuously supported through planned administrative and leadership actions. These actions were accomplished primarily through faculty and grade level meetings as well as one-to-one discussions with teachers. In contrast, many of our earlier changes were infrastructure changes, including an emphasis on uninterrupted classroom instruction, increased instructional time resulting from master schedule changes, elimination of pull-out programs, and other measures outlined earlier. We recognized that these changes in infrastructure depend on continual reminders to teachers and staff about the vision statements that guided these changes in the first place. Further, individual teachers frequently require help in solving problems that arise from these scheduling constraints so that the adaptations we made could reinforce the overall effectiveness of the instructional delivery system.

We recognized that these changes in infrastructure depend on continual reminders to teachers and staff about the vision statements that guided these changes in the first place.

Further Changes to the Reading Curriculum

The individual reading assessment program we began using the previous year showed us that many children were still leaving second grade unprepared for 3rd-grade-level work in reading. In the previous year, we had begun using the SRA Fast Cycle Reading program with our lower performing children beginning in the second semester of second grade. For the six weeks of summer school, we began to provide many of these children with two reading sessions per day using the SRA program to give them a preview and experience with the SRA Reading program, in addition to adding further substantial gains to their basic word-reading ability. Unfortunately, some of our students continued to struggle in the Fast Cycle program.

At the same time that we were attempting to strengthen reading instruction for children with the weakest skills, the use of small-group instruction was working very well to challenge our students with the strongest reading skills. At the end of the 4th grade, we had 20 of 74 students in a Level VI, grade six reading program. We also decided to add the

Accelerated Reader (1994) program for all of our students in 3rd, 4th, and 5th grades. The Accelerated Reader program is basically a way of monitoring children's outside-of-class reading so they can be encouraged and rewarded for doing more reading outside of assigned class materials. We began offering incentive awards to encourage students to read. As students read books, they took a computerized test on the content of the book. The software in the Accelerated Reader program keeps a running record of all books read and the score of each comprehension test. By the 2nd semester, we had 2nd- and 1st-grade teachers also using the program and requesting more books on their students' levels. We purchased additional disks and books for kindergarten through second grade.

One of our major concerns and an initial reason for beginning the Accelerated Reader program was reading fluency. Although we worked on fluency with students in Open Court SRA, there was an overall concern among the faculty that we needed something that involved our parents in reading. As Cunningham and Stanovich (1998) have recently underlined, once children acquire beginning reading skills, one of the keys to their becoming good readers by the end of elementary school is wide exposure to text. Thus, we began the read-at-home program for kindergarten through third grade.

Once children acquire beginning reading skills, one of the keys to their becoming good readers by the end of elementary school is wide exposure to text. Thus, we began the read-at-home program for kindergarten through third grade.

We used out-of-adoption reading series books to send home with our children. The parents signed off on the pages read nightly. This was very successful at two grade levels and had an inconsistent implementation in two others. It did improve the fluency for some students and was a great way to involve parents in their children's education.

Changes at the Kindergarten Level

At the beginning of the second semester of this school year, we administered the Test of Phonological Awareness (TOPA) (Torgesen & Bryant, 1994) to all of our kindergarten children. Using this test, we identified students with severe weaknesses in phonological awareness. For these children, we initi-

> I was able to actually see the progress Jennifer was making as we read together each night. While it wasn't always easy to stop washing dishes and doing laundry to set aside the time, it was really worth it!

ated small-group DISTAR (a language instruction program) language lessons (Engelmann & Osborn, 1987) in 20-minute sessions four days per week. We assessed these kindergarten students with the Bracken Basic Concept Scale at the end of the year to evaluate student progress and determine those needing to attend summer school.

Most of the children needed to attend. At the conclusion of summer school, we assessed kindergarten students to determine those needing the extra assistance in 1st grade. Four of the 18 students attending summer school went into the regular Open Court curriculum in 1997–1998, while the others participated in small-group instruction using the SRA Reading Mastery I curriculum. We felt that the SRA curriculum was more properly paced for these weaker students, and also that it provided more opportunities for explicit practice and skill building than did the *Collections for Young Scholars* materials. Those students receiving SRA also received the benefits of a portion of the Open Court lessons as well.

THE CHANGE PROCESS: 1997–1998

For 1997–1998, we identified some additional instructional strategies to make our students more successful. These included

- continuing to emphasize and monitor implementation of Open Court, SRA, and Accelerated Reader programs;
- providing small-group instruction to our weakest first- and second-grade children using the Reading Mastery curriculum (using Reading Mastery I and II instead of Fast Cycle) rather than the Open Court curriculum;
- implementing the Standardized Test of Assessment for Reading (1995) to determine leisure reading levels of students;

- implementing the Waterford Early Reading Program, Level 1 (Waterford Institute, 1995) in kindergarten and one 1st-grade classroom; and
- expanding instruction for language-delayed kindergarten students.

Further Changes to the Reading Curriculum

We were convinced at this point that there was conclusive research to suggest the importance of explicit phonics instruction for less advantaged children (Brown & Felton, 1990; Foorman, Francis, Fletcher, Schatschneider, & Mehta, 1998). Although this type of instruction is provided in the Open Court curriculum, and some of our students from low-income families were successful with it, many were not making adequate progress. As mentioned previously, we used the summer school data to determine which students needed SRA in first grade. Beginning this school year, these students received their small-group instruction using the Reading Mastery curriculum.

Continuing Administrative Support Actions

The principal, assistant principal, and an SRA trainer monitored the reading programs at all grade levels. One critical area we monitored was students' oral reading performance. Oral reading provides critical insight into the way children are progressing with both the accuracy and fluency of their word-reading skills. Since all of our students read in small groups daily, this was easy to accomplish.

Oral reading provides critical insight into the way children are progressing in accuracy and fluency of their word-reading skills.

In some classrooms, the teachers were grading the daily written comprehension assignments but not actual student reading. We met with the teachers, outlined the problem, and talked with them about the solution. We used this as an example of what may happen if the principal and assistant principal are not actively involved in the reading program to help keep the attention of all personnel focused on the reading goals and achievements that everyone has agreed are important.

Assessment of Reading Skills

We began the Standardized Test of Assessment for Reading (STAR) (1995) this year. Using the STAR software, we evaluated the leisure and instructional reading level for each student. All students reading at the school took the assessment on a quarterly basis. This included kindergarten children who were reading. In addition to generating individualized reading levels, it also produced a parent report and maintained a record of the results for each student.

Additions to the Kindergarten Curriculum

Given the diversity of preparation for reading among the children coming into Hartsfield, we felt the need to continue to improve the quality and power of our instruction at the kindergarten level. We made one step toward this goal by implementing the Waterford Early Reading Program, Level 1, in all our kindergarten classrooms. This program is extremely engaging for young children, and it provides 20 minutes of individualized, high-quality computer-based instruction in concepts of print, phonemic awareness, phonics, and vocabulary every day for the entire kindergarten year. An additional attractive feature of the program is that it has a set of books and video tapes that go home so parents can use them with their children.

In addition, we continued to provide small-group instruction using the DISTAR (Engelmann & Osborn, 1987) language curriculum. This year, we added an additional 10 to 15 minutes per day of specific instruction in phonemic awareness using activities from *Phonemic Awareness in Young Children: A Classroom Curriculum* that has been developed by Adams, Foorman, Lundberg, and Beeler (1997).

> I really appreciated the books and tapes the school sent home for us to use. It took the mystery out of what Josh should be doing and helped me help him.

CONCLUDING COMMENTS

The comprehensive report on the prevention of reading problems in young children published by the National Academy Press (Snow, Burns, & Griffin, 1998), as well as the later report of the National Reading Panel (2000), suggests that the first step toward ensuring that all children acquire effective reading skills involves a sound basic reading curriculum in kindergarten through 2nd grade. We would agree with that statement, but we would also emphasize that schools must be prepared to go substantially beyond that step to reach all their children (Torgesen, 2002). In our estimation, the most important additional steps are (1) identification of resources and procedures for delivering effective small-group or individual instruction to high-risk children beginning in kindergarten and extending at least through second grade; (2) regular assessment of early reading growth to ensure that the needs of all children are being met; (3) continuing administrative leadership to ensure proper coordination and execution of all elements of the preventive effort; and (4) a realistic time frame for implementation of all elements of the overall program.

Even though the reading achievement of children in first and second grades at Hartsfield Elementary School showed substantial improvement over the five-year period of the change process we have described, and these improvements were reflected in improved student performance on the CATV in 3rd grade, there were still a number of important things left to do to continue the improvement process at Hartsfield. One set of plans included making changes to the curriculum of our school-based pre-K programs to more systematically support children's acquisition of prereading skills such as vocabulary, print awareness, and sensitivity to the sound structure of language. In coordination with these school-based experiences, we also wanted to work with the pre-K parent/teacher organization to more effectively increase parental awareness of home-based activities that can support growth in emergent literacy skills.

In coordination with these school-based experiences, we also wanted to work with the Pre-K parent/teacher organization to more effectively increase parental awareness of home-based activities that can support growth in emergent literacy skills.

In addition to these improvements at the pre-K level, plans were also laid for continuing efforts in the K–5 program in three areas. First, we had begun investigating ways to more effectively use computer-assisted instruction and practice to support reading growth at all grade levels. We view computer technology as particularly effective in providing the structured and motivating practice that many of our children require to consolidate the skills they are taught in the classroom.

Second, we recognized the need for more teacher training focused on the "higher order" thinking skills that are required in the development of high levels of literacy. Our work to this point had focused primarily on word-level reading skills, and it was clear that we also needed to explore ways to expand our efforts in helping our children develop the language and thinking skills required for high-level comprehension of text.

Finally, it was clear that more effort was required to recruit high-quality teachers who shared our philosophical and research-based orientation to reading instruction for all children. We recognize the contributions of all the teachers and other school staff who contributed to the improvements noted in this chapter, and we take it as our continual goal to continue to do better than we have done before in teaching all children to read.

POSTSCRIPT: BEATING THE ODDS

At the time this chapter went to press, we had available to us data on 3rd-grade student performance on the Florida Comprehensive Assessment Test, which is a demanding test of reading comprehension for complex text. Students who attain Level 1 performance on the FCAT are regarded as seriously below grade level in reading and can be retained in third grade because of low reading performance. Although Hartsfield serves a more at-risk population of students than the state as a whole (the percentage of students receiving free or reduced lunch is 62% compared to state average of 45%), during the last three years, Hartsfield consistently had fewer students achieve Level 1 performance than the state as a whole. The figures for 2002 are 18% Hartsfield versus 27% statewide; for 2003 they are 20% Hartsfield versus 23% statewide; and for 2004 they are 14% Hartsfield versus 22% statewide. Although there remains substantial room for improvement, the effects of the school change process described in this chapter appear to be having a lasting effect on student reading outcomes at Hartsfield.

TIPS FOR PARENTS

- Ask how children with different needs and levels of achievement are being taught. If children who are behind in reading are not getting focused, intensive instruction, ask why and how the school can provide that for them.
- Check to see that skills taught at one grade level are built upon at the next grade level. Ask the principal how he makes sure that instruction is coordinated among teachers.
- Make a request for parents to become part of developing solutions along with the faculty and administration.
- Ask your child's teacher if she has sufficient time to prepare for classes.
- Ask whether textbooks are based upon research, who did the research, and how it works in schools like yours.
- Check to make sure that teachers have been given an opportunity to learn how to use these texts and other materials.
- Ask what the goals and expectations are for your child and for others in his grade. Then ask what changes have been put in place to meet those goals.
- Request copies of test scores, and ask for interpretation of your child's weaknesses and how classroom instruction will help build on her strengths and eliminate her weaknesses.
- Ask for specific advice about what you can do at home to reinforce what your child is learning in school. Correspond regularly with your child's teacher to make sure that everything is on track.

12

The Last Word

Phyllis Blaunstein and Reid Lyon

We must reform the way reading is taught in our schools. Too many of our most precious citizens continue to be disenfranchised from the joys and short- and long-term benefits afforded by being a proficient reader. We hope that you will help us make sure that our kids get what they deserve and what they need. We hope that together we can eliminate the pain and lifelong failure that accompany reading problems. We hope that the real life stories presented by parents, teachers, and scientists in this book will empower you to take up the charge to make sure that your children learn to read. In doing so, you will help all the children in your school, your community, and, through your example, the nation. The future of your children is at stake.

Until almost all children learn to read, we will continue to have a dropout rate that no individual child, group of children, or society can afford. We now know that the difference between having a high school diploma and not having one is $1 million over a lifetime. The cost of not learning to read in dollars, self-confidence, and quality of life is incalculable.

Your help is crucial. Your voices must be heard by teachers, administrators, business leaders, and policy makers to encourage them to move forward on creating research-proven reading programs in every classroom in this country. Your children need your support and advocacy because their very well-being depends on it.

We recognize that this is a difficult task. It is hard to find the time and energy and to overcome the fear of taking on a major battle. But we hope that the stories of the others who have overcome great odds will reassure and reenergize you when the going gets tough. We hope the tools and examples in this book will get you started and that you will take advantage of the many resources that are available to help you maintain your momentum.

Know that you will gain the confidence, strength, and courage you need each time you face your fears. There are many people who will help you if you ask for their assistance. Follow the lead of those who have come before you and who have mapped the way. Ask for the help you need and have faith in the fact that you will get it. Your children are depending on you.

Helen Keller, who overcame incredible odds, knew this well. She said, "Alone we can do so little; together we can do so much."

Appendix A:
What Is Scientifically Based Reading Research?

Some federal programs may have a specific statutory or regulatory definition of this term. In general, scientifically based reading research includes concepts such as those below.

Scientifically based reading research uses scientific procedures to obtain knowledge about how young children develop reading skills, how children can be taught to read, and how children can overcome reading difficulties. Scientifically based reading research has the following characteristics.

It uses clear, step-by-step methods of gathering data. These methods involve careful observations and measurements. Often, experiments are used to gather information. For example, an experiment may compare how well children learn to read when they are taught in different ways.

It uses established, acceptable ways of measuring and observing. Let's say a researcher is trying to find which type of instruction best helps children learn the meaning of new words. The researcher must decide how to measure the children's word learning. Should the children just be asked whether they know the word? Should they be able to recognize the correct definition among several choices? Or should they be able to use the new word correctly in their writing? The way the researcher chooses to measure word learning must be acceptable to other researchers as a good, or valid, measure of word learning.

It requires that researchers use established, acceptable ways of making sense of, or interpreting, the data they gather. Researchers must show that the conclusions they reach follow logically from the data they collected. Other researchers must be able to draw the same or similar conclusions from the data, and similar experiments must provide similar data.

It requires that several other researchers have carefully reviewed the report of the research. The report must include enough specific information about the research so that other researchers could repeat the research and verify the findings. These expert reviewers must agree that the research was done carefully and correctly and that the conclusions follow from the data. Usually, scientifically based reading research is published in professional journals and presented at professional meetings so that other researchers can learn from the work.

Scientifically based reading research provides the best available information about how you can help prepare young children for learning to read in school.

Source: Early Childhood-Head Start Task Force/U.S. Department of Education/ U.S. Department of Health and Human Services, 2002.

Appendix B: How Do I Know a Good Early Reading Program When I See One?

Laura Bush

Every teacher is excited about reading and promotes the value and fun of reading to students.

All students are carefully evaluated, beginning in kindergarten, to see what they know and what they need to become good readers.

Reading instruction and practice lasts 90 minutes or more a day in 1st, 2nd, and 3rd grades and 60 minutes a day in kindergarten.

All students in first, second, and third grades who are behind in reading get special instruction and practice. These students receive, throughout the day, a total of 60 extra minutes of instruction.

Before- or after-school help is given to all students beyond first grade who need extra instruction or who need to review skills. Summer school is available for students who are behind at the end of the year.

Reading instruction and practice includes work on letters, sounds, and blending sounds. Students learn to blend letters and sounds to form new words.

Learning new words and their meaning is an important part of instruction.

Students have daily spelling practice and weekly spelling tests.

The connection between reading and writing is taught on a daily basis. Students write daily. Papers are corrected and returned to the students. By the end of second grade, students write final copies of corrected papers. Corrected papers are sent home for parents to see.

All students are read to each day from different kinds of books. Students discuss what they read with teachers and other students.

All students have a chance to read both silently and aloud in school each day and at home every night.

Every classroom has a library of books that children want to read. This includes easy books and books that are more difficult.

The school library is used often and has many books. Students may check books out during the summer and over holidays.

Source: Bush, 2001.

Appendix C:
Advice to a Teacher of Beginning Reading

Sara M. Porter

If we collected all the heart-rending stories about learning to read and not learning to read, printed them in small type, and bound them, the volumes would more than likely fill several very long bookshelves.

Yet for all the suffering and all our knowledge about how to help children with reading difficulties, we continue to hear the same heartbreaking stories over and over again. Sometimes they end happily. The person learns to read after much struggle. For most, at least at this time, reading is only a dream. Students feel unfit to attend college; they lose faith in their own abilities; they lose their way in life. How can this be when the subject has been studied in such detail over so many decades? How can children still fail to learn the basic skill that lets them become readers?

Placing blame is easy. Teachers blame parents and parents blame schools. Parents and teachers blame children for not learning like everyone else. Some blame colleges because so few of them prepare teachers to teach all students.

Placing blame is easy. Teachers blame parents and parents blame schools. Parents and teachers blame children for not learning like everyone else.

We say that everyone learns differently but sometimes refuse to look at those differences in the light of science. What can we say to new teachers who enter classrooms unprepared, or ill prepared to teach beginning reading? How can we help them understand that needing to learn to read through a scientifically proven systematic and comprehensive phonics-based approach does not automatically mean a "special education" placement? How can we help teachers of beginning reading understand that they write the ending to those literacy stories, that each student's success or failure depends on them?

This is what I learned through many years of working—most times successfully—with the hard-to-teach student.

How can we help teachers of beginning reading understand that they write the ending to those literacy stories, that each student's success or failure depends on them?

BE AWARE OF YOUR OWN SHORTCOMINGS

You may believe that you are ready for anything. You aren't. Teaching reading will be just one of your challenges. Faced with all the complexities of organizing a classroom, trying to figure out reasons for seemingly small errors will seem the least of your problems. Learning why Heather can't differentiate between *b* and *d*, why Sammy can't remember the word *the* from page to page, or why he writes *p* to spell a word that begins with *b* will be the most important thing you do. Be on the lookout for these errors. Identify the children who consistently make them. They need a different approach to learning to read, and you aren't providing it. Then find out what you need to know to teach them.

BE SURE THAT *YOU* KNOW THE STRUCTURE OF LANGUAGE

It is easy to believe that we know how speech sounds are represented by the alphabet. Twenty-six letters represent at least 44 speech sounds. They spell even more speech sounds if you write dialects as Mark Twain did. Since we all talk a little differently, it is easy to dismiss phonics as being not very helpful. Nothing could be further from the truth.

Helping beginning readers translate speech into print and print into speech is easier to do when teachers know how individual sounds are formed by the lips, tongue, and breath. Letters don't actually "say" anything, they represent individual speech sounds. Phonics lessons can be confusing. Some children (and adults) question the validity of phonics. Learning that *s* represents the sound /s/ as in sister when they cannot use that knowledge to read *she* is simply confusing. Without a sequential, structured system for learning and practice in applying the skill, some reject all phonics lessons. Change the method you are using. Don't become responsible for creating or adding to their disability.

Without a sequential, structured system for learning and practice in applying the skill, some reject all phonics lessons. Change the method you are using. Don't become responsible for creating or adding to their disability.

DON'T WAIT FOR HELP TO COME FROM OUTSIDE YOUR CLASSROOM

You will know who is struggling. These children pay less attention; they act out. They may resist coming to school. You are the only one who can help right away. Blaming the student for not learning or beginning the lengthy process of getting outside help may salve your conscience, but it does nothing immediate to help the student. Put off actual changes in instruction, and you will be the teacher who is remembered as creating the problem.

INFORM YOUR SCHOOL ADMINISTRATORS

Let someone else know about your problem. Make it your problem to avoid making a six-year-old responsible for a teaching method that is way beyond his or her understanding.

Many school systems and college professors are still telling teachers that beginning reading is simply reading for meaning. This is not so. More often than not students who struggle to learn can understand stories and narratives easily when someone tells the story. However, if asked to read the same stories they are at a loss because they cannot read the words on the page accurately and quickly. There is a structure to language, and decoding is the foundation. Many children need direct, systematic, and sequential presentation of phonics skills with much practice with phonetically regular words. If these necessary materials are not available to you, or if you need more training, tell your administrators. Help your principal understand. Before you see her, arm yourself with facts. Use up-to-date research, information from professional organizations, and articles by respected authors to show that these are not "problem" children but that you have been given a "problem" curriculum. To be sure, learning phonics is absolutely necessary to become a proficient reader. However, other reading skills are critical as well. Children must be taught to read quickly and with expression. They will not be able to understand what they read if they have not been taught the meanings of the words they are reading. Even with strong phonics skills, the ability to read quickly, and well-developed vocabularies, many children must be taught how to ask themselves questions as they read so that they really understand the material. Thus, they need comprehension strategies to ensure understanding.

Enlist the aid of parents.

If these necessary materials are not available to you, or if you need more training, tell your administrators.

YOU WRITE THE ENDING TO EACH CHILD'S LITERACY STORY

With luck you will gain the respect and support of your administration and coworkers, but, more important, your student's story will end happily. She may not even remember that she had any difficulty. Because we can document failures, but not successes, you may find yourself saying, "Did she really need this change? She's doing so well." Take it from those of us who have experienced this many times. She needed what you provided. Beginning reading instruction affects your students' entire life. What you choose to do, right at the very beginning of formal reading lessons, makes the difference between success and heartbreak.

Appendix D: Tools for Parents

Sara M. Porter

SAMPLE MEDIA ADVISORY

FOR IMMEDIATE RELEASE   CONTACT: <NAME>

<DATE>   <PHONE NUMBER>

*** MEDIA ADVISORY — SATURDAY EVENT ***

ANYTOWN PARENTS ORGANIZATION TO HOLD MARCH

FOR PROVEN READING INSTRUCTION IN THE CLASSROOM

Parents Seek to End Instructional Experimentation in Schools

<ANYTOWN, USA> <DATE>

Parents and elementary school students from across Anytown will join together this Saturday, marching from Anytown Elementary School to Town Hall. The march is part of a parent-led effort to ensure that only research-proven reading instruction is being used in Anytown schools.

Prior to the march, students will be writing letters to the school board and state legislators, detailing why it is important they become strong readers.

WHO:	Anytown Concerned Parents Coalition
WHAT:	March for Proven Reading Instruction
WHEN:	Saturday, April 5, 2003
	10:00 a.m.–11:30 a.m.
WHERE:	Anytown Elementary School (start)
	442 Courthouse St.

For more information on this event, please contact
<NAME> at <PHONE> or <e-mail>.

SAMPLE PRESS RELEASE

FOR IMMEDIATE RELEASE
CONTACT:
<NAME>
<DATE>
<PHONE NUMBER>
PARENTS, STUDENTS MARCH TO IMPROVE
READING INSTRUCTION IN THE CLASSROOM
Effort Seeks to End Instructional Experimentation in Schools
<ANYTOWN, USA> <DATE>

Armed with folders stuffed with research and statistics, more than 100
parents and students from Anytown Elementary School marched from the
school to Town Hall, demanding that the city adopt proven reading instruction programs for its K–4 classrooms.

"For too long, our classrooms have been used as laboratories, with our
children exposed to the latest experiments in reading instruction," said
<NAME>. "This experimentation must come to an end. We know how to
teach reading. We know what works. Our children deserve to be taught
with proven methods, and we now demand it."

The Anytown School Board is currently debating which language arts
textbook series to adopt for kindergarten through fourth grade. With reading test scores continuing to slump, the Concerned Parents Coalition
worked to educate local officials about the wealth of research on the best
ways to teach reading.

At the conclusion of the march, parents delivered their recommendations for which textbooks to adopt. Students also provided letters to the school board, telling board members how important learning to read is to them. They also prepared similar letters for their state legislators.

"If I didn't know how to read, I couldn't go to school," said <NAME>. "How would I be able to learn about plants or dinosaurs or baseball if I couldn't read?"

The school board is expected to make its recommendations this Wednesday. The Concerned Parents Coalition is seeking to make a formal presentation to the board before that decision.

SAMPLE LETTER TO THE EDITOR

To the editor,

A few years ago, I thought nothing could be better than reading a book to my child. Now, I realize I was wrong. Having my daughter read a book to me is a far, far greater event.

I'm lucky. My daughter loves to read, and she is good at it. But after recently visiting her classroom, I realize that all children are not so blessed.

Before my daughter went off to school, I carefully researched the best ways to prepare her. It was quite clear that we know how to teach reading. We know what works. We know what doesn't work. So I was shocked to see that some of our classrooms are not using what is proven effective.

As a parent, it is my responsibility to make sure my child is getting the best education possible. As a taxpayer, it is my job to ensure that my taxes are being spent wisely. And as a citizen, it is my duty to ensure that our schools are using proven reading instruction, helping our children become strong readers.

Without reading skills, our children can never succeed in life. We all must join together to demand that our schools are doing the best jobs they can. And that comes through a strong, proven reading program that starts with learning the letters and sounds of the alphabet.

Sincerely,
Your name and address

SAMPLE LETTER TO YOUR LEGISLATOR

The Honorable Congressman/Senator
U.S. House of Representatives/U.S. Senate
Washington, DC 20150/20510

Dear Congressman/Senator,

I am writing to ask your help. My child needs to have a classroom where she can learn effectively. Currently, [state the problem here, for example] she has not learned to read and is falling behind in every subject. She says she hates school and I am really worried that she will drop out as soon as she can and throw away her future. We can't allow this to happen. Others in her school are suffering from the same problems, and we need your help to make a dramatic change to fix this problem. Will you vote for [name the bill or recommendation] that will require our schools to start testing our children at an early age and to provide the kind of instruction that is based on good research, so that my daughter and others who are struggling may more effectively learn?

Thank you for your consideration.

Sincerely,
Your name and address

CHECKLIST FOR EFFECTIVE READING INSTRUCTION

When you go to your child's school, there are some things you should look for to determine if your child is getting effective reading instruction. Following is a checklist you can use.

___ My child is learning the sounds of language. My child's teacher is helping my child practice with sounds that make up words.

___ My child is learning to put sounds together to make up words and breaking words apart into separate sounds.

___ My child is learning the letters of the alphabet.

___ My child can recognize the names and shapes of letters.

___ My child is learning and using new words.

___ My child's teacher reads to the class and talks about what the students are reading.

___ My child is learning phonics—how sounds and letters are related. My child has been continuing to learn this for about 2 years.

___ My child is practicing phonics by reading easy books that include the letter-sound relationships he or she is learning.

___ My child is practicing writing the letter-sound relationships in words, sentences, and stories.

___ My child is being asked questions to help him or her think about the meaning of what he or she is reading.

___ My child is learning the meaning of new words.

___ My child is learning to expand his or her vocabulary by using the dictionary, using known words and word parts to figure out words, and using clues from the rest of the sentence.

___ My child is being taught to think as he or she reads and to make sense of what he or she is reading.

___ My child's teacher is checking to see if my child understands what he or she is reading by asking questions about the story.

Source: The Partnership for Reading, accessed November 13, 2005, from www.nifl.gov/partnershipforreading/publications/pdf/Stanovich.

Glossary

Teachers and other educators might use some terms when you are talking to them about how your child is learning to read. The terms in this glossary will help you interpret what they are saying and communicate with them more effectively.

alphabetic knowledge: Knowing the names and shapes of the letters of the alphabet.

alphabetic principle: The understanding that written letters represent sounds. For example, the word *big* has three sounds and three letters. Assessment test scores and other data determine how well children are learning, what specific skills they have learned, and areas in which they need help.

big books: Oversized books that allow for the sharing of print and illustrations with a group of children.

blending: Putting together individual sounds to make spoken words.

comprehension: The ability to understand and gain meaning from what has been read.

decodable books: Books that are made up of words that contain only the letter-sound relationships that the children are learning, along with a few words that are taught as sight words.

decode: The ability to recognize and read words by translating the letters into speech sounds to determine the word's pronunciation and meaning.

developmental spelling: The use of letter-sound relationship information to attempt to write words.

emergent literacy: The view that literacy learning begins at birth and is encouraged through participation with adults in meaningful reading and writing activities.

environmental print: Print that is a part of everyday life, such as signs, billboards, labels, and business logos.

experimental writing: Efforts by young children to experiment with writing by creating pretend and real letters and by organizing scribbles and marks on paper.

explicit instruction: Direct, structured, systematic teaching of a task.

fluency: The ability to read text accurately and quickly and with expression and comprehension.

graphic organizers: Diagrams that visually represent the organization and relationships of ideas in a text.

invented spelling: See developmental spelling.

irregular words: Frequently used words that don't follow the letter-sound relationship rules that children are learning.

leveled books: Books that have been assigned a particular level (usually a number or letter, such as Level 1 or Level B) intended to indicate how difficult the book is for children to read.

literacy: Includes all the activities involved in speaking, listening, reading, writing, and appreciating both spoken and written language.

phonemes: The smallest parts of spoken language that combine to form words. For example, the word *hit* is made up of three phonemes (/h/ /i/ /t/) and differs by one phoneme from the words *pit*, *hip*, and *hot*.

phonemic awareness: The ability to hear and identify the individual sounds in spoken words.

phonics: The relationship between the sounds of spoken words and the individual letters or groups of letters that represent those sounds in written words.

phonological awareness: The understanding that spoken language is made up of individual and separate sounds. Phonological awareness activities can involve work with rhymes, words, sentences, syllables, and phonemes.

predictable books: Books that have repeated words or sentences, rhymes, or other patterns.

prefix: A word part such as *re-*, *un-*, or *pre-* that is added to the beginning of a root word to form a new word with a new meaning.

pretend reading: Children's attempts to "read" a book before they have learned to read. Usually children pretend to read a familiar book that they have practically memorized.

professional development: The ongoing training of teachers.

proficiency: Refers to what students are able to do at that age and grade level.

print awareness: Knowing about print and books and how they are used.

root word: A word or word part to which a prefix or suffix is added.

segmentation: Taking spoken words apart sound by sound.

sight words: Words that a reader recognizes without having to sound them out. Some sight words are "irregular," or have letter-sound relationships that are uncommon. Some examples of sight words are *you*, *are*, *have*, and *said*.

suffix: A word part such as *-ness*, *-able*, or *-er* that is added to the end of a root word to form a new word with a new meaning.

syllable: A word part that contains a vowel or, in spoken language, a vowel sound (e-vent, news-pa-per, pret-ty).

vocabulary: The words we must know to communicate effectively. Oral vocabulary refers to words that we use in speaking or recognize in listening.

reading vocabulary: Words we recognize or use in print.

word walls: Displays of word-study and vocabulary words that are posted on the classroom wall so all children can easily see them. Usually, word walls are arranged alphabetically, with words starting with a certain letter listed under that letter for easy location.

word recognition: The ability to identify printed words and to translate them into their corresponding sounds quickly and accurately so as to figure out their meanings.

Resources

WEBSITES

Following are some websites that will provide you with helpful information, materials, and contacts with other parents and officials

American Academy of Pediatrics. Read Me a Story
www.aap.org/family/readmeastory.htm

BBC. Parents Guide to Reading
www.bbc.co.uk/schools/parents/article_primary_20012003.shtml

Chateau Meddybemps
www.meddybemps.com/7.24.html

Center for the Improvement of Early Reading Achievement
www.ciera.org/

Center for Improving the Readiness of Children for Learning
www.uth.tmc.edu/circle/

Clearinghouse on Early Education and Parenting
http://ceep.crc.uiuc.edu/

Clearinghouse on Reading, English, and Communication
http://reading.indiana.edu/

Color in Colorado (Reading Rockets' Spanish site)
www.colorincolorado.org/

Early Childhood Focus
www.earlychildhoodfocus.org/index.php

Education Development Center
http://main.edc.org/

Family Education. What Works: Ideas From Parents
www.familyeducation.com/whatworks/subject/index/0,2081,1,00.html

Get Ready to Read (English and Spanish)
www.getreadytoread.org/

Haan Foundation for Children
www.haan4kids.org/home.html

Home Instruction for Parents of Preschool Youngsters
www.hippusa.org

Institute for Education Sciences, Department of Education
www.ed.gov/about/offices/list/ies/index.html

International Reading Association
www.reading.org

Literacy Connections
www.literacyconnections.com/SecondLanguage.html

National Association of State Boards of Education
www.nasbe.org/

National Center for Education Statistics. National Assessment of Educational
    Progress: Nation's Report Card
http://nces.ed.gov/nationsreportcard/reading/

National Center for Family Learning
www.famlit.org

National Center for Learning Disabilities
www.ncld.org

National Education Association
www.nea.org

National Even Start Association. Even Start Family Literacy Programs
www.evenstart.org/default.htm

National Governors Association. Reading: Overview
www.nga.org/center/topics/1,1188,C_CENTER_ISSUE^D_5029,00.html

National Governors Association. Policy Position Detail: Building Successful
Literacy Initiatives Policy
www.nga.org/nga/legislativeUpdate/1,1169,C_POLICY_POSITION^D_563,00
.html

National Governors Association. Family Literacy: A Strategy for Educational
Improvement
www.nga.org/center/divisions/1,1188,C_ISSUE_BRIEF^D_4629,00.html

National Institute for Literacy
www.nifl.gov/

National Parents Information Network
http://npin.org/

National PTA
www.pta.org/

National Reading Panel
www.nationalreadingpanel.org/Publications/subgroups.htm

National Right to Read Foundation
www.nrrf.org

Parents as Teachers
www.parentsasteachers.org

Partnership for Reading
www.nifl.gov/partnershipforreading/

PBS. Between the Lions: Get Wild About Reading
http://pbskids.org/lions/

PBS. Parents: Reading and Advice
www.pbs.org/parents/issuesadvice/reading_language.html

PBS. Reading Rainbow
http://pbskids.org/readingrainbow/

PBS. Reading Rockets: Launching Young Readers
www.pbs.org/launchingreaders/

Rand. Reading for Understanding: Toward an R&D Program in Reading
www.rand.org/publications/MR/MR1465/

Reading is Fundamental
www.rif.org

Scholastic.com Family Matters: All About Reading
www.scholastic.com/familymatters/read/index.htm

U.S. Department of Education. Especially for Parents
www.ed.gov/parents/landing.jhtml?src=pn

U.S. Department of Education. Home page
www.ed.gov/index.jhtml

U.S. Department of Education. No Child Left Behind: A Parent's Guide
(English)
www.ed.gov/parents/academic/involve/nclbguide/parentsguide.html

U.S. Department of Education. No Child Left Behind: A Parent's Guide
(Spanish)
www.ed.gov/espanol/parents/academic/involve/nclbguide/index.html

U.S. Department of Education. Reading Resources
www.ed.gov/parents/read/resources/edpicks.jhtml?src=qc

What Works Clearinghouse, Department of Education
www.whatworks.ed.gov/

STATE DEPTARTMENTS OF EDUCATION

Alabama

Alabama Department of Education
Gordon Persons Office Building
50 North Ripley Street
P.O. Box 302101
Montgomery, AL 36104-3833
Phone: (334) 242-9700
Fax: (334) 242-9708
E-mail: dmurray@alsde.edu
Website: www.alsde.edu/html/home.asp

Alaska

Alaska Department of Education and Early Development
Suite 200
801 West 10th Street
Juneau, AK 99801-1894
Phone: (907) 465-2800
Fax: (907) 465-4156
TTY: (907) 465-2800
Website: www.eed.state.ak.us/

Arizona

Arizona Department of Education
1535 West Jefferson
Phoenix, AZ 85007
Phone: (602) 542-4361
Toll-Free: (800) 352-4558
Fax: (602) 542-5440
E-mail: ADE@ade.az.gov
Website: www.ade.az.gov/

Arkansas

Arkansas Department of Education
Room 304 A
Four State Capitol Mall
Little Rock, AR 72201-1071
Phone: (501) 682-4204
Fax: (501) 682-1079
E-mail: kjames@arkedu.k12.ar.us
Website: http://arkedu.state.ar.us/

California

California Department of Education
P.O. Box 944272
1430 N Street
Sacramento, CA 95814

Phone: (916) 319-0800
Fax: (916) 319-0100
E-mail: cdewrite@cde.ca.gov
Website: www.cde.ca.gov/

Colorado

Colorado Department of Education
201 East Colfax Avenue
Denver, CO 80203-1704
Phone: (303) 866-6600
Fax: (303) 830-0793
E-mail: howerter_c@cde.state.co.us
Website: www.cde.state.co.us/

Connecticut

Connecticut Department of Education
State Office Building
165 Capitol Avenue
Hartford, CT 06106-1630
Phone: (860) 713-6548
Toll-Free: (800) 465-4014
Fax: (860) 713-7017
E-mail: thomas.murphy@po.state.ct.us
Website: www.state.ct.us/sde/

Delaware

Delaware Department of Education
John G. Townsend Building
P.O. Box 1402
Federal and Lockerman Streets
Dover, DE 19903-1402
Phone: (302) 739-4601
Fax: (302) 739-4654

E-mail: vwoodruff@doe.k12.de.us
Website: www.doe.state.de.us/

District of Columbia

District of Columbia Public Schools
Union Square
825 North Capitol Street NE
Washington, DC 20002
Phone: (202) 724-4222
Fax: (202) 442-5026
E-mail: dcpsweb@k12.dc.us
Website: www.k12.dc.us/dcps/home.html

Florida

Florida Department of Education
Turlington Building
Suite 1514
325 West Gaines Street
Tallahassee, FL 32399-0400
Phone: (850) 245-0505
Fax: (850) 245-9667
E-mail: commissioner@fldoe.org
Website: www.fldoe.org/

Georgia

Georgia Department of Education
2066 Twin Towers East
205 Jesse Hill Jr. Drive SE
Atlanta, GA 30334-5001
Phone: (404) 656-2800
Toll-Free: (800) 311-3627
Toll-Free Restrictions: GA residents only
Fax: (404) 651-8737
E-mail: kathycox@doe.k12.ga.us
Website: www.doe.k12.ga.us/index.asp

Guam

Guam Department of Education
P.O. Box DE
Hagatna, GU 96932
Phone: (671) 475-0462
Fax: (671) 472-5003
E-mail: rtaima@guam.doe.edu.gu
Website: www.gdoe.net/

Hawaii

Hawaii Department of Education
Room 309
1390 Miller Street
Honolulu, HI 96813
Phone: (808) 586-3310
Fax: (808) 586-3320
E-mail: patricia_hamamoto@notes.k12.hi.us
Website: www.k12.hi.us/

Idaho

Idaho Department of Education
Len B. Jordan Office Building
650 West State Street
P.O. Box 83720
Boise, ID 83720-0027
Phone: (208) 332-6800
Toll-Free: (800) 432-4601
Toll-Free Restrictions: ID residents only
Fax: (208) 334-2228
TTY: (800) 377-3529
E-mail: awestfal@sde.state.id.us
Website: www.sde.state.id.us/Dept/

Illinois

Illinois State Board of Education
100 North First Street

Springfield, IL 62777
Phone: (217) 782-4321
Toll-Free: (866) 262-6663
Toll-Free Restrictions: IL residents only
Fax: (217) 524-4928
TTY: (217) 782-1900
E-mail: rwatts@isbe.net
Website: www.isbe.net/

Indiana

Indiana Department of Education
State House, Room 229
Indianapolis, IN 46204-2795
Phone: (317) 232-6610
Fax: (317) 233-6326
E-mail: webmaster@doe.state.in.us
Website: www.doe.state.in.us/

Iowa

Iowa Department of Education
Grimes State Office Building
East 14th and Grand Streets
Des Moines, IA 50319-0146
Phone: (515) 281-3436
Fax: (515) 281-4122
E-mail: ted.stilwill@ed.state.ia.us
Website: www.state.ia.us/educate/

Kansas

Kansas Department of Education
120 South East 10th Avenue
Topeka, KS 66612-1182
Phone: (785) 296-3201
Fax: (785) 296-7933
TTY: (785) 296-6338
E-mail: atompkins@ksde.org or lasnider@ksde.org
Website: www.ksde.org/

Kentucky

Kentucky Department of Education
1st Floor, Capital Plaza Tower
500 Mero Street
Frankfort, KY 40601
Phone: (502) 564-3421
Toll-Free: (800) 533-5372
Fax: (502) 564-6470
Website: www.kentuckyschools.org/

Louisiana

Louisiana Department of Education
1201 North Third
P.O. Box 94064
Baton Rouge, LA 70804-9064
Phone: (225) 342-4411
Toll-Free: (877) 453-2721
Fax: (225) 342-7316
E-mail: customerservice@la.gov
Website: www.louisianaschools.net/lde/index.html

Maine

Maine Department of Education
23 State House Station
Augusta, ME 04333-0023
Phone: (207) 624-6600
Fax: (207) 624-6601
TTY: (207) 624-6800
E-mail: susan.gendron@me.gov
Website: www.state.me.us/education/homepage.htm

Maryland

Maryland Department of Education
200 West Baltimore Street
Baltimore, MD 21201

Phone: (410) 767-0100
Fax: (410) 333-6033
E-mail: rpeiffer@msde.state.md.us
Website: www.msde.state.md.us/

Massachusetts

Massachusetts Department of Education
350 Main Street
Malden, MA 02148
Phone: (781) 338-3000
Fax: (781) 338-3395
TTY: (800) 439-2370
E-mail: www@doe.mass.edu
Website: www.doe.mass.edu/

Michigan

Michigan Department of Education
Hannah Building
Fourth Floor
608 West Allegan Street
Lansing, MI 48933
Phone: (517) 373-3324
Fax: (517) 335-4565
E-mail: watkinstd@michigan.gov
Website: www.michigan.gov/mde/

Minnesota

Minnesota Department of Education
1500 Highway 36 West
Roseville, MN 55113-4266
Phone: (651) 582-8200
Fax: (651) 582-8727
TTY: (651) 582-8201
E-mail: children@state.mn.us
Website: http://education.state.mn.us

Mississippi

Mississippi State Department of Education
Central High School
359 North West Street
P.O. Box 771
Jackson, MS 39205
Phone: (601) 359-3513
Fax: (601) 359-3242
E-mail: cblanton@mde.k12.ms.us
Website: www.mde.k12.ms.us/

Missouri

Missouri Department of Elementary and Secondary Education
P.O. Box 480
Jefferson City, MO 65102-0480
Phone: (573) 751-4212
Fax: (573) 751-8613
TTY: (800) 735-2966
E-mail: pubinfo@mail.dese.state.mo.us
Website: http://dese.mo.gov/

Montana

Montana Office of Public Instruction
P.O. Box 202501
Helena, MT 59620-2501
Phone: (406) 444-2082
Toll-Free: (888) 231-9393
Toll-Free Restrictions: MT residents only
Fax: (406) 444-3924
E-mail: cbergeron@state.mt.us
Website: www.opi.state.mt.us/

Nebraska

Nebraska Department of Education
301 Centennial Mall South

P.O. Box 94987
Lincoln, NE 68509-4987
Phone: (402) 471-2295
Fax: (402) 471-0117
TTY: (402) 471-7295
E-mail: speters@nde.state.ne.us
Website: www.nde.state.ne.us/

Nevada

Nevada Department of Education
700 East Fifth Street
Carson City, NV 89701
Phone: (775) 687-9141
Fax: (775) 687-9111
E-mail: fsouth@doe.nv.gov
Website: www.doe.nv.gov

New Hampshire

New Hampshire Department of Education
101 Pleasant Street
State Office Park South
Concord, NH 03301
Phone: (603) 271-3495
Fax: (603) 271-1953
TTY: (800) 735-2964
E-mail: pbutler@ed.state.nh.us
Website: www.ed.state.nh.us/

New Jersey

New Jersey Department of Education
P.O. Box 500
100 Riverview Plaza
Trenton, NJ 08625-0500
Phone: (609) 292-4469
Fax: (609) 777-4099
Website: www.state.nj.us/education/

New Mexico

New Mexico Public Education Department
Jerry Apodaca Education Building
300 Don Gaspar
Santa Fe, NM 87501-2786
Phone: (505) 827-5800
Fax: (505) 827-6520
TTY: (505) 827-6541
Website: www.ped.state.nm.us/

New York

New York Education Department
Education Building
Room 111
89 Washington Avenue
Albany, NY 12234
Phone: (518) 474-5844
Fax: (518) 473-4909
E-mail: rmills@mail.nysed.gov
Website: www.nysed.gov/

North Carolina

North Carolina Department of Public Instruction
301 North Wilmington Street
Raleigh, NC 27601
Phone: (919) 807-3300
Fax: (919) 807-3445
E-mail: information@dpi.state.nc.us
Website: www.ncpublicschools.org/

North Dakota

North Dakota Department of Public Instruction
11th Floor
Department 201

600 East Boulevard Avenue
Bismarck, ND 58505-0440
Phone: (701) 328-2260
Fax: (701) 328-2461
E-mail: wsanstead@state.nd.us or lnorbeck@state.nd.us
Website: www.dpi.state.nd.us/

Ohio

Ohio Department of Education
25 South Front Street
Columbus, OH 43215-4183
Phone: (614) 728-6698
Toll-Free: (877) 644-6338
Fax: (614) 752-3956
E-mail: lynn.wallich@ode.state.oh.us
Website: www.ode.state.oh.us/

Oklahoma

Oklahoma State Department of Education
2500 North Lincoln Boulevard
Oklahoma City, OK 73105-4599
Phone: (405) 521-3301
Fax: (405) 521-6205
E-mail: sandy_garrett@mail.sde.state.ok.us
Website: http://sde.state.ok.us/

Oregon

Oregon Department of Education
255 Capitol Street NE
Salem, OR 97310-0203
Phone: (503) 378-3600
Fax: (503) 378-5156
TTY: (503) 378-2892
E-mail: gene.evans@state.or.us
Website: www.ode.state.or.us/

Pennsylvania

Pennsylvania Department of Education
333 Market Street
Harrisburg, PA 17126-0333
Phone: (717) 787-5820
Fax: (717) 787-7222
TTY: (717) 783-8445
E-mail: PDE@psupen.psu.edu
Website: www.pde.state.pa.us/pde_internet/site/default.asp

Rhode Island

Rhode Island Department of Elementary and Secondary Education
255 Westminster Street
Providence, RI 02903-3400
Phone: (401) 222-4600
Fax: (401) 222-2537
TTY: (800) 745-5555
E-mail: ride0777@ride.ri.net
Website: www.ridoe.net/

South Carolina

South Carolina Department of Education
1006 Rutledge Building
1429 Senate Street
Columbia, SC 29201
Phone: (803) 734-8492
Fax: (803) 734-3389
E-mail: bethrog@sde.state.sc.us
Website: www.myscschools.com/

South Dakota

South Dakota Department of Education
700 Governors Drive
Pierre, SD 57501-2291

Phone: (605) 773-3553
Fax: (605) 773-6139
TTY: (605) 773-6302
Website: www.state.sd.us/deca/

Tennessee

Tennessee State Department of Education
Andrew Johnson Tower, Sixth Floor
710 James Robertson Parkway
Nashville, TN 37243-0375
Phone: (615) 741-2731
Fax: (615) 532-4791
E-mail: Education.Comments@state.tn.us
Website: www.state.tn.us/education/

Texas

Texas Education Agency
William B. Travis Building
1701 North Congress Avenue
Austin, TX 78701-1494
Phone: (512) 463-9734
Fax: (512) 463-9838
TTY: (512) 475-3540
E-mail: teainfo@tea.state.tx.us
Website: www.tea.state.tx.us/

Utah

Utah State Office of Education
250 East 500 South
P.O. Box 144200
Salt Lake City, UT 84114-4200
Phone: (801) 538-7500
Fax: (801) 538-7521
E-mail: mpeterso@usoe.k12.ut.us
Website: www.usoe.k12.ut.us/

Vermont

Vermont Department of Education
120 State Street
Montpelier, VT 05620-2501
Phone: (802) 828-3135
Fax: (802) 828-3140
TTY: (802) 828-2755
E-mail: edinfo@education.state.vt.us
Website: www.state.vt.us/educ/

Virginia

Virginia Department of Education
P.O. Box 2120
101 North 14th Street
Richmond, VA 23218-2120
Phone: (804) 225-2023
Toll-Free: (800) 292-3820
Toll-Free Restrictions: VA residents only
Fax: (804) 371-2455
E-mail: cmakela@pen.k12.va.us
Website: www.pen.k12.va.us/go/VDOE/

Washington

Office of Superintendent of Public Instruction (Washington)
Old Capitol Building
600 South Washington
P.O. Box 47200
Olympia, WA 98504-7200
Phone: (360) 725-6000
Fax: (360) 753-6712
TTY: (360) 664-3631
E-mail: mdaybell@ospi.wednet.edu
Website: www.k12.wa.us/

West Virginia

West Virginia Department of Education
Building 6, Room 346

1900 Kanawha Boulevard East
Charleston, WV 25305-0330
Phone: (304) 558-0304
Fax: (304) 558-2584
E-mail: wvde@access.k12.wv.us
Website: http://wvde.state.wv.us/

Wisconsin

Wisconsin Department of Public Instruction
125 South Webster Street
P.O. Box 7841
Madison, WI 53707-7841
Phone: (608) 266-3390
Toll-Free: (800) 441-4563
Fax: (608) 267-1052
TTY: (608) 267-2427
E-mail: kay.ihlenfeldt@dpi.state.wi.us
Website: www.dpi.state.wi.us/

Wyoming

Wyoming Department of Education
Hathaway Building
Second Floor
2300 Capitol Avenue
Cheyenne, WY 82002-0050
Phone: (307) 777-7675
Fax: (307) 777-6234
TTY: (307) 777-8546
E-mail: tblank@educ.state.wy.us
Website: www.k12.wy.us/

STATE LITERACY RESOURCES

Alabama

Alabama Adult Literacy Resource Center
Department of Postsecondary Education
GED Testing

P.O. Box 302130
Montgomery, AL 36130-2130
Phone: (334) 353-4889
Toll-Free: (800) 392-8086
Toll-Free Restrictions: AL residents only
Fax: (334) 353-4884
E-mail: macaluso@sdenet.alsde.edu

Alaska

Alaska State Literacy Resource Center
Nine Star Enterprises
125 West Fifth Avenue
Anchorage, AK 99501
Phone: (907) 279-7827
Fax: (907) 279-3299
E-mail: davida@ninestar.com
Website: www.ninestar.com/lincs/

Arizona

Division of Adult & Family Literacy Education
Bin 26
1535 West Jefferson Street
Phoenix, AZ 85007
Phone: (602) 258-2410
Toll-Free: (800) 352-4558
Toll-Free Restrictions: AZ residents only
Fax: (602) 258-4986
E-mail: kliersc@ade.az.gov
Website: www.ade.state.az.us/Adult-Ed/

Arkansas

Arkansas Adult Learning Resource Center
Suite D
3905 Cooperative Way
Little Rock, AR 72209
Phone: (501) 907-2490

Toll-Free: (800) 832-6242
Toll-Free Restrictions: AR residents only
Fax: (501) 907-2492
E-mail: info@aalrc.org
Website: www.aalrc.org/

California

None

Colorado

Colorado State Literacy Resource Center
State Department of Education
201 East Colfax Avenue
Denver, CO 80203
Phone: (303) 866-6914
Fax: (303) 866-6947
E-mail: Fawcett_D@cde.state.co.us
Website: www.cde.state.co.us/cdeadult/adultslrcindexnew.htm

Connecticut

Connecticut Literacy Resource Center
Adult Training and Development Network
Capitol Region Education Council
111 Charter Oak Avenue
Hartford, CT 06106
Phone: (860) 524-4034
Fax: (860) 524-4050
E-mail: khanaway@crec.org
Website: www.crec.org/atdn/

New England Literacy Resource Center/World Education
44 Farnsworth Street
Boston, MA 02210-1211
Phone: (617) 482-9485
Fax: (617) 482-0617
E-mail: skallenbach@worlded.org

Website: www.nelrc.org/
States Served: Connecticut, Maine, Massachusetts, New Hampshire,
Rhode Island, Vermont

Delaware

Delaware State Literacy Resource Center
ACE Network
P.O. Box 639
Dover, DE 19903
Phone: (302) 739-5556
Fax: (302) 739-5565
E-mail: acedir@yahoo.com
Website: www.acenetwork.org/

District of Columbia

District of Columbia Literacy Resource Center
Room 300
901 G Street NW
Washington, DC 20001
Phone: (202) 727-1616
Fax: (202) 727-0193
TTY: (202) 727-2145
E-mail: dclrc@yahoo.com
Website: www.dclibrary.org/

Florida

Florida Literacy Coalition
Suite 104
934 North Magnolia Avenue
Orlando, FL 32803-3854
Phone: (407) 246-7110
Toll-Free: (800) 237-5113
Toll-Free Restrictions: FL residents only
Fax: (407) 246-7104
E-mail: info@floridaliteracy.org or sparkss@floridaliteracy.org
Website: www.floridaliteracy.org/

Georgia

Georgia Department of Technical and Adult Education
Office of Adult Literacy
Suite 400
1800 Century Place, NE
Atlanta, GA 30345-4304
Phone: (404) 679-1635
Fax: (404) 679-1630
E-mail: mdelaney@dtae.org or klee@dtae.org
Website: www.dtae.org/adultlit.html

Hawaii

Hawaii Literacy Office
Library Development Office
Suite 205
3225 Salt Lake Boulevard
Honolulu, HI 96818
Phone: (808) 831-6878
Fax: (808) 831-6882
E-mail: susann@lib.state.hi.us
Website: http://literacynet.org/hawaii/home.html

Idaho

ABLE Network Literacy Resource Center
P.O. Box 42496
Olympia, WA 98504-2496
Phone: (360) 586-3527
Fax: (360) 586-3529
E-mail: able@sbctc.ctc.edu
Website: www.sbctc.ctc.edu/able/default.asp
States Served: Idaho, Montana, Oregon, Washington, Wyoming

Illinois

Secretary of State Literacy Office (Illinois)
300 South Second Street
Springfield, IL 62701

Phone: (217) 785-6921
Toll-Free: (800) 665-5576
Toll-Free Restrictions: IL residents only
Fax: (217) 785-6927
TTY: (800) 528-0844
E-mail: ccolletti@ilsos.net
Website: http://literacy.kent.edu/illinois/

Indiana

Indiana Literacy Foundation
1920 West Morris
Indianapolis, IN 46221
Phone: (317) 639-6106, Ext. 211
Toll-Free: (800) 217-1839
Fax: (317) 639-2782
E-mail: psiemant@indianaliteracy.org or director@indianaliteracy.org
Website: www.indianaliteracy.org/index.asp

Iowa

Iowa Literacy Resource Center
415 Commercial Street
Waterloo, IA 50701
Phone: (319) 233-1200
Toll-Free: (800) 772-2023
Fax: (319) 233-1964
E-mail: riesberg@neilsa.org or luppen@neilsa.org
Website: www.readiowa.org/

Kansas

Kansas State Literacy Resource Center
Kansas Board of Regents
Suite 520
1000 SW Jackson Street
Topeka, KS 66612-1368
Phone: (785) 296-7159
Fax: (785) 296-0983

E-mail: dglass@ksbor.org or dwhitley@ksbor.org
Website: www.kansasregents.org/adult_ed/kslrc.html

Kentucky

Kentucky Department for Adult Education and Literacy
Suite 250
1024 Capital Center Drive
Frankfort, KY 40601
Phone: (502) 573-5114
Toll-Free: (800) 928-7323
Fax: (502) 573-5436
TTY: (800) 928-7323
E-mail: reecie.stagnolia@ky.gov
Website: http://adulted.state.ky.us/index.htm

Louisiana

Louisiana State Literacy Resource Center
State Department of Education
Office of School and Community Support
Division of Family, Career, and Technical Ed
P.O. Box 94064
Baton Rouge, LA 70804-9064
Phone: (225) 342-3340
Toll-Free: (877) 453-2721
Fax: (225) 219-4439
E-mail: mbryant@la.gov
Website: www.louisianaschools.net/lde/index.html

Maine

Center for Adult Learning and Literacy (Maine)
University of Maine
5749 Merrill Hall
Orono, ME 04469-5766
Phone: (207) 581-2498
Fax: (207) 581-9322
E-mail: shannon.cox@umit.maine.edu or rosanna.libby@umit.maine.edu
Website: www.umaine.edu/call/

New England Literacy Resource Center/World Education
44 Farnsworth Street
Boston, MA 02210-1211
Phone: (617) 482-9485
Fax: (617) 482-0617
E-mail: skallenbach@worlded.org
Website: www.nelrc.org/
States Served: Connecticut, Maine, Massachusetts, New Hampshire, Rhode Island, Vermont

Maryland

Maryland Adult Literacy Resource Center
UMBC, Education Department
1000 Hilltop Circle
Baltimore, MD 21250
Phone: (410) 455-6725
Toll-Free: (800) 358-3010
Fax: (410) 455-1139
E-mail: ira@umbc.edu
Website: www.research.umbc.edu/~ira/

Massachusetts

Massachusetts System for Adult Basic Education Support
SABES/World Education
44 Farnsworth Street
Boston, MA 02210-1211
Phone: (617) 482-9485
Toll-Free: (800) 447-8844
Fax: (617) 482-0617
TTY: (800) 447-8844
E-mail: sabes@theworld.com
Website: www.sabes.org/

New England Literacy Resource Center/World Education
44 Farnsworth Street
Boston, MA 02210-1211
Phone: (617) 482-9485
Fax: (617) 482-0617

E-mail: skallenbach@worlded.org
Website: www.nelrc.org/
States Served: Connecticut, Maine, Massachusetts, New Hampshire, Rhode
Island, Vermont

Michigan

None

Minnesota

Literacy Training Network
University of St. Thomas
Mail #MOH217
1000 LaSalle Avenue
Minneapolis, MN 55403
Phone: (651) 962-4440
Fax: (651) 962-4438
E-mail: dasimmons@stthomas.edu

Mississippi

Mississippi State Literacy Resource Center
The University of Southern Mississippi
Center for Adult Learning and Education
118 College Drive, #10062
Hattiesburg, MS 39406
Phone: (601) 266-5089
Toll-Free: (800) 325-7323
Fax: (601) 266-5141
E-mail: w.pierce@usm.edu
Website: www.ihl.state.ms.us/gol/usm.edu

Missouri

LIFT—Literacy Investment for Tomorrow (Missouri)
Suite 601
500 Northwest Plaza
Saint Ann, MO 63074

Phone: (314) 291-4443
Toll-Free: (800) 729-4443
Fax: (314) 291-7385
E-mail: todea@webster.edu
Website: www.lift-missouri.org/

Montana

ABLE Network Literacy Resource Center
P.O. Box 42496
Olympia, WA 98504-2496
Phone: (360) 586-3527
Fax: (360) 586-3529
E-mail: able@sbctc.ctc.edu
Website: www.sbctc.ctc.edu/able/default.asp
States Served: Idaho, Montana, Oregon, Washington, Wyoming

Nebraska

None

Nevada

Nevada Literacy Coalition
Nevada State Library and Archives
100 North Stewart Street
Carson City, NV 89701-4285
Phone: (775) 684-3340
Toll-Free: (800) 445-WORD (9673)
Toll-Free Restrictions: NV residents only
Fax: (775) 684-3344
TTY: (775) 684-3321
E-mail: sfgraf@clan.lib.nv.us or jgoena@clan.lib.nv.us
Website: www.nevadaliteracy.org/

New Hampshire

Adult Learning Center (New Hampshire)
4 Lake Street

Nashua, NH 03060
Phone: (603) 882-9080, Ext. 207
Fax: (603) 882-0069
E-mail: Dowen@adultlearningcenter.org
Website: www.adultlearningcenter.org/

New England Literacy Resource Center/World Education
44 Farnsworth Street
Boston, MA 02210-1211
Phone: (617) 482-9485
Fax: (617) 482-0617
E-mail: skallenbach@worlded.org
Website: www.nelrc.org/
States Served: Connecticut, Maine, Massachusetts, New Hampshire, Rhode
Island, Vermont

New Jersey

None

New Mexico

New Mexico Coalition for Literacy/New Mexico Literacy Resource Center
3209-B Mercantile Court
Santa Fe, NM 87507
Phone: (505) 982-7997
Toll-Free: (800) 233-7587
Toll-Free Restrictions: NM residents only
Fax: (505) 982-4095
E-mail: literacy@swcp.com
Website: www.nmcl.org/

New York

New York State Literacy Hotline
10th Floor
32 Broadway
New York, NY 10004
Phone: (212) 803-3333

Toll-Free: (888) 683-7323
Fax: (212) 785-3685
E-mail: dianep@lac.nyc.org
Website: www.lacnyc.org/

North Carolina

North Carolina Community College Literacy Resource Center
Caswell Building, Fifth Floor
200 West Jones Street
5025 Mail Service Center
Raleigh, NC 27699-5025
Phone: (919) 807-7144
Toll-Free: (800) 553-9759
Toll-Free Restrictions: NC residents only
Fax: (919) 807-7164
E-mail: allenb@ncccs.cc.nc.us
Website: www.ncccs.cc.nc.us/basic_skills/nccliteracyresourcecenter2.htm

North Dakota

North Dakota Adult Education and Literacy Resource Center
1609 Fourth Avenue, NW
Minot, ND 58703
Phone: (701) 857-4467
Fax: (701) 857-4489
E-mail: deb.sisco@sendit.nodak.edu
Website: www.dpi.state.nd.us/adulted/index.shtm

Ohio

Ohio Literacy Resource Center (The)
Kent State University
Research 1 — 1100 Summit Street
P.O. Box 5190
Kent, OH 44242-0001
Phone: (330) 672-2007
Toll-Free: (800) 765-2897
Toll-Free Restrictions: OH residents only

Fax: (330) 672-4841
TTY: (330) 672-2379
E-mail: olrc@literacy.kent.edu or dbaycich@literacy.kent.edu
Website: http://literacy.kent.edu/

Oklahoma

Oklahoma Literacy Resource Office
Oklahoma Department of Libraries
200 Northeast 18th Street
Oklahoma City, OK 73105-3298
Phone: (405) 522-3205
Toll-Free: (800) 522-8116
Fax: (800) 397-8116
E-mail: lgelders@oltn.odl.state.ok.us or rbarker@oltn.odl.state.ok.us
Website: www.odl.state.ok.us/literacy/

Oregon

ABLE Network Literacy Resource Center
P.O. Box 42496
Olympia, WA 98504-2496
Phone: (360) 586-3527
Fax: (360) 586-3529
E-mail: able@sbctc.ctc.edu
Website: www.sbctc.ctc.edu/able/default.asp
States Served: Idaho, Montana, Oregon, Washington, Wyoming

Pennsylvania

Advance State Literacy Resource Center (Pennsylvania)
Pennsylvania Department of Education
11th Floor
333 Market Street
Harrisburg, PA 17126-0333
Phone: (717) 783-9192
Toll-Free: (800) 992-2283
Toll-Free Restrictions: PA residents only
Fax: (717) 783-5420

TTY: (717) 783-8445
E-mail: lstasiulat@state.pa.us
Website: www.statelibrary.state.pa.us/libraries/cwp/view.asp?a=4&Q=4035

Rhode Island

Literacy Resources (Rhode Island)
Brown University
P.O. Box 1974
Providence, RI 02912
Phone: (401) 863-2839
Fax: (401) 863-3094
E-mail: lrri@brown.edu or janet_isserlis@brown.edu
Website: www.brown.edu/Departments/Swearer_Center/Literacy_Resources/

New England Literacy Resource Center/World Education
44 Farnsworth Street
Boston, MA 02210-1211
Phone: (617) 482-9485
Fax: (617) 482-0617
E-mail: skallenbach@worlded.org
Website: www.nelrc.org/
States Served: Connecticut, Maine, Massachusetts, New Hampshire, Rhode
Island, Vermont

South Carolina

None

South Dakota

South Dakota Literacy Resource Center
State Library
800 Governor's Drive
Pierre, SD 57501
Phone: (605) 773-3131
Toll-Free: (800) 423-6665
Toll-Free Restrictions: SD residents only
Fax: (605) 773-6962

E-mail: dan.boyd@state.sd.us
Website: http://literacy.kent.edu/~sdakota/

Tennessee

Center for Literacy Studies (Tennessee)
University of Tennessee — Knoxville
Suite 312
600 Henley Street
Knoxville, TN 37996-4135
Phone: (865) 974-4109
Toll-Free: (877) 340-0546
Toll-Free Restrictions: TN residents only
Fax: (865) 974-3857
E-mail: jjstephe@utk.edu
Website: http://cls.coe.utk.edu/

Texas

Texas Center for Adult Literacy and Learning
Texas A&M University
4477 TAMU
College Station, TX 77843-4477
Phone: (979) 845-6615
Toll-Free: (800) 441-7323
Fax: (979) 845-0952
E-mail: tcall@coe.tamu.edu or dseaman@tamu.edu
Website: www-tcall.tamu.edu/

Utah

None

Vermont

New England Literacy Resource Center/World Education
44 Farnsworth Street
Boston, MA 02210-1211
Phone: (617) 482-9485

Vermont Department of Education
120 State Street
Montpelier, VT 05620
Phone: (802) 828-3134
E-mail: srobinson@doe.state.vt.us
Website: http://www.state.vt.us/educ/

Fax: (617) 482-0617
E-mail: skallenbach@worlded.org
Website: www.nelrc.org/
States Served: Connecticut, Maine, Massachusetts, New Hampshire, Rhode Island, Vermont

Virginia

Adult Learning and Resource Center (Virginia)
Virginia Commonwealth University
Box 842020
1015 West Main Street
Richmond, VA 23284-2020
Phone: (804) 828-6521
Toll-Free: (800) 237-0178
Fax: (804) 828-7539
E-mail: vdesk@vcu.edu
Website: www.aelweb.vcu.edu/

Washington

ABLE Network Literacy Resource Center
P.O. Box 42496
Olympia, WA 98504-2496
Phone: (360) 586-3527
Fax: (360) 586-3529
E-mail: able@sbctc.ctc.edu
Website: www.sbctc.ctc.edu/able/default.asp
States Served: Idaho, Montana, Oregon, Washington, Wyoming

West Virginia

Office of Adult Education and Workforce Development (West Virginia)
West Virginia Department of Education

Building 6, Room 230
1900 Kanawha Boulevard, East
Charleston, WV 25305-0330
Phone: (304) 558-0280
Fax: (304) 558-3946
E-mail: bwilcox@access.k12.wv.us or dvarner@access.k12.wv.us
Website: www.wvabe.org/

Wisconsin

Wisconsin Literacy Resource Network
345 West Washington
Madison, WI 53703
Phone: (608) 266-1272
Fax: (608) 266-1690
TTY: (608) 267-2483
E-mail: mark.johnson@wtcsystem.org
Website: www.wtcsystem.org/wlrn

Wyoming

ABLE Network Literacy Resource Center
P.O. Box 42496
Olympia, WA 98504-2496
Phone: (360) 586-3527
Fax: (360) 586-3529
E-mail: able@sbctc.ctc.edu
Website: www.sbctc.ctc.edu/able/default.asp
States Served: Idaho, Montana, Oregon, Washington, Wyoming

STATE PTAS

Alabama

Alabama PTA
470 South Union Street
Montgomery, AL 36104-4330
Phone: (334) 834-2501
Toll-Free: (800) 328-1897
Fax: (334) 834-2504

E-mail: al_office@pta.org
Website: www.alabamapta.org/

Alaska

Alaska PTA
P.O. Box 201496
Anchorage, AK 99520-1496
Phone: (907) 279-9345
Fax: (907) 222-2401
E-mail: ak_office@pta.org
Website: www.alaska.net/~akpta/

Arizona

Arizona PTA
2721 North Seventh Avenue
Phoenix, AZ 85007-1102
Phone: (602) 279-1811
Fax: (602) 279-1814
E-mail: az_office@pta.org or az_pres@pta.org
Website: www.azpta.org/

Arkansas

Arkansas PTA
P.O. Box 1015
North Little Rock, AR 72115
Phone: (501) 753-5247
Toll-Free: (800) PTA-4PTA (782-4782)
Fax: (501) 753-6168
E-mail: ar_office@pta.org
Website: www.arkansaspta.org/

California

California PTA
930 Georgia Street
Los Angeles, CA 90015-1322

Phone: (213) 620-1100
Toll-Free: (888) 564-6182
Fax: (213) 620-1411
E-mail: info@capta.org
Website: www.capta.org/

Colorado

Colorado PTA
7859 West 38th Avenue
Wheat Ridge, CO 80033
Phone: (303) 420-7820
Toll-Free: (888) 225-8234
Toll-Free Restrictions: CO residents only
Fax: (303) 420-7703
E-mail: office@copta.org
Website: www.copta.org/

Connecticut

Connecticut PTA
Wilbur Cross Commons
Building 12
60 Connolly Parkway
Hamden, CT 06514-2519
Phone: (203) 281-6617
Fax: (203) 281-6749
E-mail: connecticut.pta@snet.net
Website: www.ctpta.org/

Delaware

Delaware PTA
92 South Gerald Drive
Newark, DE 19713-3299
Phone: (302) 737-4750
Fax: (302) 737-7450
E-mail: dpta@delawarepta.org
Website: http://delawarepta.org/Default.htm

District of Columbia

District of Columbia PTA
Hamilton Administration Building
1401 Brentwood Parkway, NE
Washington, DC 20002
Phone: (202) 543-0333
Fax: (202) 543-4306
E-mail: dc_office@pta.org

Florida

Florida PTA
1747 Orlando Central Parkway
Orlando, FL 32809-5757
Phone: (407) 855-7604
Toll-Free: (800) 373-5782
Fax: (407) 240-9577
E-mail: info@floridapta.org or janice@floridapta.org
Website: www.floridapta.org/

Georgia

Georgia PTA
114 Baker Street, NE
Atlanta, GA 30308-3366
Phone: (404) 659-0214
Toll-Free: (800) 782-8632
Fax: (404) 525-0210
E-mail: gapta@bellsouth.net
Website: www.georgiapta.org/

Hawaii

Hawaii State PTSA
Suite 209
1350 South King Street
Honolulu, HI 96814-2008

Phone: (808) 593-2042
Toll-Free: (877) 834-7872
Toll-Free Restrictions: HI residents only
Fax: (808) 593-2041
E-mail: hi_office@pta.org or dhayman@aol.com
Website: www.hawaiiptsa.org/

Idaho

Idaho PTA
500 West Washington
Boise, ID 83702-5965
Phone: (208) 344-0851
Fax: (208) 342-8585
E-mail: idahopta@mindspring.com or id_office@pta.org

Illinois

Illinois PTA
901 South Spring Street
Springfield, IL 62704-2790
Phone: (217) 528-9617
Toll-Free: (800) 877-9617
Toll-Free Restrictions: IL residents only
Fax: (217) 528-9490
E-mail: il_office@pta.org
Website: www.illinoispta.org/

Indiana

Indiana PTA
2525 North Shadeland Avenue, D4
Indianapolis, IN 46219-1787
Phone: (317) 357-5881
Fax: (317) 357-3751
E-mail: pta@indianapta.org or office@ptamail.com
Website: www.indianapta.org/

Iowa

Iowa PTA
Suite F-1
8345 University Boulevard
Des Moines, IA 50325-1169
Phone: (515) 225-4197
Toll-Free: (800) 475-4782
Fax: (515) 225-6363
E-mail: ia_office@pta.org
Website: www.nevada.k12.ia.us/iowapta/iowapta.htm

Kansas

Kansas PTA
715 Southwest 10th Street
Topeka, KS 66612-1686
Phone: (785) 234-5782
Fax: (785) 234-4170
E-mail: ks_office@pta.org
Website: www.ptasonline.org/kspta/

Kentucky

Kentucky PTA
P.O. Box 654
Frankfort, KY 40602-1169
Phone: (502) 564-4378
Fax: (502) 564-2599
E-mail: ky_office@pta.org
Website: www.kypta.org/

Louisiana

Louisiana PTA
Suite 13
1543 Del Plaza
Baton Rouge, LA 70815

Phone: (225) 927-7382
Fax: (225) 927-9497
E-mail: la_office@pta.org
Website: www.lapta.org/

Maine

Maine PTA
28 Webb Road
Windham, ME 04062
Phone: (207) 892-5700
Fax: (207) 892-7454
E-mail: info@mainepta.org or jpierce@mainepta.org
Website: www.mainepta.org/

Maryland

Maryland PTA
5 Central Avenue
Glen Burnie, MD 21061-3441
Phone: (410) 760-6221
Toll-Free: (800) 707-7972
Fax: (410) 760-6344
E-mail: mdpta@mdpta.org or office@mdpta.org
Website: www.mdpta.org/

Massachusetts

Massachusetts PTA
484 Main Street
P.O. Box 710
Fiskdale, MA 01518-0710
Phone: (508) 347-7055
Toll-Free: (888) 404-4PTA (4782)
Fax: (508) 347-7090
E-mail: masspta@aol.com
Website: www.masspta.org/

Michigan

Michigan PTSA
1011 North Washington Avenue
Lansing, MI 48906-4897
Phone: (517) 485-4345
Fax: (517) 485-0012
E-mail: info@michiganpta.org or donnar@michiganpta.org
Website: www.michiganpta.org/

Minnesota

Minnesota PTA/PTSA
Suite 111
1667 Snelling Avenue North
St. Paul, MN 55108
Phone: (651) 999-7320
Toll-Free: (800) 672-0993
Fax: (651) 999-7321
E-mail: mnptaofc@mnpta.org
Website: www.mnpta.org/

Mississippi

Mississippi PTA
P.O. Box 1937
Jackson, MS 39215-1937
Phone: (601) 352-7383
Toll-Free: (800) 795-6123
Toll-Free Restrictions: MS residents only
Fax: (601) 352-8600
E-mail: ms_office@pta.org
Website: www.myschoolonline.com/site/0,1876,-105132-153,00.html

Missouri

Missouri PTA
2100 I-70 Drive SW
Columbia, MO 65203-0099

Phone: (573) 445-4161
Toll-Free: (800) 328-7330
Toll-Free Restrictions: MO residents only
Fax: (573) 445-4163
E-mail: mo_office@pta.org or mcptoffice@aol.com
Website: www.mopta.org

Montana

Montana PTA
P.O. Box 6448
Great Falls, MT 59406
Phone: (406) 268-7475
E-mail: montanapta@montanapta.org
Website: www.montanapta.org/

Nebraska

Nebraska PTA
3534 South 108th Street
Omaha, NE 68144
Phone: (402) 390-3339
Toll-Free: (800) 714-3374
Toll-Free Restrictions: NE residents only
Fax: (402) 390-3338
E-mail: ne_office@pta.org
Website: www.nebraskapta.org/

Nevada

Nevada PTA
6134 West Charleston Boulevard
Las Vegas, NV 89146
Phone: (702) 258-7885
Toll-Free: (800) 782-7201
Toll-Free Restrictions: NV residents only
Fax: (702) 258-7836
E-mail: nv_office@pta.org or support@nevadapta.org
Website: www.nevadapta.org/

New Hampshire

New Hampshire PTA
47 Kendall Hill Road
Mont Vernon, NH 03057
Phone: (603) 673-7555
Toll-Free: (877) 701-4782
Toll-Free Restrictions: NH residents only
Fax: (603) 673-7555
E-mail: NHPTA1@aol.com

New Jersey

New Jersey PTA
900 Berkeley Avenue
Trenton, NJ 08618
Phone: (609) 393-5004
Fax: (609) 393-8471
E-mail: nj_office@pta.org
Website: www.njpta.org/

New Mexico

New Mexico PTA
Montgomery Complex
3315 Louisiana Boulevard NE
Albuquerque, NM 87110
Phone: (505) 881-0712
Fax: (505) 884-0793
E-mail: nmpta@aol.com
Website: www.nmpta.org/

New York

New York State PTA
One Wembley Court
Albany, NY 12205-3830
Phone: (518) 452-8808

Toll-Free: (877) 569-7782
Fax: (518) 452-8105
E-mail: office@nypta.com
Website: www.nypta.com/

North Carolina

North Carolina PTA
3501 Glenwood Avenue
Raleigh, NC 27612-4934
Phone: (919) 787-0534
Toll-Free: (800) 255-0417
Toll-Free Restrictions: NC residents only
Fax: (919) 787-0569
E-mail: office@ncpta.org
Website: www.ncpta.org/

North Dakota

North Dakota PTA
#106A
623 Maine Avenue
West Fargo, ND 58078
Phone: (701) 297-9168
Fax: (701) 297-9168
E-mail: ndptaoffice@aol.com or nd_office@pta.org
Website: www.myschoolonline.com/site/0,1876,0-34-1215,00.html

Ohio

Ohio PTA
40 Northwoods Boulevard
Columbus, OH 43235
Phone: (614) 781-6344
Fax: (614) 781-6349
E-mail: oh_office@pta.org or PTA40@aol.com
Website: www.ohiopta.org/

Oklahoma

Oklahoma PTA
Suite 214
2801 North Lincoln Boulevard
Oklahoma City, OK 73105
Phone: (405) 681-0750
Fax: (405) 681-0736
E-mail: oklahomapta@earthlink.net or ok_office@pta.org
Website: www.okpta.org/

Oregon

Oregon PTA
P.O. Box 4569
Portland, OR 97208-4569
Phone: (503) 234-3928
Fax: (503) 234-6024
E-mail: or_office@pta.org or or_pres@pta.org
Website: www.oregonpta.org/

Pennsylvania

Pennsylvania PTA
4804 Derry Street
Harrisburg, PA 17111-3440
Phone: (717) 564-8985
Fax: (717) 564-9046
E-mail: info@papta.org or infopta717@aol.com
Website: www.papta.org/

Rhode Island

Rhode Island PTA
RIC East Campus-Building 6
600 Mount Pleasant Avenue
Providence, RI 02908-1924
Phone: (401) 272-6405
Fax: (401) 272-6409
E-mail: ri_office@pta.org or ri_pres@pta.org

South Carolina

South Carolina PTA
1826 Henderson Street
Columbia, SC 29201-2619
Phone: (803) 765-0806
Toll-Free: (800) 743-3782
Fax: (803) 765-0399
E-mail: sc_office@pta.org
Website: www.myschoolonline.com/site/0,1876,-110242-48-1146,00.html

South Dakota

South Dakota PTA
411 East Capitol
Pierre, SD 57501
Phone: (605) 224-0144
Fax: (605) 224-5810
E-mail: sd_office@pta.org

Tennessee

Tennessee PTA
1905 Acklen Avenue
Nashville, TN 37212-3788
Phone: (615) 383-9740
Toll-Free: (888) 782-5712
Toll-Free Restrictions: TN residents only
Fax: (615) 383-9741
E-mail: tn_office@bellsouth.net or BetsyBug4@aol.com
Website: www.tnpta.org/

Texas

Texas PTA
408 West 11th Street
Austin, TX 78701-2199
Phone: (512) 476-6769
Toll-Free: (800) TALKPTA (825-5782)
Toll-Free Restrictions: TX residents only
Fax: (512) 476-8152

E-mail: txpta@txpta.org or ctounget@txpta.org
Website: www.txpta.org/

Utah

Utah PTA
5192 South Greenpine Drive
Salt Lake City, UT 84123
Phone: (801) 261-3100
Toll-Free: (866) 782-8824
Toll-Free Restrictions: UT residents only
Fax: (801) 261-3110
E-mail: kids@utahpta.org
Website: www.utahpta.org/

Vermont

Vermont PTA
P.O. Box 284
Richmond, VT 05477
Phone: (802) 892-0782
E-mail: vt_office@pta.org or vt_pres@pta.org
Website: www.vermontpta.org/

Virginia

Virginia PTA
1027 Wilmer Avenue
Richmond, VA 23227-2419
Phone: (804) 264-1234
Toll-Free: (866) 482-5437
Toll-Free Restrictions: VA residents only
Fax: (804) 264-4014
E-mail: info@vapta.org
Website: www.vapta.org/

Washington

Washington PTA
2003 65th Avenue West
Tacoma, WA 98466-6215

Phone: (253) 565-2153
Toll-Free: (800) 562-3804
Fax: (253) 565-7753
E-mail: wapta@wastatepta.org or jcarpenter@wastatepta.org
Website: www.wastatepta.org/

West Virginia

West Virginia PTA
P.O. Box 3557
Parkersburg, WV 26103-3557
Phone: (304) 420-9576
Fax: (304) 420-9577
E-mail: wv_office@pta.org or wv_pres@pta.org

Wisconsin

Wisconsin PTA
Suite 102
4797 Hayes Road
Madison, WI 53704-3256
Phone: (608) 244-1455
E-mail: wi_office@pta.org
Website: www.wisconsinpta.org/

Wyoming

Wyoming PTA
1821 Spruce Drive
Cheyenne, WY 82001
Phone: (307) 630-1007
E-mail: jmschnmn@aol.com or lbrandon@trib.com
Website: http://w3.trib.com/~lbrandn/wyopta.html

STATE LEGISLATURES

Alabama

Senate: State House, 11 S. Union St., Montgomery, AL 36130, (334) 242-7800
House: State House, 11 S. Union St., Montgomery, AL 36130, (334) 242-7600
Website: www.legislature.state.al.us

Alaska

Senate: State Capitol, Juneau, AK 99801-1182, (907) 465-3701
House: State Capitol, Juneau, AK 99801-1182, (907) 465-3725
Website: www.legis.state.ak.us

Arizona

Senate: Capitol Complex, 1700 W. Washington St., Phoenix, AZ 85007, (602) 542-3559
House: Capitol Complex, 1700 W. Washington St., Phoenix, AZ 85007, (602) 542-4221
Website: www.azleg.state.az.us

Arkansas

Senate: 320 State Capitol Bldg., Little Rock, AR 72201, (501) 682-2902
House: 320 State Capitol Bldg., Little Rock, AR 72201, (501) 682-7771
Website: www.arkleg.state.ar.us

California

Senate: State Capitol, Sacramento, CA 95814, (916) 445-4311
House: State Capitol, Sacramento, CA 95814, (916) 445-2323
Website: www.leginfo.ca.gov

Colorado

Senate: State Capitol, 200 E. Colfax Avenue, Denver, CO 80203, (303) 866-2316
House: State Capitol, 200 E. Colfax Avenue, Denver, CO 80203, (303) 866-2904
Website: www.colorado.gov

Connecticut

Senate and House: Legislative Office Building, Hartford, CT 06106-1591, (860) 240-0100
Website: www.cga.state.ct.us

Delaware

Senate: Legislative Hall, P.O. Box 1401, Dover, DE 19903, (302) 739-4129
House: Legislative Hall, P.O. Box 1401, Dover, DE 19903, (302) 739-4087
Website: www.legis.state.de.us/Legislature.nsf

District of Columbia

Council of the District of Columbia, 441 Fourth St. NW, Ste. 716, Washington, DC 20001, (202) 724-8000
Website: www.dccouncil.washington.dc.us

Florida

Senate: The Capitol, Tallahassee, FL 32399, (850) 487-5270
House: The Capitol, Tallahassee, FL 32399, (850) 488-1234
Website: www.leg.state.fl.us

Georgia

Senate: State Capitol, Atlanta, GA 30334, (404) 656-5040
House: State Capitol, Atlanta, GA 30334, (404) 656-5082
Website: www.state.ga.us/legis

Hawaii

Senate: State Capitol, 415 Beretania St., Honolulu, HI 96813, (808) 586-6720
House: State Capitol, 415 Beretania St., Honolulu, HI 96813, (808) 587-0666
Website: www.capitol.hawaii.gov

Idaho

Senate: State Capitol Bldg., P.O. Box 83720, Boise, ID 83720-0081, (208) 332-1300
House: State Capitol Bldg., P.O. Box 83720, Boise, ID 83720-0038, (208) 332-1300
Website: www2.state.id.us/legislat

Illinois

Senate: State House, Springfield, IL 62706, (217) 782-4517
House: State House, Springfield, IL 62706, (217) 782-8223
Website: www.state.il.us/state/legis

Indiana

Senate: State House, Indianapolis, IN 46204, (317) 232-9400
House: State House, Indianapolis, IN 46204, (317) 232-9600
Website: www.state.in.us/legislative

Iowa

Senate: State Capitol, Des Moines, IA 50319, (515) 281-3371
House: State Capitol, Des Moines, IA 50319, (515) 281-3221
Website: www.legis.state.ia.us

Kansas

Senate: Statehouse, 300 SW 10th Ave., Topeka, KS 66612, (785) 296-2456
House: Statehouse, 300 SW 10th Ave., Topeka, KS 66612, (785) 296-2391
Website: www.kslegislature.org

Kentucky

Senate: State Capitol, Frankfort, KY 40601, (502) 564-3120
House: State Capitol, Frankfort, KY 40601, (502) 564-8100
Website: www.lrc.state.ky.us

Louisiana

Senate: State Capitol, Baton Rouge, LA 70804, (225) 342-2040
House: State Capitol, Baton Rouge, LA 70804, (225) 342-6945
Website: www.legis.state.la.us

Maine

Senate: 3 State House Station, Augusta, ME 04333-0003
House: 2 State House Station, Augusta, ME 04333-0002
Website: http://janus.state.me.us/legis

Maryland

Senate and House: State House, Annapolis, MD 21401, (410) 841-3000
Website: http://mlis.state.md.us

Massachusetts

Senate: State House, Boston, MA 02133, (617) 722-1455
House: State House, Boston, MA 02133, (617) 722-2000
Website: www.state.ma.us/legis/legis.htm

Michigan

Senate: State Capitol, P.O. Box 30036, Lansing, MI 48909, (517) 373-2400
House: State Capitol, P.O. Box 30036, Lansing, MI 48909, (517) 373-0135
Website: www.michiganlegislature.org

Minnesota

Senate: State Capitol, 75 Constitution Ave., St. Paul, MN 55155, (651) 296-0504
House: State Capitol, 100 Constitution Ave., St. Paul, MN 55155, (651) 296-2146
Website: www.leg.state.mn.us

Mississippi

Senate: New Capitol, P.O. Box 1018, Jackson, MS 39215-1018, (601) 350-3770
House: New Capitol, P.O. Box 1018, Jackson, MS 39215-1018, (601) 359-3358
Website: www.ls.state.ms.us

Missouri

Senate: State Capitol, Jefferson City, MO 65101, (573) 751-2745
House: State Capitol, Jefferson City, MO 65101, (573) 751-3659
Website: www.moga.state.mo.us

Montana

Senate and House: Capitol Station, Helena, MT 59620, (406) 444-4800
Website: www.leg.state.mt.us

Nebraska

Senate and House: State Capitol, P.O. Box 94604, Lincoln, NE 68509-4604, (402) 471-2271
Website: www.unicam.state.ne.us

Nevada

Senate: 401 S. Carson St., Carson City, NV 89710, (702) 687-5742
Assembly: 401 S. Carson St., Carson City, NV 89710, (702) 684-8555
Website: www.leg.state.nv.us

New Hampshire

Senate: State House, Concord, NH 03301, (603) 271-2111
House: State House, Concord, NH 03301, (603) 271-3661
Website: http://gencourt.state.nh.us

New Jersey

Senate and House: State House Annex, P.O. Box, 068, Trenton, NJ 08625-0068, (609) 292-4840
Website: www.njleg.state.nj.us

New Mexico

Senate: State Capitol, Santa Fe, NM 87501, (505) 986-4714
House: State Capitol, Santa Fe, NM 87501, (505) 986-4751
Website: www.legis.state.nm.us

New York

Senate: Legislative Office Building, Albany, NY 12247, (518) 455-2800
Assembly: Legislative Office Building, Albany, NY 12247, (518) 455-4100
Website: www.assembly.state.ny.us

North Carolina

Senate and House: State Legislative Building, Raleigh, NC 27603-2808, (919) 733-7928
Website: www.ncleg.net

North Dakota

Senate: State Capitol, 600 E. Boulevard Ave., Bismarck, ND 58505-0360, (701) 328-3373
House: State Capitol, 600 E. Boulevard Ave., Bismarck, ND 58505-0360, (701) 328-2916
Website: www.state.nd.us/lr

Ohio

Senate: State House, Columbus, OH 43215, (614) 466-4900
House: State House, Columbus, OH 43215, (614) 466-3357
Website: www.ohio.gov/ohio/legislat.htm

Oklahoma

Senate: State Capitol, 2300 N. Lincoln Blvd., Oklahoma City, OK 73105, (405) 524-0126
House: State Capitol, 2300 N. Lincoln Blvd., Oklahoma City, OK 73105, (405) 521-2711
Website: www.lsb.state.ok.us

Oregon

Senate and House: State Capitol, Salem, OR 97310, (503) 986-1187
Website: www.leg.state.or.us

Pennsylvania

Senate: Capitol Building, Harrisburg, PA 17120, (717) 787-5920
House: Capitol Building, Harrisburg, PA 17120, (717) 787-2372
Website: www.legis.state.pa.us

Rhode Island

Senate: State House, Providence, RI 02903, (401) 222-6655
House: State House, Providence, RI 02903, (401) 222-2466
Website: www.rilin.state.ri.us

South Carolina

Senate: Gressette Bldg., P.O. Box 142, Columbia, SC 29202, (803) 212-6700
House: Blatt Bldg., P.O. Box 11867, Columbia, SC 29211, (803) 734-2010
Website: www.lpitr.state.sc.us

South Dakota

Senate: Capitol Building, Pierre, SD 57501-5070, (605) 773-3821
House: Capitol Building, Pierre, SD 57501-5070, (605) 773-3851
Website: http://legis.state.sd.us/sessions/2001/index.cfm

Tennessee

Senate: State Capitol, Nashville, TN 37243, (615) 741-2730
House: State Capitol, Nashville, TN 37243, (615) 741-2901
Website: www.legislature.state.tn.us

Texas

Senate: State Capitol, P.O. Box 12068, Austin, TX 78711, (512) 463-0100
House: State Capitol, P.O. Box 12068, Austin, TX 78711, (512) 463-4630
Website: www.capitol.state.tx.us

Utah

Senate: State Capitol, Salt Lake City, UT 84114, (801) 538-1035
House: State Capitol, Salt Lake City, UT 84114, (801) 538-1029
Website: www.le.state.ut.us

Vermont

Senate: State House, Montpelier, VT 05602, (802) 828-2241
House: State House, Montpelier, VT 05602, (802) 828-2228
Website: www.leg.state.vt.us

Virginia

Senate: General Assembly Building, P.O. Box 396, Richmond, VA 23218, (804) 698-7410
House: State Capitol, P.O. Box 406, Richmond, VA 23218, (804) 698-1500
Website: http://legis.state.va.us

Washington

Senate: P.O. Box 40482, Olympia, WA 98504-0482, (360) 786-7550
House: P.O. Box 40600, Olympia, WA 98504-0600, (360) 786-7573
Website: www.leg.wa.gov

West Virginia

Senate: State Capitol, Charleston, WV 25305, (304) 357-7800
House: State Capitol, Charleston, WV 25305, (304) 340-3200
Website: www.legis.state.wv.us

Wisconsin

Senate: P.O. Box 7882, Madison, WI 53707-7882, (608) 266-2517
House: P.O. Box 8952, Madison, WI 53708, (608) 266-1501
Website: www.legis.state.wi.us

Wyoming

Senate: State Capitol, Cheyenne, WY 82002, (307) 777-7711
House: State Capitol, Cheyenne, WY 82002, (307) 777-7852
Website: http://legisweb.state.wy.us

STATE GOVERNORS

Office of the Governor
State Capitol
600 Dexter Avenue
Montgomery, AL 36130-2751
(334) 242-7100

Office of the Governor
State Capitol
P.O. Box 110001
Juneau, AK 99811-0001
(907) 465-3500

Office of the Governor
Executive Office Building
Third Floor
Pago Pago, AS 96799
(011-684) 633-4116

Office of the Governor
1700 West Washington
Phoenix, AZ 85007
(602) 542-4331

Office of the Governor
State Capitol
Room 250
Little Rock, AR 72201
(501) 682-2345

Office of the Governor
State Capitol
Sacramento, CA 95814
(916) 445-2841

Office of the Governor
136 State Capitol
Denver, CO 80203-1792
(303) 866-2471

Office of the Governor
210 Capitol Avenue

Hartford, CT 06106
(800) 406-1527

Office of the Governor
Tatnall Building
William Penn Street
Dover, DE 19901
(302) 744-4101

Office of the Governor
The Capitol
Tallahassee, FL 32399-0001
(850) 488-2272

Office of the Governor
203 State Capitol
Atlanta, GA 30334
(404) 656-1776

Office of the Governor
Executive Chamber
P.O. Box 2950
Hagatna, GU 96932
(671) 472-8931

Office of the Governor
State Capitol
Executive Chambers
Honolulu, HI 96813
(808) 586-0034

Office of the Governor State Capitol
700 West Jefferson, 2nd Floor
Boise, ID 83720
(208) 334-2100

Office of the Governor
State Capitol
207 Statehouse
Springfield, IL 62706
(217) 782-6830

Office of the Governor
206 State House
Indianapolis, IN 46204
(317) 232-4567

Office of the Governor
State Capitol
Des Moines, IA 50319-0001
(515) 281-5211

Office of the Governor
State Capitol
2nd Floor
Topeka, KS 66612-1590
(785) 296-3232

Office of the Governor
The Capitol Building
700 Capitol Avenue, Suite 100
Frankfort, KY 40601
(502) 564-2611

Office of the Governor
P.O. Box 94004
Baton Rouge, LA 70804-9004
(225) 342-7015

Office of the Governor
1 State House Station
Augusta, ME 04333
(207) 287-3531

Office of the Governor
State House
100 State Circle
Annapolis, MD 21401
(410) 974-3901

Office of the Governor
State House
Room 360
Boston, MA 02133
(617) 725-4000

Office of the Governor
Governor's Office
P.O. Box 30013
Lansing, MI 48909
(517) 373-3400

Office of the Governor
130 State Capitol
75 Rev. Dr. Martin Luther King Jr.
Boulevard
St. Paul, MN 55155
(651) 296-3391

Office of the Governor
P.O. Box 139
Jackson, MS 39205
(601) 359-3150

Office of the Governor
Missouri Capitol Building
Room 216
Jefferson City, MO 65101
(573) 751-3222

Office of the Governor
P.O. Box 200801
State Capitol
Helena, MT 59620-0801
(406) 444-3111

Office of the Governor
P.O. Box 94848
Lincoln, NE 68509-4848
(402) 471-2244

Office of the Governor
State Capitol
101 North Carson Street
Carson City, NV 89701
(775) 684-5670

Office of the Governor
State House, Room 208

107 North Main Street
Concord, NH 03301
(603) 271-2121

Office of the Governor
125 West State Street
P.O. Box 001
Trenton, NJ 08625
(609) 292-6000

Office of the Governor
State Capitol
Fourth Floor
Santa Fe, NM 87501
(505) 476-2200

Office of the Governor
State Capitol
Albany, NY 12224
(518) 474-7516

Office of the Governor
20301 Mail Service Center
Raleigh, NC 27699-0301
(919) 733-5811

Office of the Governor
State Capitol
600 East Boulevard Avenue,
Department 101
Bismarck, ND 58505-0001
(701) 328-2200

Office of the Governor
Caller Box 10007
Capitol Hill
Saipan, MP 96950
(670) 664-2280

Office of the Governor
77 South High Street
30th Floor

Columbus, OH 43215-6117
(614) 466-3555

Office of the Governor
State Capitol Building
Suite 212
Oklahoma City, OK 73105
(405) 521-2342

Office of the Governor
900 Court Street NE
Room 160
Salem, OR 97301-4047
(503) 378-3111

Office of the Governor
Room 225
Main Capitol Building
Harrisburg, PA 17120
(717) 787-2500

Office of the Governor
La Fortaleza
P.O. Box 9020082
San Juan, PR 00902-0082
(787) 721-7000

Office of the Governor
State House
Providence, RI 02903-1196
(401) 222-2080

Office of the Governor
P.O. Box 12267
Columbia, SC 29211
(803) 734-2100

Office of the Governor
500 East Capitol Avenue
Pierre, SD 57501
(605) 773-3212

Office of the Governor
State Capitol
Nashville, TN 37243-0001
(615) 741-2001

Office of the Governor
P.O. Box 12428
Austin, TX 78711
(512) 463-2000

Office of the Governor
Utah East Office Building, Suite E220
P.O. Box 142220
Salt Lake City, UT 84114-2220
(801) 538-1000

Office of the Governor
109 State Street
Montpelier, VT 05609
(802) 828-3333

Office of the Governor
Government House, 21-22 Kongens
Gade
Charlotte Amalie
St. Thomas, VI 00802
(340) 774-0001

Office of the Governor
State Capitol
Richmond, VA 23219
(804) 786-2211

Office of the Governor
P.O. Box 40002
Olympia, WA 98504-0002
(360) 753-6780

Office of the Governor
State Capitol Complex
Charleston, WV 25305-0370
(304) 558-2000

Office of the Governor
State Capitol
115 East
Madison, WI 53702
(608) 266-1212

Office of the Governor
State Capitol Building
Room 124
Cheyenne, WY 82002
(307) 777-7434

References

Adams, M. J. (2000). *Beginning to read: Thinking and learning about print.* Cambridge, MA: MIT Press.

Adams, M. J., Foorman, B. R., Lundberg, I., & Beeler, T. (1997). *Phonemic awareness in young children: A classroom curriculum.* Baltimore: Brooks Publishing.

August, D., & Hakuta, K. (1998). *Educating language-minority children.* Washington, DC: National Academy Press.

Bloom, J. (1990). *Help me to help my child: A sourcebook for parents of learning disabled children.* Boston: Little, Brown.

Bracken, B. A. (1984). Bracken Basic Concept Scale. San Antonio: The Psychological Corporation.

Brown, I. S., & Felton, R. H. (1990). Effects of instruction on beginning reading skills in children at risk for reading disability. *Reading and Writing: An Interdisciplinary Journal, 2,* 223–241.

Bush, L. (2001, February 26). *A guide for parents: How do I know a good early reading program when I see one? Ready to read, ready to learn initiative.* Washington, DC: U.S. Department of Education.

Chall, J. (1967). *Learning to read: The great debate.* New York: McGraw Hill, Inc.

Clay, M. M. (1985). *The early detection of reading difficulties.* Portsmouth, NH: Heinemann.

Cunningham, A. E., & Stanovich, K. E. (1998). What reading does for the mind. *American Educator, 22,* 8–15.

Departments of Labor, Health and Human Services, and Education and Related Agencies. (1997, July 24). Calendar No. 125, 105th Congress 1st Session SENATE Report 105-58. Appropriation Bill, 1998.

Early Childhood-Head Start Task Force/U.S. Department of Education/U.S. Department of Health and Human Services. (2002). *Teaching our youngest: A guide for preschool teachers and child-care and family providers.* Washington, DC: Author.

Englemann, S., & Bruner, E. C. (1995). Science Research Associates' Reading Mastery Rainbow Edition program. Chicago, IL: SRA/McGraw-Hill.

Englemann, S., & Osborn, J. (1987). DISTAR Language I. Chicago: SRA/McGraw-Hill.

Flesch, R. (1986). *Why Johnny can't read: And what you can do about it.* New York: Harper.

Foorman, B. R., Francis, D. J., Fletcher, J. M., Schatschneider, C., & Mehta, P. (1998). The role of instruction in learning to read: Preventing reading failure in at-risk children. *Journal of Educational Psychology, 90,* 37–55.

Francis, D. J., Shaywitz, S. E., Steubing, K. K., Shaywitz, B. A., & Fletcher J. M. (1994). The measurement of change: Assessing behavior over time and within a developmental context. In G. R. Lyon (Ed.), *Frames of reference for the assessment of learning disabilities: New views on measurement issues* (pp. 29–58). Baltimore: Paul H. Brookes.

Hall, S., & Moats, L. C. (2002). *Parenting a struggling reader: A guide to diagnosing and finding help for your child's reading difficulties.* New York: Broadway Books.

Honig, B. (1995). *Teaching our children to read: The role of skills in a comprehensive reading program.* Thousand Oaks, CA: Corwin Press.

Moats, L. C. (2000). *Speech to print: Language essentials for teachers.* New York: Broadway Books.

National Institute of Child Health and Human Development (NICHD). (2000). Report of the National Reading Panel. *Teaching children to read: An evidence-based assessment of the scientific research literature on reading and its implications for reading instruction* [NIH Publication No. 00-4754]. Washington, DC: U.S. Government Printing Office.

National Reading Panel. (2000). *Teaching children to read: An evidence-based assessment of the scientific research literature on reading and its implications for reading instruction.* Washington, DC: National Institute of Child Health and Human Development.

Neuhaus News. (2002, Fall). Vol. XXII, No. 2. Bellaire, TX: Neuhaus Education Center.

Olson, R. (1998, April). *Report of the National Research Council on Early Reading: Implications for practice.* Presented at the Urban Symposium on Literacy, Los Angeles, CA.

Open Court Reading. (1995). *Collections for young scholars*. Peru, IL: SRA/ McGraw-Hill.

The Partnership for Reading. *Put reading first: Helping your child learn to read*. Accessed November 13, 2005, from www.nifl.gov/partnershipforreading/ publications/pdf/Stanovich.

Shaywitz, S., (2003). *Overcoming dyslexia: A new and complete science-based program for reading problems at any level*. New York: Knopf.

Slavin, R. E., & Madden, N. (1989). What works for students at risk: A research synthesis. *Educational Leadership, 64*, 4–13.

Smith, F. (1992, February). Learning to read: The never-ending debate. *Phi Delta Kappan*, 432–441.

Snow, C. E., Burns, M. S., & Griffin, P. (1998). *Preventing reading difficulties in young children*. Washington, DC: National Academy Press.

Stahl, S. A., Osborn, J., & Lehr, F. (1990). *Beginning to read: Thinking and learning about print*. Urbana-Champaign, IL: Center for the Study of Reading.

Standardized Test of Assessment for Reading. (1995). Wisconsin Rapids, WI: Advantage Learning Systems, Inc.

Stanovich, P. J., & Stanovich, K. E. (2003). *Using research and reason in education: How teachers can use scientifically based research to make curricular and instructional decisions*. Washington, DC: U.S. Department of Education. Retrieved June 19, 2005, from www.nifl.gov/partnershipforreading/publications/pdf/ Stanovich.

Stevens, S. H. (1980). *The learning disabled child: Ways that parents can help*. Winston-Salem, NC: John F. Blair, Publisher.

Torgesen, J. K. (2002). The prevention of reading difficulties. *Journal of School Psychology, 40*, 7–26.

Torgesen, J. K., & Bryant, B. (1994). Test of Phonological Awareness. Austin, TX: Pro-Ed Publishers, Inc.

Walt, K. (1996, February 2). The crisis at hand: Governor wants $65 million to ensure that Texas schoolchildren learn to read. *Houston Chronicle*.

Waterford Institute. (1995). Waterford Early Reading Program, Level I. Menlo Park, CA: Electronic Education, Inc.

Woodcock, R. W., & Johnson, M. B. (1989). Woodcock-Johnson Psycho-Educational Battery-Revised. Allen, TX: DLM/Teaching Resources.

About the Contributors

Teresa Ankney, PhD, currently serves as head of the Friendship School in Eldersburg, Maryland, which was founded as a parent cooperative school to serve the needs of dyslexic children. She is also the chairperson and a cofounder of the Margaret Byrd Rawson Institute, a nonprofit organization providing teacher education and community outreach. In 1999, she cofounded the Parent Advocacy Group for Educational Rights. In addition to her extensive advocacy efforts, Ankney teaches sociology courses at Hood College in Frederick, Maryland. She is a parent of two dyslexic sons.

Diane Badgley Lyon serves as the project manager for the Research and Evaluation program at the American College of Education in Dallas, Texas. She has spent the majority of her adult life working to bring about changes in education, first as a parent, then as a project specialist in the Office of Special Education Programs within the U.S. Department of Education, where she oversaw the work of the Parent Information Training Centers. She has traveled throughout the nation providing the public with information on effective research-based education programs for students with reading disabilities.

Diane struggled throughout her life as a result of her poor reading skills and then relived that struggle with her son, who has dyslexia. She used that determination to build partnerships between educators and community leaders to meet the needs of children who were unable to learn to read in the state of Indiana. She is committed to ensuring that all students have the opportunity to learn to read.

Phyllis Blaunstein is a national leader in education policy and public engagement. She worked extensively with state boards of education to develop state policies to ensure an effective education for all children as the former executive director of the National Association of State Boards of Education, was an education policy fellow with the Institute for Education Leadership, and was a member of the regulations writing team for the first law that guaranteed the right to an education for children with disabilities, P.L. 94-142, the Education for All Handicapped Children Act.

Trained as a speech and language pathologist, Blaunstein directed the Speech and Hearing Clinic at the University of Tennessee Research Hospital, where she worked with physicians, medical students, and high-risk infants and their parents and staffed the Birth Defects Clinic. She was a member of the faculty of the Department of Audiology and Speech Pathology at the University of Tennessee. Her work in language disorders is the precursor of her interest in providing children research-based skills for learning to read.

Blaunstein started her career as a secondary school English teacher and was shocked to learn that her class of high school juniors was unable to read. This was her first indication that students could get through the education system without the most fundamental skill—reading. She specializes in social marketing, using commercial marketing techniques to promote social issues.

Blaunstein received a BA from the State University of New York, Albany, and an MA from the University of Tennessee and was a vocational rehabilitation fellow.

Norma Garza is a graduate of Southern Methodist University in Dallas, Texas, with an undergraduate business degree, and has practiced as a certified public accountant for 16 years. She became interested in reading when she discovered that one of her three sons was having difficulty reading. This experience catapulted her from her practice as a certified public accountant to a community leader.

In 1996, Garza cofounded the Brownsville Reads Task Force, a nonprofit organization of community members and educators who joined together to promote research-based reading instruction in the public and private schools of Brownsville, Texas, with the overall goal of creating a more literate community. At Saint Joseph Academy, in Brownsville, Texas, a 7 through 12 grade Marist college prep school, she helped inaugurate a learning center for students who struggled with their academic work. From 2001 through 2005, she served as the coordinator for the United Way of Southern Cameron County Success By 6 Initiative, a program for children birth to six years of age that focuses on community system reform to prepare children to succeed when they enter school. In 2002, Garza was appointed as a member of the White House Educational Excellence for Hispanic Americans Commission and a member of the National Reading Panel. In Texas she was a member of the Governor's Focus on Reading Task Force, Governor's Special Education Committee, and Academics Goals 2000 Texas Panel. She has received several awards and recognitions for her advocacy work in literacy. In 2005, she began serving as a presidential appointee to the U.S. Department of Education as senior advisor to secretary of education, Margaret Spellings, in the area of early childhood education.

Marion Joseph has been credited with turning the tide in reading instruction by promoting a research-based program in California at a time when the reading scores of children in that state were the worst in the country. Her relentless fight to change the way children are taught to read was spurred by her grandson's struggles. When she began, she knew nothing about reading instruction, but she did some research and found that there was evidence to demonstrate that there was an effective way to teach reading and that children in California were not being taught that way.

Joseph successfully convinced the state legislature to pass two bills in 1995 that mandated the use of a systematic and comprehensive phonics-based approach in reading instruction. She was subsequently appointed to the California Board of Education, where she helped oversee the development of rigorous standards for the teaching of reading. This grandmother continues to travel the country to help other states accomplish what California has done.

Joseph holds a bachelor's degree in political science from the University of California, Berkeley, and the University of California, Los Angeles.

Raymond King became principal at Hartsfield Elementary School in 1992 and dramatically raised reading scores in that school before going on to two other schools, where he also instituted changes that turned around these schools and dramatically improved the achievement scores of his students. In each of these schools the students were poor and had consistent high rates of failure before King instituted changes described in his chapter. Hartsfield Elementary School became an "A" school for three consecutive years, and their program was named the Model Reading Program in the state of Florida. King worked in special education for 15 years with students who had multiple handicaps and were classified as severely or profoundly impaired, and he supervised juvenile justice programs and gifted programs for six years.

He holds a BS in secondary education social sciences from the University of Tennessee, an MS in special education from George Peabody College at Vanderbilt, and an MS in education leadership from Florida State University.

Richard Long has helped shape federal education policy for two decades. As director of government relations for the International Reading Association, he has worked with both the House and Senate to fashion laws such as the Individuals with Disabilities Act (IDEA) and the Elementary and Secondary Education Act (ESEA) and to shepherd these laws through the rule-making process of the Department of Education. He is a valuable resource on reading issues for both houses when key federal education laws come up for reauthorization. He works tirelessly to keep the reading community's message alive on the Hill.

He has been with the International Reading Association since 1978. He began as a part-time employee after serving on the staff of Congressman James W. Symington and working as coordinator of multidisciplinary interventions at the George Washington University (GWU) Reading Center. While with the association he completed his doctoral work at GWU, focusing on counseling, reading, and public policy, and began consulting with *USA Today*, the World Health Organization, and several U.S. government agencies and education groups. He was president of the U.S. Coalition for Education for All and chaired the North American Consultation for the Education for All program. Dr. Long is also the executive director of the National Association of State Title I Directors.

Reid Lyon is the executive vice president for research and evaluation at the American College of Education in Dallas, Texas. Dr. Lyon also serves on the Whitney International University team, part of Global Education's mission to create high-quality institutions in key regions of the world to make postsecondary education accessible for all qualified students. He was a research psychologist and chief of the Child Development and Behavior Branch within the National Institute of Child Health and Human Development at the National Institutes of Health. In that capacity, he was responsible for the direction and management of research programs in developmental psychology, cognitive neuroscience, behavioral pediatrics, reading and human learning, and learning disorders. He was also responsible for translating NIH scientific discoveries relevant to the development and education of children to Congress and other government agencies.

Lyon has authored, coauthored, and edited over 120 journal articles, books, and book chapters addressing learning differences and disabilities in children and the development of evidence-based education policies at the national level. He was a member of the President's Commission on Excellence in Special Education and served as an advisor to President George W. Bush and First Lady Laura Bush on child development and education research and policies from 2000 through 2005.

Sara M. Porter was an elementary school teacher who believes that a person who has developed a love of reading can always learn, regardless of his or her formal education. As a consumer of research-based methods of teaching, she was a pioneer in advocating for a structured, explicit, and systematic phonics-based program in the school systems in which she taught.

Porter retired after more than 40 years as an elementary school teacher, reading teacher, and tutor. She was the chair of the Education committee of the Maryland branch of the International Dyslexia Association and was responsible for encouraging a major newspaper to run a three-year series of articles called "Reading by Nine" to inform parents about effective reading instruction. Porter has a BSc and an MEd from Towson State University.

Patrick Riccards has built and executed successful media relations and integrated communications campaigns for public- and private-sector organizations for more than a dozen years. As project director for the federal Partnership for Reading, Patrick has worked closely with parents and teachers on the best ways to improve classroom reading instruction through scientifically based instruction. He also served as senior advisor to the National Reading Panel, helping shepherd its landmark *Teaching Children to Read* report. Recognized as one of the top PR professionals in the field by both *PR Week* and *PR News* magazines, Patrick is an award-winning writer and communications strategist. He began his career as a press secretary and strategist on Capitol Hill.

Benjamin Sayeski is the senior project director with the Darden/Curry Partnership for Leaders in Education. The partnership provides executive education for school leaders by combining the expertise of faculty members from the Darden School of Business and the Curry School of Education at the University of Virginia.

Prior to joining the Partnership for Leaders in Education, Sayeski was the principal of Johnson Elementary School in Charlottesville, Virginia, from 2000 to 2004. At the completion of his 2nd year at Johnson Elementary, the school achieved full state accreditation for the first time in the school's history. The school retained full state accreditation and met federal adequate yearly progress (AYP) standards under No Child Left Behind for the remainder of his tenure. In 2002, the Virginia Association of School Superintendents recognized Johnson as a high performing/high poverty school.

For the past three years, Sayeski has taught the course The School Principalship as an adjunct professor for the School of Continuing and Professional Studies at the University of Virginia. He has also served on a number of committees and guest lectured for a variety of administrative and teacher education courses at the University of Virginia. Sayeski earned his PhD from the University of Virginia in administration and supervision, his MA from the Ohio State University in Secondary Education, and his BA from Furman University in Political Science.

Bennett A. Shaywitz, MD, is professor of pediatrics and neurology and chief of pediatric neurology at the Yale University School of Medicine. Dr. Shaywitz received his AB from Washington University, where he was elected to Phi Beta Kappa, and his MD from Washington University School of Medicine. He completed his pediatric training and then a postdoctoral fellowship in child neurology at the Albert Einstein College of Medicine. Together with his wife, Dr. Sally Shaywitz, Dr. Bennett Shaywitz established and is currently codirector of the Yale Center for the Study of Learning, Reading, and Attention. Dr. Shaywitz has a long-standing interest in disorders of learning and attention in children and young adults. Recently he has used functional magnetic resonance imaging (fMRI) to discover differences in brain organization and function in children and adults with dyslexia, and he is now using fMRI to study how the brain changes as children with dyslexia are taught to read.

The author of over 300 scientific papers, Dr. Shaywitz's honors include election to membership in the Institute of Medicine of the National Academy of Sciences; he was selected to deliver the 2005 New York University Medical Scientist Training Program Honors Lecture and was the recipient of the 2003 Distinguished Alumni Award from Washington University. Dr. Shaywitz has been chosen as "One of the Best Doctors in America" and "One of America's Top Doctors." He currently serves on the Scientific Advisory Board of the March of Dimes and on the Functional Brain Imaging Advisory Board of the Haan Foundation for Children and has served on the Institute of Medicine Immunization Safety Review Committee. Dr. Shaywitz also serves on the editorial board of *Pediatrics in Review, Learning Disabilities: A Contemporary Journal*, and *Child Neuropsychology*.

Sally E. Shaywitz, MD, is professor of pediatrics at the Yale University School of Medicine. Dr. Shaywitz received her AB (with honors) from the City University, where she was elected to Phi Beta Kappa, and her MD from Albert Einstein College of Medicine. She is currently, with her husband, Dr. Bennett A. Shaywitz, codirector of the Yale Center for the Study of Learning, Reading, and Attention. Dr. Sally Shaywitz has devoted her career to better understanding reading and dyslexia; her research provides the basic framework: conceptual model, epidemiology, and neurobiology for the scientific study of learning disabilities, particularly dyslexia. Dr. Shaywitz is the author of 200 scientific articles, chapters, and books, including *Overcoming Dyslexia: A New and Complete Science-Based Program for Reading Problems at Any Level* (2003), which received the 2004 Margo Marek Book Award and the 2004 NAMI Book Award.

Dr. Shaywitz, a member of the Institute of Medicine of the National Academy of Sciences, was awarded an honorary degree by Williams College in June 2005. She received the 2004 Townsend Harris Medal of the City College of New York and was also the 1998 recipient of the Achievement Award in Women's Health of the Society for the Advancement of Women's Health Research and the 1995 Distinguished Alumnus Award of the Albert Einstein College of Medicine. Dr. Shaywitz has been chosen as "One of the Best Doctors in America" and "One of America's Top Doctors" and "One of New York's Top Doctors." Dr. Shaywitz currently serves on the Advisory Council of the National Institute of Neurological Diseases and Stroke (NINDS), the National Research Council Committee on Women in Science and Engineering, the National Board for Education Sciences, and the Scientific Advisory Board of the March of Dimes. Dr. Shaywitz cochairs the National Research Council Committee on Gender Differences in the Careers of Science, Engineering, and Mathematics Faculty; she served on the National Reading Panel and on the Committee to Prevent Reading Difficulties in Young Children of the National Research Council. Dr. Shaywitz also serves on the editorial board of the *Journal of Learning Disabilities* and *Learning Disabilities: A Contemporary Journal.*

Joseph Torgesen is the Robert M. Gagne Professor of Psychology and Education at Florida State University and the director of the Florida Center for Reading Research. He also is currently serving as the director of the Eastern Regional Reading First Technical Assistance Center. He has been conducting research with children who have learning problems for over 25 years and is the author of over 170 articles, book chapters, books, and tests related to reading and learning disabilities. Throughout his career, Dr. Torgesen's work has been continuously supported by research grants from private foundations, the state of Florida, the U.S. Office of Education, and the National Institute of Child Health and Human Development (NICHD). For the last 15 years, he has been part of the effort supported by the NICHD to learn more about the nature of reading difficulties and ways to prevent and remediate reading problems in children. His current professional service includes membership on the editorial boards of six research journals as well as membership on the professional advisory board for the National Center for Learning Disabilities and the Scientific Advisory Board of the Haan Foundation for Children. He has also recently been appointed by President Bush to the board of directors of the Institute for Education Sciences in Washington, DC.